THE APPLAUSE SCREENPLAY SERIES
Mark Mixson, General Editor

# Jacob's Ladder

by
## Bruce Joel Rubin

with over 100 photographs from the film
and including
an appendix of deleted scenes

Jacob's Chronicle by Bruce Joel Rubin
and the complete credits

APPLAUSE
THEATRE BOOK PUBLISHERS

An Applause Original
JACOB'S LADDER

**Library of Congress Cataloging-in-Publication Data:**

Rubin, Bruce Joel.
    Jacob's ladder : an original screenplay / by Bruce Joel Rubin.
        p.      cm.
    "An Applause original" -- T.p. verso.
    ISBN 1-55783-086-X
    1. Jacob's ladder (Motion picture)     I. Title
PN1997.J27    1990
791.43'72 -- dc20                                                90-19365
                                                                      CIP

APPLAUSE THEATRE BOOK PUBLISHERS
211 West 71st Street
New York, NY  10023
Phone (212) 595-4735

First Applause Printing, 1990

*For Blanche with all my love*

# Contents

# Introduction

It is a screenwriter's continuing frustration that, with the exception of some relatives, a few studio executives, and the director, almost nobody ever sees the original script for a feature film. It is assumed by most people that in film, like theatre, the script is being performed on the screen. But that is rarely true. Unlike theatre, where no one can change a line of dialogue without the playwright's consent, in motion pictures a script cannot only be changed, it can be altered and mutilated beyond all recognition.

The operating rule in Hollywood is that selling a screenplay is like selling a house. Once sold, the new owner can do with it as he pleases, redecorating, adding on, or even tearing it down. That you spent a lifetime dreaming this home into existence, designing it, constructing it, decorating it, has no significance. That your children were born there and that your own life is bound up with the mortar of its walls, has no bearing on the rights of the new owner. You cannot tell the director or the studio that they have no right to change the living room. They own it. It doesn't matter that you put your soul into designing the bedroom. It's not your house any more. It's theirs. This is very difficult for writers to comprehend.

Most people who write do so because they have something to say, an urge to tell a story, to communicate an idea, to express something deep and gnawing within themselves. In their naiveté many writers think that by selling their script to be made into a "major motion picture" they will actually get an opportunity to present their stories, ideas, and emotions to the world.

Unfortunately, after the initial excitement of actually being paid for something he wrote, a writer often discovers that the studio bought his work not because they liked the script but because they liked one of the characters ("It'd be a great part for Harrison Ford"), or a particular story concept. Suddenly all of the effusions of love accompanying the purchase of the screenplay have been tempered into pages of notes, telling the writer how the script can be improved. One is often shocked at this point to discover that everyone at the studio wants the main character to be changed from a man to a woman ("Cher is available"), or that the childhood neighborhood you have so lovingly detailed is too ethnic and should be moved from East L.A. to Connecticut.

And so it goes. Directors, actors, executives and their secretaries all begin to have enormous input into the creation and recreation of the movie you wrote. If you are very lucky, a brilliant director or compassionate studio executive will enhance your script, taking your simple words and fashioning them into indelible cinema. This is every screenwriter's fantasy. But usually, just the opposite occurs. Screenwriters often find themselves being judged for work that bears only slight resemblance to what they originally write. Rarely does a screenplay have an opportunity to stand on its own. I wanted that chance.

The script presented here is not my initial screenplay but the final draft completed just before shooting. While close to the original, some significant scenes have been changed or cut. You will find them in the final chapter. It is also important to understand that this script is not necessarily what you will see on the screen, but the inspiration for it.

*Bruce Joel Rubin*

# Jacob's
# Ladder

1   **EXT.   VIETNAM — DUSK**

A swarm of helicopters swoops out of a yellow sky and
deposits an army of men over a Vietnamese hillside.

The SOLDIERS scramble over the terraced rice paddies
for the protection of the jungle. Falling into
columns, like strands of soldier ants, seventy-five
men, at combat readiness, assemble on the edge of a
sweltering wilderness.

It is dusk. The mood is lazy, soporific. Members of
one platoon huddle close to the ground smoking a
joint.

                    JERRY
          Strong stuff.

                    ROD
               (to JACOB, a soldier
               squatting several yards
               away)
          Hey, Professor, how many times can
          you shit in an hour?

                    GEORGE
          Don't bug 'im.

                    DOUG
          Where are those gooks already?

                    FRANK
          Some offensive. I don't even think
          they're out there.

                    PAUL
          Jesus, this grass is something else.

JACOB SINGER returns to the group, pulling up his
pants.

                    ROD
          Why even bother to pull 'em up?

                    FRANK
          You jackin' off out there again, huh
          Jake?

                    PAUL
          Hey, get off his back.

                    ROD
          It's called philosophizing, right
          Professor?

JACOB gives them the finger.

                    JACOB
          Up yours, you adolescent scum.

                                        (CONTINUED)

1    CONTINUED:

Laughter.

> SERGEANT (V.O.)
> Mount your bayonets.

> FRANK
> (frightened)
> Oh shit!

> PAUL
> Goddam!

> ROD
> Gimme that joint!

> JERRY
> Hey, something's wrong.

> GEORGE
> What is it?

> JERRY
> My head.

> GEORGE
> It's nerves. Take another toke.

GEORGE reaches out, extending a joint. Suddenly he
gasps and falls to the ground, his body convulsing
uncontrollably. The others stand back, startled. JACOB
grabs him and shoves a rifle barrel between his
chattering teeth.

> ROD
> What's going on?

Before anyone can answer JERRY grabs his head,
screaming. He turns frantically in all directions.

> JERRY
> Help me! Help me!

> PAUL
> What the hell ... ?

In seconds JERRY is spinning wildly out of control,
his head shaking into a terrific blur. He crashes into
FRANK with the force of a truck. FRANK slams into the
ground as all the air rushes from his lungs. He begins
gasping and hyperventilating. His eyes grow wide and
frenzied as he gulps for air. Fear and confusion sweep
across his face. The MEN watch, horrified, as FRANK's
terror escalates beyond reason into all-out panic.

Suddenly FRANK begins howling. He lunges for his
bayonet and, without warning, attacks the MEN around
him.

> PAUL
> God Almighty!

(CONTINUED)

2

1    CONTINUED:

PAUL spins out of the way as FRANK's bayonet impales
the ground. JACOB jumps on top of FRANK and wrestles
him into the tall grass. PAUL rushes to his
assistance.

JACOB stares at FRANK's face as FRANK struggles
beneath him. It is the face of a madman.

                         PAUL
          Good God! What's happening?

The sudden chaos is intensified by the sound of
fighting erupting behind them. Guns crackle and bursts
of light penetrate the darkening sky.

                         ROD
          Behind you! Look out! This is it!

The MEN spin around. PAUL panics and jumps to his
feet, leaving JACOB alone with FRANK. FRANK's eyes
burn with demonic force as he gathers his strength.

                        JACOB
          Don't leave me.

Dark figures, silhouetted by the setting sun, are
storming at them. SOLDIERS squint to see. It is a
horrifying vision.

                         PAUL
          They're coming!

Gunfire explodes on all sides. Suddenly PAUL flips
out. He begins screaming uncontrollably, ripping at
his clothes and skin. FRANK is struggling like four
men and JACOB is weakening in his effort to restrain
him. Bayonets glimmer in the exchange of fire. Bodies
fall. More bodies keep coming. The first wave is upon
them.

ROD shoots into the air. Shadowy forms hurl forward
screaming like banshees. ROD, squinting, jabs with his
bayonet, piercing the belly of his attacker. Agonizing
cries accompany his fall. ROD yanks the bayonet out
and stabs again.

In the midst of this madness FRANK shoots to his feet,
and slams the butt of his rifle into JACOB's back.
There is a cracking sound. JACOB's eyes freeze with
pain. His hands rush for his spine. As he spins around
one of the ATTACKERS jams all eight inches of his
bayonet blade into JACOB's stomach. JACOB screams. It
is a loud and piercing wail.


2    CUT ON THE SOUND OF THE SCREAM to a sudden rush
     through a long dark tunnel. There is a sense of

                                        (CONTINUED)

2    CONTINUED:

enormous speed accelerating toward a brilliant light.
The rush suggests a passage between life and death,
but as the light bursts upon us we realize that we are
passing through a SUBWAY STATION far below the city of
NEW YORK.


2A  INT.    SUBWAY — NIGHT

THE WHEELS OF AN EXPRESS TRAIN screech through the
station. JACOB SINGER, sitting alone in the last car,
wakes up. The sounds of the scream and the grating
wheels merge. He is dazed and confused, not certain
where he is.

JACOB glances around the empty car. His eyes gravitate
to overhead advertisements for hemorrhoid preparations
and savings banks. Gradually his confusion subsides.
Shifting uncomfortably he pulls a thick book out of
his back pocket, "The Stranger" by Albert Camus. He
begins reading. Another station blurs by.

JACOB is a good-looking man, of obvious intelligence.
He is in his mid-thirties. It is surprising that he is
wearing a mailman's uniform. He doesn't look like one.

The subway ride seems to go on interminably. JACOB is
restless and concerned. He glances at his watch. It is
3:30 A.M. Putting his book in his back pocket, JACOB
stands up, and makes his way through the deserted car.


3   INT.    SUBWAY TRACKS — NIGHT

JACOB enters the rumbling passageway between the cars.
The wheels spark against the rails. The dark tunnel
walls flash by. He pulls the handle on the door to the
next car. It is stuck. He struggles with it. A LADY
sitting alone inside turns to look at him. She seems
threatened by his effort. He motions for her to help.
She turns away.

A look of disgust crosses JACOB's face. He kicks the
door. It slides open. The WOMAN seems frightened as he
approaches her.


4                        JACOB
                Excuse me, do you know if we've
                passed Nostrand Avenue yet?
                     (she doesn't answer)
                Excuse me.
                     (she does not
                     acknowledge his
                     existence)

                                        (CONTINUED)

                         4

                              JACOB (CONT.)
          Look, I'm asking a simple question.
          Have we hit Nostrand Avenue? I fell
          asleep.
                              WOMAN
                       (speaking with a Puerto
                       Rican accent)
          I no from around here.

                              JACOB
                       (glad for a response)
          Yeah, you and everyone else.

JACOB walks to the other end of the car and sits down.
The only other passenger is an OLD MAN lying asleep on
the fiberglass bench. Occasionally his body shudders.
It is the only sign of life in him.

The train begins to slow down. JACOB peers out of the
window. Nostrand Avenue signs appear. He is relieved.
He gets up and grabs hold of the overhead bar.

The OLD MAN shudders and stretches out on the seat. As
he adjusts his position, tugging at his coat, JACOB
catches a brief glimpse of something protruding from
beneath the coat's hem. His eyes fixate on the spot,
waiting for another look. There is a slight movement
and it appears — a long, red, fleshy protuberance. The
sight of it sends shivers up JACOB's spine. It looks
strangely like a tail. Only the stopping of the train
breaks JACOB's stare.


5   INT.   SUBWAY STATION — NIGHT

JACOB is the only passenger getting off. The doors
close quickly behind him. He glances at the LADY
sitting by the window. There is a fearful expression
on her face as the train carries her back into the
dark tunnel, out of his sight.

JACOB reaches the exit, a huge metal revolving door
surrounded by floor to ceiling gates. He is about to
push when he notices a chain locking it shut. He
stares at it in disbelief.

                              JACOB
          Goddam it.

He turns in a huff and hikes to the other end of the
platform. As he approaches the far exit, his eyes
widen. The gate there is also locked. His hands reach
for his hips as he studies an impossible situation.

CUT TO JACOB stepping cautiously onto the ladder going
down to the tracks. A rat scampers by and he gasps.

                                          (CONTINUED)

5    CONTINUED:

                              JACOB
              No way!

He starts to climb back up the ladder but sees that
there is nowhere else to go. He juts out his jaw and
steps back down.
JACOB is not comfortable on the tracks. He cannot see
where he is stepping. His shoes splash in unseen
liquid which make him grimace. The steel girders are
coated in subway grime. The oily substance coats his
hands as he reaches for support.

                              JACOB
              Goddamn fucking city!

He wipes the grime on his postal uniform as he steps
toward the center track. He reaches for another girder
when it starts to vibrate. Two pinpoints of light hurl
toward him. Then the noise arrives confirming his
fear. A train is bearing down on him. JACOB looks
frightened, not sure which way to go. He steps
forward, up to his ankle in slime. He cannot tell
which track the train is on. It is moving at
phenomenal speed. The station is spinning. The train's
lights merge into one brilliant intensity.

In near panic JACOB jumps across the track as the
train spins by. Its velocity blows his hair straight
up as though it is standing on end. He clings to a
pillar for support, gasping in short breaths.

A few PEOPLE are staring at JACOB from the train.
Their faces, pressed up against the glass, seem
deformed. A lone figure waves at him from the rear
window. The train bears them all away. Then it is
quiet again. For a moment JACOB is afraid to move but
slowly regains his composure. He continues to the
other side of the tracks and stumbles up the ladder to
the UPTOWN PLATFORM.

                                                  CUT TO:

6    JACOB smiling.The smile, however, is one of irony, not
     amusement. This exit too is locked. A heavy chain is
     wrapped through the bars. JACOB stares at it with an
     expression of total bewilderment.


7    A sudden muffled scream alerts JACOB that he is not
     alone. His head turns but sees no one. He hears the
     scream again. He senses its direction and walks toward
     the MEN'S ROOM. A crack of light appears under the
     door. He can hear someone moaning inside. JACOB knocks
     softly and the moaning stops. The lights click off.

                                              (CONTINUED)

                         JACOB
            Hey, is someone in there?

There is no answer. JACOB stands silently for a
moment, not sure what to do. He can hear whispering.
He chews his lower lip nervously and then reaches for
the door. It pushes open.

The light from the station penetrates the darkness. He
gasps. He sees a MAN tied naked to the stall with
ANOTHER NAKED MAN grabbing quickly for his clothes.
The BOUND MAN screams.

                       BOUND MAN
            Fuck off! Mind your own business!

A THIRD MAN spins out of the shadows, pointing a knife
at JACOB's throat.

                          MAN
            You cocksucker! Get outta here.

The MAN's face is barely human. Before JACOB can even
react the door slams shut. The lock engages. The crack
of light reappears. JACOB can hear laughter coming
from inside, followed by a scream. He backs away from
the door. His face is white.

JACOB turns with full fury and storms the gate. The
chain gives way to his anger. It flies apart and the
gate flings open. He stands in amazement, observing
the chain as it slides from between the bars and drops
to the concrete below. The gate squeaks loudly as
JACOB pushes it aside and clangs with an almost
painful burst as he slams it shut.


8   EXT.   **WILMINGTON TOWERS — DAWN**

     JACOB walks toward the towering shadows of a massive
     PUBLIC HOUSING PROJECT. It is dark and the moonlight
     silhouettes the huge monolithic structures. JACOB
     passes through a vast COURTYARD dominated by the
     imposing shapes. Aside from his moving body everything
     is still.


9   INT.   **HALLWAY — DAWN**

     JACOB steps off a graffiti-festooned ELEVATOR into a
     long impersonal HALLWAY. He uses three keys to unlock
     the door to his APARTMENT.

10 **INT.   JACOB'S APT. — DAWN**

JACOB enters the darkness without turning on the light
He tries to navigate his way to the BATHROOM,
illuminated by a tiny nightlight in the distance. His
effort is unsuccessful. He bangs loudly into a table.
A WOMAN's voice calls out.

>                    JEZZIE (V.O.)
>           Jake, is that you?

>                    JACOB
>           What the hell did you do, move all
>           the furniture?

>                    JEZZIE (V.O.)
>           Why didn't you turn on the light?

>                    JACOB
>           I didn't want to wake you.

>                    JEZZIE (V.O.)
>                (sleepy but pleasant)
>           Gee, thanks a lot.

>                    JACOB
>           Where is the lamp?

>                    JEZZIE (V.O.)
>           Where are you?

>                    JACOB
>           If I knew I wouldn't have to ask.
>           What did you do? I was happy the way
>           it was.

>                    JEZZIE (V.O.)
>           I moved the couch. That's all.

>                    JACOB
>           Where to?

JACOB crashes into it. A light suddenly goes on.
JEZEBEL "JEZZIE" PIPKIN, 33, is standing in the
BEDROOM door tying a man's terrycloth bathrobe around
her waist. Although sleepy, disheveled, and not
looking her best, it is obvious that JEZZIE is a beefy
woman, juicy and sensual.

>                    JEZZIE
>           That help?

>                    JACOB
>                (nearly sprawled over
>                the couch)
>           Thanks.

He pushes himself up.

                                        (CONTINUED)

                              JEZZIE
          What do you think?

                              JACOB
          What do you mean?

                              JEZZIE
          The room!

                              JACOB
          Oh God, Jezzie, ask me tomorrow.

                              JEZZIE
          It is tomorrow. Four A.M. How come
          you're so late?

                              JACOB
          Roberts didn't show up. What could I
          say? Besides, it's double time.

                              JEZZIE
                    (seeing the grease on
                    his uniform)
          What happened to you?

                              JACOB
                    (unbuttoning his shirt
                    as he walks to the
                    BATHROOM)
          Don't ask.

JACOB steps into the BATHROOM and pulls at his
clothes, leaving them in a pile on the floor. He
reaches for the faucet and sends a stream of water
pounding against the porcelain tub. JEZZIE enjoys
JACOB's nakedness. She reaches out to his chest and
squeezes one of his nipples. His body tenses slightly.
JEZZIE drops her robe. They enter the shower together.


11  EXT.    VIETNAM — NIGHT

A DENSE RAIN falls on a dark night filling puddles of
water. JACOB is crawling through the underbrush in the
Vietnamese JUNGLE. His shirt is bloodsoaked. He moves
slowly, creeping on his right forearm. His left hand
is holding his intestines from spilling onto the
grass.

                              JACOB
          Help me. Someone.

Suddenly a flashlight beam can be seen in the
distance. It dances around the bamboo trees and draws
closer to JACOB. It is impossible to see who is
carrying it. The light darts near the ground where
JACOB is lying and then bursts directly into his eyes.

                                        (CONTINUED)

12  INT.   JACOB'S APT. — DAY

SUNLIGHT pours through the BEDROOM window. JACOB is
sleeping fitfully as a bar of light saturates his
face. His hand rushes up to cover and protect his eyes
but the damage is done. He is awake.

JACOB lies in bed for a few moments, dazed. Slowly his
hand gropes along the shelf at the head of the bed,
searching for his glasses. He has trouble finding
them. As his hand sweeps blindly across the headboard
it hits the telephone and sends it crashing to the
floor. He sits up with a disgusted look on his face
and searches the out-of-focus shelf behind him.
Suddenly JEZZIE enters.

                    JEZZIE
          You up?

                    JACOB
          No. Have you seen my glasses?

                    JEZZIE
               (shaking her head)
          Where'd you leave 'em?

                    JACOB
          I don't know.

                    JEZZIE
          Did you look around the headboard?

                    JACOB
               (wearily)
          Jezzie, I can't see.

                    JEZZIE
               (she scans the shelf)
          Maybe you left 'em in the bathroom.

She leaves and returns moments later with his glasses
and a large paper bag. She tosses them both onto the
bed.

                    JACOB
          Thanks.
               (he puts on his glasses
               and notices the bag)
          What's that?

                    JEZZIE
          Your kid dropped it off.

                    JACOB
          Who? Jed?

                    JEZZIE
               (stooping to pick up the
               phone)
          No. The little one.

                                        (CONTINUED)

10

                         JACOB
          Eli. Why can't you remember their
          names?

                         JEZZIE
          They're weird names.

                         JACOB
          They're Biblical. They were prophets.

                         JEZZIE
          Well, personally, I never went for
          church names.

                         JACOB
          And where do you think Jezebel comes
          from?

                         JEZZIE
          I don't let anybody call me that.

                         JACOB
                (shaking his head)
          You're a real heathen, you know that,
          Jezzie? Jesus, how did I ever get
          involved with such a ninny?

                         JEZZIE
          You sold your soul, remember? That's
          what you told me.

                         JACOB
          Yeah, but for what?

                         JEZZIE
          A good lay.

                         JACOB
          And look what I got.

                         JEZZIE
          The best.

                         JACOB
          I must have been out of my head.

                         JEZZIE
          Jake, you are never out of your head!

                         JACOB
                (ignoring the criticism
                and reaching for the
                paper bag)
          What's in here?

                         JEZZIE
          Pictures. Your wife was gonna toss
          'em so "what's his name" brought 'em
          over on his way to school.

                                        (CONTINUED)

JACOB lifts the bag and pours the photographs onto the
bed. There are hundreds of them. He examines them with
growing delight.

                    JACOB
          Look at these, will ya? I don't
          believe it. Jesus, these are
          fantastic. Look, here's my Dad ...
          And here's my brother, when we were
          down in Florida.

                    JEZZIE
          Lemme see.

                    JACOB
               (rummaging excitedly
               through the pile)
          Here. Look. This is me and Sarah when
          I was still at City College.

                    JEZZIE
               (looking closely)
          That's Sarah?
               (she studies the photo)
          I can see what you mean.

                    JACOB
          What?

                    JEZZIE
          Why you left.

                    JACOB
          What do you mean you can see?

                    JEZZIE
          Look at her face. A real bitch.

                    JACOB
          She looked good then.

                    JEZZIE
          Not to me.

                    JACOB
          Well, you didn't marry her.

He digs through some more photos. Suddenly he stops.

                    JEZZIE
          What's wrong?

To JEZZIE's surprise and his own, tears well up in his
eyes. For a moment JACOB is unable to speak. He just
stares at one of the photos. JEZZIE looks at the
picture. It is an image of JACOB carrying a small
child on his shoulders.

                    JEZZIE
          Is that the one who died?

                                        (CONTINUED)

                         JACOB
                    (nodding)
          Gabe.

JEZZIE is silent. JACOB grabs a Kleenex and blows his
nose.

                         JACOB
                    (continuing)
          Sorry. It just took me by surprise. I
          didn't expect to see him this morning
          ... God, what I wouldn't ... He was
          the cutest little guy. Like an angel,
          you know. He had this smile ...
                    (choking up again)
          Fuck, I don't even remember this
          picture.

Hiding his emotions, JACOB scrambles over the bed and
reaches for a pair of pants. He pulls out his wallet
and then carefully puts the photo of GABE inside. It
joins photos of his two other boys. JEZZIE begins
shoving the remaining pictures back into the paper bag.

                         JACOB
          Wait. Don't.

                         JEZZIE
          I don't like things that make you
          cry.

                         JACOB
          I just want to look ...

He reaches into the pile for other snapshots. We see
an array of frozen moments, happy, unfocused, obscure.
Suddenly he stops and stares at a yellowing snapshot.

                         JACOB
          God, this is me!
                    (he holds up a baby
                    photo)
          Look. It's dated right after I was
          born.
                    (he stares at it
                    intently)
          What a kid. Cute, huh? So much
          promise.

JEZZIE surveys the scene.

                         JEZZIE
          It's amazing, huh Jake? Your whole
          life ... right in front of you.
                    (she pauses before
                    making her final
                    pronouncement)
          What a mess!

                         13

13  INT.   HALLWAY — DAY

JEZZIE carries the garbage to an INCINERATOR ROOM down
the hall. She is carrying several bags. Two of them
are tossed instantly down the chute. She hesitates
with the third. After a moment she reaches into it and
pulls out a handful of photos. They are pictures of
JACOB and SARAH. With cool deliberation she drops them
down the chute. An apartment door slams shut. Quickly
she disposes of the pictures remaining in her hand.
JACOB opens the door to the tiny room as the bag
filled with the memories of his life falls to the fire
below.

                    JACOB
          Ready?

                    JEZZIE
          Just gettin' rid of the garbage.

JACOB and JEZZIE, both wearing postal uniforms, head
for the ELEVATOR. They are surprised that it has
arrived promptly. JEZZIE reaches out and playfully
sticks her tongue into JACOB's ear. He pulls her into
the ELEVATOR. They disappear, laughing, behind its
closing doors.


14  EXT.   NEW YORK CITY — DAY

JACOB is driving a mail truck through the crowded
streets of midtown Manhattan. As he drives he is
humming to himself a rendition of Al Jolson's "Sonny
Boy."

JACOB stops his truck in front of a LAUNDRY on West
46th Street. He opens the back door and pulls a stack
of boxes toward him. He lifts them with effort and
slams the door with his foot. It doesn't close. He
considers giving it another whack but the boxes are
heavy. He turns instead and waddles toward the store.


15  INT.   LAUNDRY — DAY

A heavyset WOMAN with a dark tan is standing behind a
counter cluttered with laundry. A picture of Richard
Nixon is still stapled to the wall. She looks at
JACOB.

                    WOMAN
          Where do you expect me to put those?
          I don't have any room.

She tries clearing the counter, but it doesn't help.

                                        (CONTINUED)

>                    WOMAN
>                  (continuing)
>     How 'bout over there?
>           (she points to a table)
>     No wait. Do me a favor. Bring 'em to
>     the back room.

>                    JACOB
>     They're awfully heavy.

>                    WOMAN
>     I know. That's why I'm asking.

JACOB waddles reluctantly toward the back of the store.
CHINESE LAUNDERERS are hovering over piles of clothes.
Steam from the pressing machines shoots into the air.

>                    JACOB
>              (huffing and puffing)
>     Where's Wong?

>                    WOMAN
>     That's what I'd like to know. If you
>     see him on the street somewhere, tell
>     him he's fired.

JACOB stoops to put the boxes on the shelf. There is a
snapping sound and he winces in pain. Massaging his
back, JACOB unfolds some papers for the WOMAN's
signature.

>                    JACOB
>     How was Palm Springs?

>                    WOMAN
>     Hot. Where do I sign?

>                    JACOB
>              (pointing to the line)
>     You got a nice tan, though.

>                    WOMAN
>     Tan? What tan? It faded on the
>     airplane. I'd try to get my money
>     back, but who do you ask?
>           (she looks heavenward)
>     Two hundred dollars a night, for
>     what?

She hands JACOB the wrong sheet.

>                    JACOB
>     No. I'll take the other one.
>           (he takes it)
>     Right. Well it's good to have you
>     back. See you tomorrow, probably.

>                    WOMAN
>     If you're lucky.

(CONTINUED)

JACOB smiles to himself as he leaves the store. He walks carefully. His back is out.


## 16  INT.    MAIL TRUCK — DAY

ANGLE ON THE MAIL TRUCK stuck in traffic. Nothing is moving. Horns are blaring and drivers are agitated. JACOB reaches for a newspaper lying on top of his mail bags. To his shock one of the bags appears to move. Curious, JACOB pokes at it. Instantly a terrifying figure pops out from beneath it and stares at him with a frightening glare. JACOB jumps back, stunned. It is a moment before he realizes that he is looking at an old WINO who has been sleeping in the truck. The man's face is covered in strange bumps.

> JACOB
> Goddamn it! What the hell ... ?

> WINO
> (pleading)
> I didn't take nothin'. I was just napping. Don't hit me. I was cold.

> JACOB
> (lifting the man up)
> What the hell do you think you're doing? You can't do this. This is government property.

He begins opening the door. The WINO begs.

> WINO
> Don't throw me out. They're gonna get me. They'll tear me to pieces.

He holds on to JACOB's leg. JACOB tries to pull away.

> JACOB
> Come on. You can't stay here.

> WINO
> Please! I never hurt anybody when I was alive. Believe me. I don't belong here.

JACOB gives the WINO a strange look and then escorts him from the truck. A hundred eyes peer out of motionless cars and follow him as he leads the WINO to the sidewalk. JACOB pulls a dollar bill from his pocket and places it in the WINO's hand. The OLD MAN crumples it into a ball and turns away. He has a frightened look on his face. JACOB returns to the truck shaking his head.

> JACOB
> New York!

(CONTINUED)

16 CONTINUED:

He climbs into his seat and glances into his rear view
mirror. He notices the WINO edging fearfully along the
side of a building. A horn honks and traffic begins
moving. When JACOB looks back the WINO is no longer
there.

17  INT.   GARAGE — DAY

JACOB drives his mail truck into the huge POST OFFICE
PARKING GARAGE on 34th Street. His mind seems
distracted. He has difficulty parking.

18  INT.   POST OFFICE — DAY

We see a vast room filled with hundreds of PEOPLE
sorting and moving mail.

JACOB, carrying a bag of McDonald's hamburgers, walks
stiffly through the aisles, his left hand rubbing his
back. Several workers greet him and grab for his
french fries. He offers them around.

ANGLE ON a conveyor belt sorting mail. A hand reaches
in, correcting mistakes. Suddenly a hamburger passes
by. JEZZIE looks up and smiles.

                    JEZZIE
          Jake!

                    JACOB
          How's it going?

She takes the hamburger and shrugs.

                    JACOB
                 (continuing)
          I'm going home.

                    JEZZIE
          What's wrong?

                    JACOB
          I don't know. One of these days, I'm
          gonna see Louis. My back's killing
          me.

                    JEZZIE
          Now? What about the boss? He's not
          gonna like it.

JACOB shrugs.

                    JEZZIE
                 (continuing)
          Well, I'll miss riding home with you.
          I was looking forward to it.

                                        (CONTINUED)

> JACOB
> I'll be glad to avoid the crush.

> JEZZIE
> I enjoy crushing into you.

She grabs him and hugs him tightly.

> JACOB
> Gently. My back.

JEZZIE ignores him and squeezes again.

## 19 INT.    CHIROPRACTIC OFFICE — DAY

CUT ON A SCREAM to JACOB in a CHIROPRACTOR'S OFFICE.
He is lying on a long leather padded device that looks
like an instrument of torture. LOUIS, the Chiropractor, is a giant of a man, 280 pounds.  He is
adjusting JACOB's spine.

> LOUIS
> Come on, Jake. That didn't hurt.

> JACOB
> How do you know?

> LOUIS
> I know you. How come you're so tense
> today?

> JACOB
> What can I tell you?

> LOUIS
> I saw Sarah the other day.

> JACOB
> Her knee acting up?

> LOUIS
> A bit.

> JACOB
> What did she have to say?

> LOUIS
> Turn on your right side.
>         (he turns on his left)
> How about the other "right"?
>         (JACOB turns back)
> I don't understand you philosophers.
> You've got the whole world figured
> out but you can't remember the
> difference between right and left.

> JACOB
> I was absent the day they taught that
> in school. What did she say?

(CONTINUED)

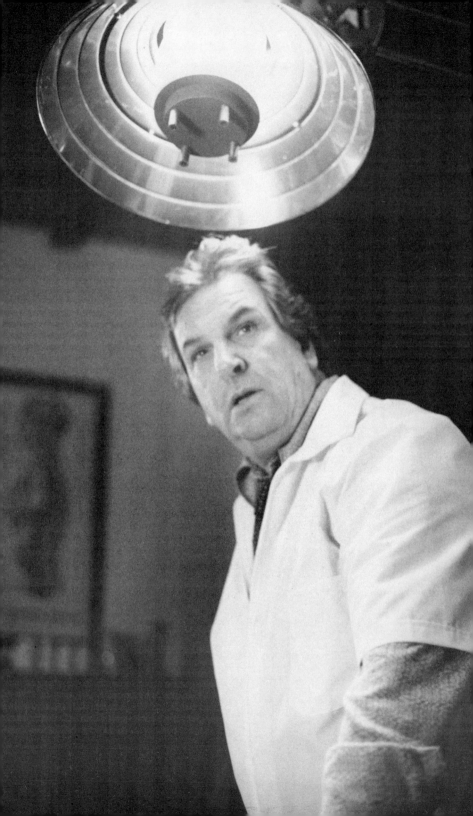

> LOUIS

Who?

> JACOB

Sarah.

> LOUIS

Not much. She's like you that way.
Two clams. No wonder your marriage
didn't last. Put your hand under your
head. Take a breath and then let it
out.

He makes a rapid adjustment pushing down on JACOB's
thigh. JACOB groans.

> LOUIS
> (continuing)

Ah, good. Now turn to your left.

> JACOB

She talk about the boys?

> LOUIS

She says she can't get them new coats
because you haven't sent the alimony
for three months.

> JACOB

She told you that?
> (he shakes his head)
Did she tell you about the $2,000 I'm
still paying for the orthodontist?
I'll bet she didn't mention that.

> LOUIS

She said you were a son of a bitch
and she regrets the day she set eyes
on you.

> JACOB

I thought you said she didn't say
much.

> LOUIS

She didn't. That's about all she
said. Put your hand up. Good. I think
she still loves you. Take a breath
and let it out.

He makes an adjustment. JACOB screams.

> JACOB

Loves me!? She hasn't said a kind
word about me in years.

> LOUIS

Right. She doesn't stop talking about

(CONTINUED)

19

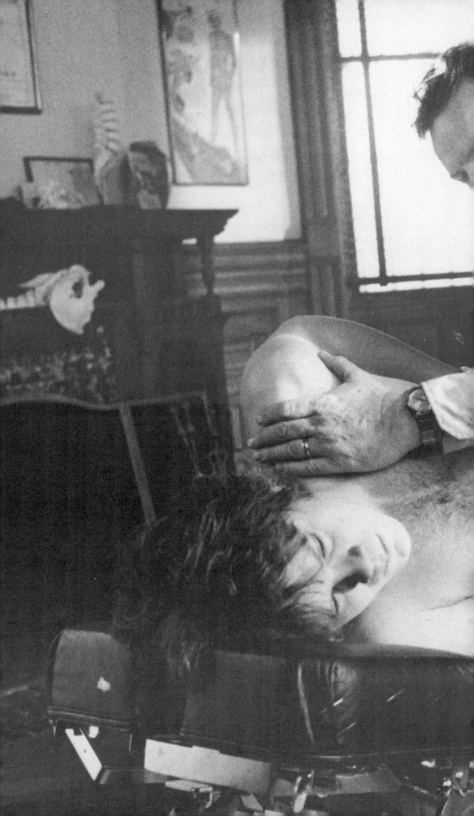

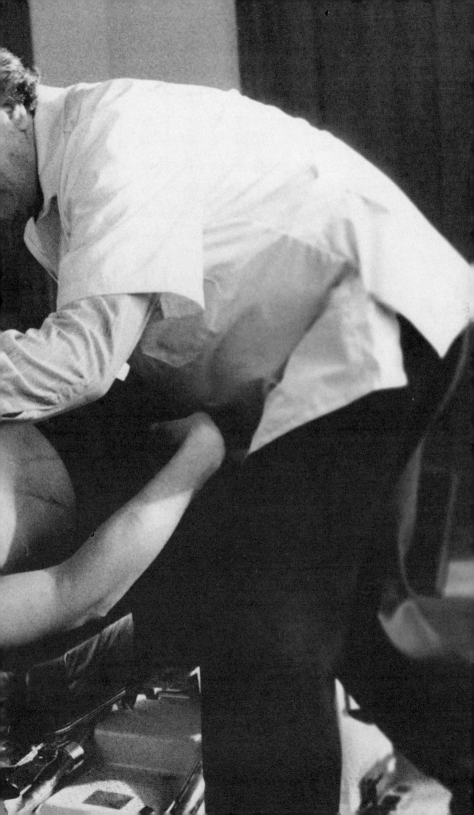

> > > LOUIS (CONT.)
> >
> > you. You're always on her mind.
> > That's love, Jake.

> > > JACOB
> >
> > She hates me, Louis.

> > > LOUIS
> >
> > You should go back to her.

> > > JACOB
> >
> > What? She threw me out, remember. She
> > wanted some professor to carry her
> > far away from Brooklyn. Only we
> > didn't make it. She can't forgive me
> > that she still lives in the same
> > house she grew up in.

> > > LOUIS
> >
> > Her problem is that you spent eight
> > years getting a PhD and then went to
> > work for the post office.

> > > JACOB
> >
> > What can I tell you, Louis? After Nam
> > I didn't want to think anymore. I
> > decided my brain was too small an
> > organ to comprehend this chaos.

> > > LOUIS
> > > (looking at JACOB with
> > > affection)
> >
> > If it was any other brain but yours,
> > I might agree. Relax, this is going
> > to be strong.

> > > JACOB
> >
> > I can't relax.

> > > LOUIS
> >
> > Wiggle your toes.

JACOB wiggles his toes. At that instant, LOUIS twists
JACOB's neck rapidly. There is a loud cracking sound.


20  **EXT.    VIETNAM — NIGHT**

THERE IS A FLASH OF LIGHT. A MAN rushes at the camera
yelling.

> > > MAN
> >
> > I found one. He's alive.

He shines a flashlight into the lens creating rings
and halos.

## 21  CHIROPRACTIC OFFICE — DAY

Suddenly LOUIS reappears, a halo effect still visible
behind his head.

> JACOB
> God almighty. What did you do to me?

> LOUIS
> I had to get in there. A deep
> adjustment. Rest a moment and let it
> set a bit.

> JACOB
> I had this weird flash just then.

> LOUIS
> What?

> JACOB
> I don't know. I've been having them
> recently.
> > (he thinks a moment,
> > then changes the
> > subject)
> You know, you look like an angel,
> Louis, an overgrown cherub. Anyone
> ever tell you that?

> LOUIS
> Yeah. You. Every time I see you. No
> more Errol Flynn, okay? Your back
> won't take it. You tell your girl
> friend to calm down if she knows
> what's good for you.

> JACOB
> Louis, you're a life saver.

> LOUIS
> I know.


## 22  EXT.   BROOKLYN STREETS — EVENING

JACOB is walking down Nostrand Avenue. He is singing
to himself and imitating Al Jolson.

> JACOB
> When there are gray skies, I don't
> mind the gray skies, as long as
> there's you ...

He hums. It is near dusk and lights are just coming
on. The shop windows have a particularly garish look
about them. The mannequins are dressed in inexpensive,
almost tawdry, clothes and have a pathetic appearance.
A few shops have set up their Christmas decorations.

(CONTINUED)

21

The ornamentation seems strangely out of place: almost blasphemous.

JACOB passes a street gang standing in the doorway of a local drug store. They chortle and make taunting sounds.

>                    GIRL
>              (shaking her tits,
>              singing)
>         "Hey, Mr. Postman ... "

JACOB stops and stares at them. To their surprise, he begins to sing with them. He knows the words. They like that. It is a sweet moment.

JACOB continues walking. He comes to a cross street. The light is green. He is still singing to himself and does not notice a BLACK CAR charging around the corner. The car is moving at full speed, heading straight toward him. A YOUNG MAN walking a few steps behind yells out.

>                    YOUNG MAN
>         Look out!

JACOB turns and sees the car. He scoots out of the way but it swerves in his direction. The YOUNG MAN calls out again.

>                    YOUNG MAN
>         Jump!

With a huge thrust, JACOB hurls himself onto the curb as the car shoots by. Two MEN are peering at him from the back seat. They are laughing like madmen and shaking their heads. They do not look human. JACOB yells and waves his fist, to no effect. After a moment he turns to thank the YOUNG MAN whose scream had saved him, but he is gone.


23  **INT.   JACOB'S APT. — DUSK**

JACOB and JEZZIE are lying in bed. They are a sensual couple and even in quiet, reflective moments such as this, their positioning is erotic and stimulating. Both of them are nude. JACOB's hands are clasped behind his neck and he is staring mournfully at the ceiling. JEZZIE is lying on her side, her left leg draped across JACOB's pelvis. Her head is propped up on her right arm while her left hand strokes the bayonet scar on JACOB's stomach. Neither are talking. Suddenly, out of the blue, JEZZIE speaks.

>                    JEZZIE
>         Maybe it's all the pressure, Jake.

(CONTINUED)

23 CONTINUED:

> JEZZIE (CONT.)
> The money. Things like that. Or your
> wife.

> JACOB
> Why do you bring her up?

> JEZZIE
> 'Cause she's always on your mind.

> JACOB
> When was the last time I said a word?

> JEZZIE
> It has nothin' to do with talkin'.

She pauses for a while, long enough to suppose that
the conversation is over. Then she continues.

> JEZZIE
> (continuing)
> Or maybe it's the war.

JACOB closes his eyes.

> JEZZIE
> (continuing)
> It's still there, Jake.
> (she points to his
> brain)
> Even if you never say a word about
> it. You can't spend two years in
> Vietnam ...

> JACOB
> (annoyed)
> What does that have to do with
> anything? Does it explain the
> barricaded subway stations? Does it
> explain those Godforsaken creatures?

> JEZZIE
> New York is filled with creatures.
> Everywhere. And lots of stations are
> closed.

> JACOB
> They're like demons, Jez.

> JEZZIE
> Demons, Jake? Come on. They're winos
> and bag ladies. Low life. That's all
> they are. The streets are crawling
> with 'em. Don't make 'em into
> somethin' they're not.
> (she rubs his forehead)
> It's the pressure, honey. That's all
> it is.

(CONTINUED)

23

                    JACOB
        Those guys tried to kill me tonight.
        They were aiming right at me.

                    JEZZIE
        Kids on a joy ride. Happens all the
        time.

                    JACOB
        They weren't human!

                    JEZZIE
        Come on. What were they, Jake?

JACOB doesn't answer. He turns over on his stomach.
JEZZIE stares at his naked back and drags her finger-
nails down to his buttocks. Scratch marks follow in
their wake.

                    JEZZIE
        You still love me?

He does not respond.


24  INT.   JACOB'S KITCHEN — DAY

JACOB and JEZZIE are sitting at the breakfast table.
JEZZIE is reading the National Enquirer and chewing at
her lip. Suddenly a drop of blood forms and falls onto
the formica table top. Staring at it for a moment, she
wipes it with her finger and then licks it with her
tongue.

JACOB is nursing a cup of coffee and staring out the
window at the housing project across the way. The
toaster pops. JEZZIE jumps. She gets up, butters her
toast, and returns to her paper.

                    JEZZIE
        Says here the world's comin' to an
        end. The battle of heaven and hell
        they call it. Should be quite a show;
        fireworks, H bombs, and everything.
        You believe them, Jake?

JACOB doesn't answer.

                    JEZZIE
                 (continuing)
        Me neither ... God, look at this. Two
        heads. Only lived two days. A day for
        each head. Could you imagine me with
        two heads? We'd probably keep each
        other up all night — arguing and
        whatnot. You wanna see the picture?

He does not respond. JEZZIE gets up and walks over to

(CONTINUED)

JACOB. Standing in front of him she slowly unties her
robe and lets it fall apart. She is naked underneath it.
Sensuously she leans forward, unbuttons his shirt, and
strokes his chest. She waits for a response from him,
but there is none. He sits silently, disinterested.

Furious, JEZZIE turns away. Grabbing the vacuum
cleaner from the broom closet she angrily unravels the
cord and switches it on. Breasts flash from beneath
her gown as the vacuum roars back and forth across the
floor.

> JEZZIE
> (continuing)
> Goddamn you son-of-a-bitch! My
> uncle's dogs used to treat me better
> than you do. At least they'd lick my
> toes once in a while. At least they
> showed some fucking interest.

A NEIGHBOR bangs on the wall, shouting.

> JEZZIE
> All right! All right! All right!

JACOB peers at the courtyard eighteen stories below
and watches the patterns of early morning movement.
Tiny figures drift purposefully over the concrete.

Suddenly the vacuum cleaner goes off. In the silence,
JACOB realizes that JEZZIE is crying and turns to see
her curled over the kitchen table. He walks to her
side and strokes her hair. JEZZIE begins to sob. After
a moment she looks at him with puffy eyes.

> JEZZIE
> You love me?

He nods his head "yes". She smiles coyly and rubs her
hair like a kitten against his crotch. After a few
moments she speaks.

> JEZZIE
> (continuing)
> Della's party's tonight.Why don't we
> go? It'll take your mind offa things.
> And I won't make you dance. I
> promise. Huh?
> > (he nods his head in
> > consent. JEZZIE hugs
> > him)
> You still love me, Jake?

He nods his head again, only heavily, as though the
question exhausts him.

25  INT.  **BELLEVUE HOSPITAL — DAY**

JACOB is in the "Mental Health Clinic" at BELLEVUE HOSPITAL walking through the PSYCHIATRIC EMERGENCY ROOM. It is overflowing with people. Some are hand-cuffed to their chairs. POLICEMEN are with them. JACOB approaches the main RECEPTION DESK. He speaks nervously.

>                   JACOB
>         I'd like to speak to Dr. Carlson,
>         please.
>
>                   RECEPTIONIST
>         Carlson? Is he new here?
>
>                   JACOB
>         New? He's been here for years.

She shrugs and looks at a log book.

>                   RECEPTIONIST
>         Not according to my charts. Do you
>         have an appointment?
>
>                   JACOB
>             (shaking his head)
>         Look, I need to see him. I know where
>         his room is. Just give me a pass. I
>         won't be long. Ten minutes.
>
>                   RECEPTIONIST
>         Our doctors are seen by appointment
>         only.
>
>                   JACOB
>         Damn it. I was in the veterans' out-
>         patient program. He knows me.
>
>                   RECEPTIONIST
>             (not happy)
>         What's your name?
>
>                   JACOB
>         Jacob Singer.

She walks over to a file drawer and goes through it several times before coming back over to JACOB.

>                   RECEPTIONIST
>         I'm sorry but there's no record of a
>         Jacob Singer in our files.
>
>                   JACOB
>         Whataya mean, no record?
>
>                   RECEPTIONIST
>         You want me to spell it out? There's
>         nothing here.

(CONTINUED)

                    JACOB
          That's ridiculous. I've been coming
          here for years. Listen to me. I'm
          going out of my fucking mind here. I
          need to see him.

                    RECEPTIONIST
          If this is an emergency we have a
          staff of psychiatric social workers.
          There's about an hour's wait. I'll be
          glad to take your name. Why don't you
          just fill out this form?

                    JACOB
          Goddamn it! I don't want a social
          worker. Carlson knows me.

JACOB pounds the desk, rattling a tiny African Violet
and knocking the RECEPTIONIST's forms onto the floor.
She grunts angrily and stoops to retrieve them.
Standing up her cap hits a drawer handle and slips
off. TWO KNUCKLE-LIKE HORNS protrude from her skull
where the cap had been. JACOB's eyes lock on them like
radar. He backs away. She immediately replaces her cap
and breaks the spell, but her eyes glare at him with
demonic intensity. JACOB, freaked, angry, turns and
runs toward the "In Patient" door.

                    RECEPTIONIST
          Hey! You can't go in there!

JACOB doesn't stop. A POLICEMAN, guarding the
entrance, runs after him.


26  JACOB charges through the interior corridors of the
    aging institution. A LINE OF MENTAL PATIENTS, all
    holding hands, is moving down the hall. They break
    ranks as he charges by and begin to scream. Their
    ATTENDANT tries to calm them down but the sight of the
    POLICEMAN increases their hysteria. They grab hold of
    him as he tries to get by.

                    POLICEMAN
          LET GO! GET AWAY!


27  INT.  GROUP ROOM — DAY

    JACOB dashes out of view. He runs down another
    corridor, wildly searching for a specific room. He
    finds it and rushes inside. He is surprised to find A
    GROUP OF MEN AND WOMEN seated in a circle. They all
    look up at him.

                    LEADER
          Can I help you?

(CONTINUED)

> JACOB
>
> I'm looking for Dr. Carlson. Isn't
> this his office?

The LEADER stares at him uncomfortably. After a moment
he gets up and takes JACOB into a corner of the room.
Everyone is watching them. The LEADER speaks quietly.

> LEADER
>
> I'm so sorry. Obviously you haven't
> ... Dr. Carlson died.

> JACOB
> (stunned)
>
> Died?

> LEADER
>
> A car accident

> JACOB
>
> Jesus, Jesus! ... When?

> LEADER
>
> Last month, before Thanksgiving.

> JACOB
>
> How did it happen?

> LEADER
>
> No one knows. They say it blew up.

> JACOB
> (growing pale)
>
> Blew up? What do you mean it blew up?

The LEADER shrugs and tries to put his arm around
JACOB, but he pulls away.

> LEADER
>
> Do you want me to get someone?

> JACOB
>
> No. No. It's okay. I'm okay.

He backs quickly to the door. As he turns to leave he
realizes that all of the PEOPLE in the group are
watching him intently.

28  Unsettled, JACOB hurries back into the hallway. He is
frightened and confused. Suddenly a voice calls out.

> POLICEMAN
>
> HEY YOU! MAILMAN!

JACOB turns and sees the POLICEMAN waiting for him.
His gun is drawn.

(CONTINUED)

>                        POLICEMAN
>           Hold it. Just hold it. Where the hell
>           do you think you are? This is
>           Bellevue, for God's sake. People
>           running around here get shot.

The GROUP LEADER pokes his head out of the door and motions to the POLICEMAN.

>                         LEADER
>           It's alright. He's okay.

>                        POLICEMAN
>                (nodding, reholstering
>                 his gun)
>           Come on, get out of here. I wouldn't
>           want to interfere with the U.S. Mail.

He leads JACOB toward the lobby. JACOB does not look back.


## 29  INT.   DELLA'S APT. — NIGHT

WE HEAR LOUD DANCE MUSIC, SLY AND THE FAMILY STONE. JACOB is with some POST OFFICE EMPLOYEES at a crowded party in a small apartment. A DRUNK is telling a bad joke and trying to hold a glass of wine at the same time. It is constantly on the verge of spilling. JACOB is fixated on it. In the background, we see JEZZIE dancing and motioning for JACOB to join her. He nods no. The DRUNK, who keeps asking people if they "get it," takes JACOB's head nodding as a sign of confusion and keeps trying to re-explain the joke.

JACOB hears a strange noise and looks around. It seems to be coming from a covered bird cage. He goes over to it and lifts the cover. The BIRD is flapping its wings wildly as if trying to get out. The sound, loud and insistent, startles him. He lowers the cover.

In the DINING ROOM, several people are gathered around ELSA, an attractive black woman who is reading palms. She sees JACOB and calls over the music.

>                         ELSA
>           Hey, you! Let me look at your hand.

JACOB shrugs. DELLA, dancing near by, calls out.

>                         DELLA
>           Go on Jake. She reads 'em like a
>           book.

>                         JACOB
>           No, thanks.

>                                              (CONTINUED)

>                    DELLA
>         It's fun.

CUT TO A CLOSE UP OF JACOB'S HAND. ELSA is squeezing
the mounds and examining the lines. What begins as a
playful expression on her face turns suddenly serious.
She reaches for his other hand and compares the two of
them. JEZZIE looks over from her dancing and eyes the
scene jealously.

>                    ELSA
>         You have an unusual hand.

>                    JACOB
>         I could have told you that.

>                    ELSA
>         You see this line here? It's your
>         life line. Here's where you were
>         born. And this is where you got
>         married. You're a married man, huh?
>         Oh oh. Nope. Divorce. See this split.

She studies his life line with growing concern. JEZZIE
tries to get JACOB's attention. He ignores her.

>                    ELSA
>              (continuing)
>         You know, you got a strange line
>         here.

>                    JACOB
>              (examining it)
>         It's short, huh?

>                    ELSA
>         Short? It's ended.

>                    JACOB
>              (laughing)
>         Oh, terrific.

>                    ELSA
>         It's not funny. According to this ...
>         you're already dead.

>                    JACOB
>              (smiling)
>         Just my luck.

>                                        CUT TO:

THE DANCERS. Their movements are loose and getting
looser. The music is strong and insistent. The smokey
atmosphere disfigures the dancers and gives them a
strange, distorted appearance. Suddenly JEZZIE breaks
from the crowd and reaches for JACOB. He pulls away.
Some of the MALE DANCERS call out to him.

>                                   (CONTINUED)

DANCERS
Come on man, show your stuff.

JACOB is easily intimidated. Relenting, he glares at
JEZZIE and nods apologetically to ELSA. It is obvious
that he is embarrassed at his inadequacy on the dance
floor.

MAN
Come on professor. You got feet, too.

JACOB tries to smile but it is pained and unconvinc-
ing. JEZZIE is playing with him, mimicking his
movement. A number of DANCERS notice and laugh, which
only increases his discomfort. JEZZIE's taunting has a
strange effect on JACOB. He grows distant and with-
drawn, even though his body is still going through the
motions of the dance.

A MAN taps JEZZIE on the shoulder. She spins around,
smiling, and begins dancing with him. JACOB is left
alone, dancing by himself. He looks away, uncomfortable.

In the shadows a WOMAN kneels close to the floor. She
seems to be urinating on the carpet. JACOB is shocked.
Several DANCERS obscure his view. He turns around.

A PREGNANT WOMAN stands half naked in the kitchen.
JACOB cannot believe what he sees.

In the next room, past JEZZIE, JACOB glimpses a
terrifying image, a MAN whose head seems to be
vibrating at such enormous speed that it has lost all
definition. Something about the image compels and
frightens JACOB. Slowly he approaches it. As he draws
nearer to it the tortured image lets out a scream of
such pain and unearthly terror that JACOB backs away.

A WOMAN, laughing, grabs JACOB, spins him around, and
begins dancing with him. He is totally disoriented.

WOMAN
Hold me, baby!

She takes JACOB's arm and guides it to her back. THE
CAMERA follows his hand as it reaches the smooth skin
beneath her sexy, loose fitting dress. He runs his
fingers up to her shoulder blades. Then, suddenly, he
recoils. Her back is a mass of shoulder blades,
hundreds of strange, bony protrusions. JACOB gasps.
Out of the blue, JEZZIE leans into him and wiggles her
tongue in his ear. JACOB, startled, jerks his head and
his glasses go flying to the floor.

JACOB
Shit!

(CONTINUED)

31

He stoops down blindly to pick them up. Shoes just miss his fingers as he digs between dancing legs trying to recover them. Miraculously, he grabs the spectacles just before they are crushed and slips them back on. Instantly his world comes back into focus.

As he stands, JACOB is surprised to find JEZZIE facing him, gyrating in wild abandon. There is a huge, satisfied smile on her face. She grabs his hand as if encouraging him to dance but it is obvious that she is dancing to her own rhythm. JACOB stares at her, confused. It takes him a moment to realize that her smile is not for him.

Standing behind JEZZIE is another DANCER, his hands around her waist. They are moving together, locked in erotic embrace. It appears that he is mounting her from behind. Looking down we see that the DANCER's feet are deformed. They have a bizarre clubbed appearance and look very much like hooves. They skid and career amidst the dancing feet.

Something horrible and winglike flaps behind JEZZIE's back. We cannot make out what it is, but it elicits a primal terror. Before JACOB can react, JEZZIE opens her mouth. With a roaring sound, a spiked horn erupts from her throat. It juts menacingly from between her teeth and thrusts into the air. A CIRCLE OF DANCERS scream out in excited approval.

CUT TO JACOB's face as it registers terror and disbelief. He stares at the DANCERS who are crowding around him. They have become perverse, corrupt aspects of their normal selves.

JACOB grabs his eyes as though trying to pull the vision from his head but it won't go away. The music throbs. His actions become spastic, almost delirious.

JACOB is out of control. His frenzy becomes a kind of exorcism, a desperate attempt to free himself from his body and his mind. WE MOVE IN ON HIM as his eyes pass beyond pain. The dark walls of the APARTMENT fade away.

30  **EXT.   VIETNAM — NIGHT**

Strange faces in infantry helmets appear in the darkness, outlined by a bright moon that is emerging from behind a cloud. The faces are looking down and voices are speaking.

> VOICE
> He's burning up.

> VOICE
> Total delirium.

(CONTINUED)

> VOICE
> That's some gash. His guts keep
> spilling out.
>
> VOICE
> Push 'em back.
>
> JACOB (V.O.)
> Help me!

His eyes focus on the moon. Rings of light emanate
from it filling the sky with their sparkling
brilliance. The rings draw us forward with a
quickening intensity that grows into exhilarating
speed. The rush causes them to flash stroboscopically
and produces a dazzling, almost sensual, surge of
color. The display is spectacular and compelling.

Music can be heard in the distance, growing hard and
insistent, like a heart beat. Heavy breathing
accompanies the sound. The stroboscopic flashes are
replaced by intense flashes of red and blue light. The
music grows louder and reaches a thundering crescendo.
Then silence.

31  INT.  DELLA'S APT. — NIGHT

The APARTMENT reappears in all its normalcy. The neon
sign is still flashing outside the window. DANCERS are
smiling and sweating.

Cheers and applause ring out for JACOB and JEZZIE but
JACOB barely hears them. JEZZIE hugs him tightly.
PEOPLE smack him on the back.

> ADMIRER
> You are out of your mind, man. Out of
> your fuckin' mind.
>
> WOMAN
> Jake, you little devil. You never
> told me you could dance like that.
>
> MAN
> Jezzie, what did you put in his
> drink?

JEZZIE smiles while pulling JACOB to a corner chair.
He plops down. His chest is heaving and he is grabbing
hold of his stomach. His face is frightened and
distorted.

> JEZZIE
> You okay?
>
> JACOB
> I wanna leave. Get me out of here.

(CONTINUED)

                         JEZZIE
          Oh, come on. It's early.

                         JACOB
                    (pulling JEZZIE close to
                    him, his voice filled
                    with paranoia)
          Where are we?
                         JEZZIE
                    (surprised by the
                    question)
          We're at Della's.

                         JACOB
          Where?

                         JEZZIE
          What do you mean? Where do you think?

                         JACOB
          Where's Della? Bring her here.

                         JEZZIE
          Why? What for?

                         JACOB
          *Show me Della!*

                         JEZZIE
                    (confused)
          Hey, *I'm* here.

JACOB eyes her with a pleading look. Annoyed, JEZZIE
leaves JACOB and crosses the room. He watches her as
she goes. JACOB is holding his stomach and rocking
painfully. Moments later JEZZIE returns with DELLA.

                         DELLA
          Hiya Jake. That was some dance.

                         JACOB
                    (staring at her closely)
          Della?

                         DELLA
                    (feeling the
                    strangeness)
          You want to see me? Well, here I am.

                         JACOB
          I see.

                         DELLA
          What do you want?

                         JACOB
          Just to see you. That's all.

                                        (CONTINUED)
                         34

>                           DELLA
>                    (a bit uncomfortable)
>            Well, how do I look?

>                           JACOB
>            Like Della.

Suddenly JACOB breaks out in a dense sweat and begins
shaking. His entire body is convulsive.

>                           JEZZIE
>            Are you feeling all right? Shit,
>            you're burning up. Feel his forehead.

>                           DELLA
>                    (checking his forehead
>                    and cheeks)
>            Damn, that's hot. Maybe from dancing.

>                           JEZZIE
>            I think you should lie down.

JACOB is shaking uncontrollably. People are gathering
around.

>                           JEZZIE
>                    (continuing)
>            Can't you stop it?

>                           JACOB
>            If I could stop it, I'd stop it.

>                           WOMAN
>            Is he sick?

>                           DELLA
>            He's on fire.

>                           ELSA
>            Let me help you.

She reaches out to JACOB. Unexpectedly he recoils,
jumping to his feet like a wild man. He begins to
scream.

>                           JACOB
>            Stay away from me! Don't you come
>            near me! All of you. Go to hell! Go
>            to hell, goddamn you! Stay away!

JEZZIE stares at JACOB with a confused and embarrassed
look. A MAN whispers to her.

>                           MAN
>            I'll call a cab.

32 INT.   JACOB'S APT — NIGHT

JACOB is lying in bed in his own BEDROOM with a
thermometer in his mouth. JEZZIE is pacing the floor
with great agitation.

                    JEZZIE
          I've never been so mortified in my
          whole life. Never! Screaming like
          that. I don't understand what's
          gotten into you, Jake, to make you do
          a thing like that. You're not acting
          normal. I've lived with too many
          crazies in my life. I don't want it
          anymore. I can't handle it. I'm tired
          of men flipping out on me. Shit,
          you'd think it was my fault. Well you
          picked me, remember that. I don't
          need this.

The NEIGHBOR pounds on the wall.

                    JEZZIE
                 (continuing)
          All right! All right!

JEZZIE jabs her finger at the wall.

                    JEZZIE
                 (continuing)
          If you go crazy on me you're goin'
          crazy by yourself. You understand?

JEZZIE reaches for his mouth and pulls out the thermometer. She looks at it closely and then squints to
see it better.

                    JACOB
          What's it say? A hundred and two?

                    JEZZIE
          I don't believe this. I'm calling the
          doctor.

She runs out of the room. JACOB calls after her.

                    JACOB
          What does it say?

                    JEZZIE (V.O.)
          It's gone to the top.

                    JACOB
          How high is that?

                    JEZZIE (V.O.)
          The numbers stop at 107.

JEZZIE is on the phone to the doctor in the next room.

                                        (CONTINUED)

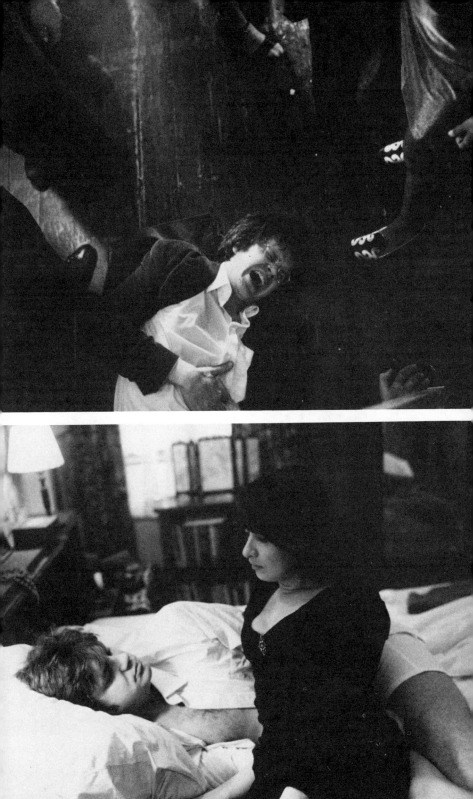

JACOB begins shaking again and reaches for the extra
blanket at the foot of the bed. He pulls it up around
his shoulders. The whole bed vibrates with his
shivering. Suddenly JEZZIE rushes through the BEDROOM
and into the BATHROOM. She turns on the bath water.

> JACOB
> What the hell are you doin'?

> JEZZIE
> Get your clothes off.

> JACOB
> What are you talking about? I'm
> freezing.

> JEZZIE
> Get your clothes off!

JACOB gives her a confused look as she rushes back to
the KITCHEN.

> JACOB
> What'd the doctor say?

> JEZZIE (V.O.)
> That you'd die on the way to the
> hospital. Now get into that tub.

JACOB stares at her as she bursts back into the
BEDROOM carrying four trays of ice cubes. She hurries
into the BATHROOM and dumps them in the tub.

> JEZZIE (V.O.)
> He's coming right over.

> JACOB
> Coming here?

> JEZZIE (V.O.)
> Goddamn it. Get in here. I can't
> stand around waiting.

She rushes out of the BATHROOM and pulls JACOB out of
bed. He is shaking violently and she has difficulty
navigating across the room and undressing him at the
same time. She maneuvers him into the BATHROOM next to
the tub. He looks down at the ice cubes floating in
the water.

> JACOB
> You're out of your mind. I'm not
> getting in there. I'd rather die.

> JEZZIE
> That's your decision.

> JACOB
> Look at me. I'm ice cold.

(CONTINUED)

37

32  CONTINUED:

> JEZZIE
> You're red hot, damn it. Get in
> there. I've got to get more ice.

She runs out of the room. The door to the apartment
slams shut. JACOB sticks his toe into the water and
pulls it out again instantly.

> JACOB
> Oh Jesus!

He sticks his whole foot in and grits his teeth as the
ice cold water turns his foot bright red. He keeps it
in as long as he can and then yanks it out, quickly
wrapping it in a towel. JACOB rubs his foot vigorously
to get rid of the sting and stares at the water,
afraid of its pain.


33  **INT.   CORRIDOR — NIGHT**

JEZZIE is running up and down the CORRIDOR knocking on
doors and collecting ice cubes from those who will
answer. She hurries back to the BATHROOM with several
PEOPLE behind her carrying additional ice trays. One
of the MEN is shifting the trays in his hands to avoid
the burning cold.


34  **INT.   JACOB'S BATHROOM**

As JEZZIE enters the BATHROOM, JACOB is sitting on the
rim of the tub with the water up to his calves,
shivering vigorously.

> JACOB
> I can't do it.

> JEZZIE
> What kind of man are you?

She unloads two trays into the water.

> JACOB
> Don't gimme that.

> JEZZIE
> Lie down!

> JACOB
> (pleading)
> Jezzie! My feet are throbbing!

> JEZZIE
> (calling out)
> Sam, Tony, come in here.

(CONTINUED)

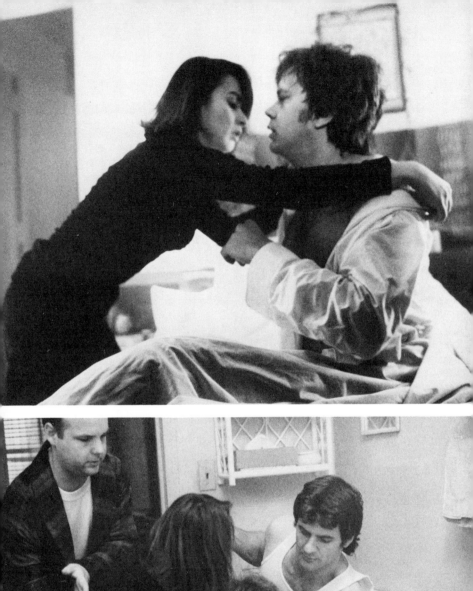
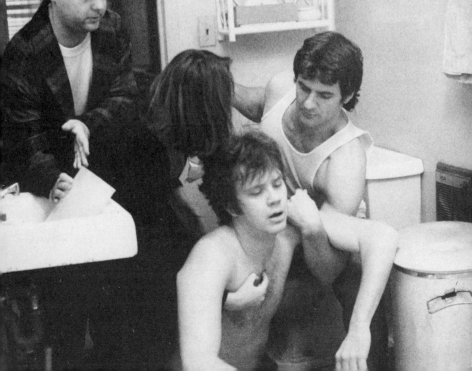

> JACOB
> Hey, I'm not dressed.

> SAM
> You got nothin' we ain't seen before.

SAM and TONY grab hold of JACOB who wrestles to get away.

> JACOB
> Get the hell off me.

> TONY
> He's like a hot coal.

> SAM
> It's for your own good, Jake.

> JACOB
> Let go of me, you sons of bitches.

The TWO MEN struggle with JACOB and force him into the water. TONY winces when the water hits his arm. JACOB nearly flies out of the tub. The TWO MEN fight to hold him down. JACOB screams and cries for the MEN to let him go but they keep him flat on his back.

> JACOB
> (continuing)
> I'm freezing! I'm freezing! Goddamn you!

> TONY
> (his hand turning red)
> Sam, I can't take it.

> SAM
> Don't you let go.

> TONY
> Jez, get help. My hands are killing me.

> JACOB
> Help me! Help me!

> JEZZIE
> (To TONY)
> Here. I'll do it.

> TONY
> Take his legs.

> SAM
> Run your hands under hot water.

MRS. CARMICHAEL comes in.

> MRS. CARMICHAEL
> I have some ice from the machine.

(CONTINUED)

                         JEZZIE
        Bring it in.

                    MRS. CARMICHAEL
        Is he all right?

                         JEZZIE
        He doesn't like it.

                    MRS. CARMICHAEL
        I don't blame him. What should I do
        with the ice?

                         JEZZIE
        Pour it in.

                    MRS. CARMICHAEL
        On top of him?

                         JEZZIE
        He's melting it as fast as we dump it
        in.

                    MRS. CARMICHAEL
        Okay. My husband's got two more bags.
        He's coming. They're heavy.

TONY helps her pour the ice into the water. JACOB
yells.

                         JACOB
        Oh God! You're killing me! Stop!


35  INT.   A BEDROOM — NIGHT

CUT TO JACOB lying in a BEDROOM we have not seen
before. He is tossing and turning in his bed as though
struggling to get out. Suddenly he sits up and looks
over at the window. It is open and the shade is
flapping. Cold air is blowing in and he is shivering.

                         JACOB
        Damn! You and your fresh air.

He jumps out of bed and goes over to the window. He
pushes at the frame and it comes flying down with a
loud bang. A woman in the bed sits up. It is SARAH.

                         SARAH
        What was that?

                         JACOB
        It's freezing.

                         SARAH
        I'm not cold.

                                        (CONTINUED)
                         40

                         JACOB
          Of course not. You have all the
          blankets. It must be ten degrees in
          here. I'm telling you, Sarah, if you
          want to sleep with fresh air, you
          sleep on the fire escape. From now on
          that window is closed.

                         SARAH
          It's not healthy with it closed.

                         JACOB
          This is healthy? I'll probably die of
          pneumonia tomorrow and this is
          healthy.

He settles back into bed and pulls the covers back
over to his side. He lies quietly for a moment,
thinking.

                         JACOB
                    (continuing)
          What a dream I was having. I was
          living with another woman ... You
          know who it was?

                         SARAH
          I don't want to know.

                         JACOB
          Jezebel, from the post office. You
          remember, you met her that time at
          the Christmas party. I was living
          with her. God, it was a nightmare.
          There were all these demons and I was
          on fire. Only I was burning from ice.

                         SARAH
          Guilty thoughts. See what happens
          when you cheat on me, even in your
          mind?

                         JACOB
          She was good in bed, though.

                         SARAH
          Go to sleep.

                         JACOB
          She had these real beefy thighs.
          Delicious.

                         SARAH
          I thought you said it was a
          nightmare?

Suddenly, out of nowhere, we hear the tinkling sound
of a music box. A YOUNG BOY enters the room, carrying

                                        (CONTINUED)

35 CONTINUED:

a musical LUNCH BOX in his arms. He is wearing a long
T shirt nearly down to his ankles. We recognize him
from his photograph. It is GABE.

                    GABE
         Daddy, what was that noise?

                    JACOB
              (surprised to see him)
         Gabe?
              (he stares curiously at
              his son)
         What are you doing ... ?

                    GABE
         There was a bang.

                    JACOB
         It was the window.

                    GABE
         It's cold.

                    JACOB
         Tell your mother.

                    GABE
         Mom, it's ...

                    SARAH
         I heard you. Go back to sleep.

                    GABE
         Will you tuck me in?

                    SARAH
              (not happily)
         Oh ... all right.

She starts to rise. JACOB stops her and gets up
instead. He whisks GABE upside down and carries him
into his

36  **GABE'S BEDROOM — NIGHT**

BEDROOM, licking his belly and tickling him all the
way. GABE laughs and snuggles into his pillow as soon
as he hits the bed. JED, 9, and ELI, 7, are in bunk
beds across the room. JED looks up.

                    JED
         Dad?

                    JACOB
         Jed. It's the middle of the night.
              (he kisses GABE and goes
              over to JED in the lower
              bunk)
         What's up?

                                    (CONTINUED)

                              JED
              You forgot my allowance.

                             JACOB
              Your allowance? It's five A.M. We'll
              talk at breakfast.

                              JED
              Okay, but don't forget.

Suddenly another voice pipes in from the top bunk.

                              ELI
              I love you, Dad.

JACOB smiles.

                             JACOB
              What is this, a convention? I love
              you, too, Pickles. Now go back to
              sleep.

He turns to leave.

                             GABE
              Wait ... Daddy,

                             JACOB
              Now what?

                             GABE
              Don't go.

                             JACOB
              Don't go?
                   (he smiles)
              I'm not going anywhere. I'm right
              here, Gabe.
                   (he looks at his son
                   tenderly)
              Come on, go back to sleep. You can
              still get a couple of hours.

He hugs him warmly and then walks to the door.

                             GABE
              ... I love you.

There is deep emotion and seriousness in GABE's words.
JACOB is struck by them.

                             GABE
                   (continuing)
              Don't shut the door.

JACOB nods and leaves it a tiny bit ajar.

                             GABE
                   (continuing)
              A bit more ... a bit more.

                                        (CONTINUED)
                        43

36  CONTINUED:

JACOB adjusts the opening enough to please GABE and
make him secure. GABE smiles and cuddles in his bed.


37  INT.    SARAH'S BEDROOM — NIGHT

JACOB settles back in bed. SARAH turns over and gets
comfortable. JACOB lies on his back facing the
ceiling. He pulls the blankets up to his neck. He is
overcome with feelings of sadness and longing.

                    JACOB
          I love you, Sarah.

She smiles warmly. His eyes close and in a matter of
seconds he is back asleep.


38  EXT.    VIETNAM — PRE DAWN

WE HEAR SUMMER MORNING SOUNDS, CRICKETS and BIRDS.
The image of trees materializes overhead and a
beautiful pink sky, just before sunrise, can be seen
through the branches. It is an idyllic setting.

Suddenly a strange sound can be heard in the distance,
a metallic humming, growing louder. There is a
scramble of feet and a sound of heavy boots moving
through the tall grass. Voices can be heard. Men's
voices.

                    VOICE
          They're here.

                    VOICE
          Thank God. Move 'em out!

                    VOICES
          Bust your balls!

                    VOICE
          Move it! Move it!

There is an instant swell of activity. Trees and
branches blur and speed by overhead. The idyllic image
of moments before reveals itself as a P.O.V. SHOT. The
CAMERA races out of a JUNGLE covering and into a huge
CLEARING.

High overhead a helicopter appears. Its blades whirl
with a deafening whine. Long lines drop from its belly
and dangle in mid-air. SOLDIERS leap up into the air
reaching for them. The air is filled with turbulence.
Tarps fly off dead bodies. SOLDIERS hold them down.
Voices yell but the words are not clear. They are
filled with urgency.

                                        (CONTINUED)

44

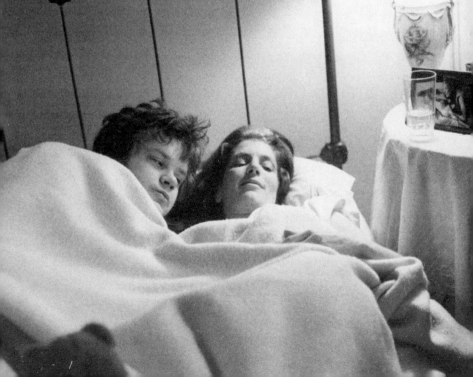

The CAMERA leaves the ground. The edges of the sky disappear as the helicopter's gray mass fills the frame. It grows larger and darker as the CAMERA approaches. Rivets and insignia dotting the underbelly come into view. Suddenly the stretcher begins spinning, out of control. Hands emerge from inside, reaching out to grab it.

Watery, womb-like sounds rise out of nowhere, the rippling of water, a heart beating. Gradually voices can be heard mumbling; distant sounds, warm and familiar.

39 INT.   BATHROOM — NIGHT

JACOB's DOCTOR reaches down to help him out of the tub. Surprisingly JEZZIE and MRS. CARMICHAEL are standing there too. JACOB stares at them in total confusion.

>                    DOCTOR
>           You are a lucky man, my friend. A
>           lucky man. You must have friends in
>           high places, that's all I can say.

SAM and TONY appear next to the DOCTOR. They are extending their hands to the P.O.V. CAMERA. JACOB's arms, nearly blue, reach out to them.

Slowly they lift him from the icy water. JACOB takes one step onto the tile and collapses to the floor.

CUT TO BLACK:

40 INT.   JACOB'S BEDROOM — DAY

FADE IN sounds of feet shuffling across the carpet. A glass rattles on a tray. A television is on low in the background. Slowly the CAMERA LENS opens from JACOB's P.O.V. and we see JEZZIE puttering around the BEDROOM. Suddenly she is aware that JACOB is watching her. She smiles.

>                    JEZZIE
>     Jake.
>               (she places her hand on
>               his head and strokes his
>               hair)
>     You're gonna be all right, Jake.
>     You're gonna be fine.

>                    JACOB
>     Am I home?

(CONTINUED)

40  CONTINUED:

                              JEZZIE
            You're here. Home. The doctor said
            you're lucky your brains didn't boil.
                         (she smiles)
            What a night, Jake. It was crazy. You
            kept sayin' "Sarah, close the
            window," over and over. And talkin'
            to your kids. Even the dead one.
            Weird. You know you melted 200 pounds
            of ice in 8 hours. Amazing, huh?

                              JACOB
            Are we in Brooklyn?

                              JEZZIE
            You're right here, Jake. You just
            rest.
                         (she puffs up his
                         pillow)
            The doctor said you had a virus.
            That's what they say when they don't
            know what it is. You can't do
            anything for a week. He says you
            gotta recuperate.
                         (she strokes his
                         forehead, and gets up)
            Now you just lie here. Mrs. Sandelman
            made you some chicken soup. It'll
            warm you up.

JEZZIE leaves the room. JACOB watches her as she goes.
He seems lost and confused.


41  INT.    JACOB'S KITCHEN — DAY

    JACOB, unshaven, wearing his bathrobe, is sitting at
    the KITCHEN TABLE. PILES OF BOOKS on demonology are
    spread out before him. He studies them to distraction.
    JEZZIE is standing by the counter making sandwiches.
    She wraps them in plastic Baggies and puts one in a
    lunch box, another in the refrigerator. She is dressed
    in her postal uniform.

                              JEZZIE
            You know, you really ought to get out
            today. You can't just sit around like
            this all the time. It's not healthy.
            It's not good for your mind. Go take
            a walk, or somethin'. Go to a movie.
            Christ, who's gonna know? You think I
            care? I don't give a shit. Go. Enjoy
            yourself. One of us should be having
            a good time.
                         (JEZZIE knocks on
                         JACOB's head)

                                          (CONTINUED)
                        46

> JEZZIE (CONT.)
> Hello! Anybody home?
>> (she looks in his ear)
> Anybody in there?

> JACOB
> What?

JEZZIE just stares at him. She does not respond. JACOB returns to his books.

CUT TO CLOSE UP IMAGES OF WINGED DEMONS, real demons, with spindly horns and long tails. JACOB's huge finger, magnified, scans page after page of ancient images and archaic text. JEZZIE, enraged at his lack of attention, returns to packing her lunch box. Suddenly she spins around.

> JEZZIE
> Goddamn it! I can't stand it anymore.
> I've had it up to here. Go ahead and
> rot if you want ... You son-of-a-
> bitch, I'm talking to you.

CUT BACK to the DEMONS. Suddenly a crashing sound catches JACOB's attention as a KITCHEN POT flies by his head. He looks up to see JEZZIE knocking pots and pans off the kitchen counter and kicking them wildly across the room. The noise is terrible. The intensity of her rage is shocking. The pots crash into every surface, knocking all his books onto the floor. And then, suddenly, she stops.

JEZZIE stoops down to the floor and picks up her sandwich, stuffs it back in its plastic Baggie, and puts it back in her lunch box. She is about to leave when she stops and looks at JACOB.

> JEZZIE
>> (continuing, her anger
>> in check)
> I made you a tuna fish sandwich. It's
> in the fridge. Eat a carrot with it.
> The aspirin's on the bottom shelf.
> We're out of soap so, if for some
> reason you decide to wash yourself
> again, use the dishwashing stuff.
>> (she walks out of the
>> room and returns with
>> her coat.)
> I'm sorry I yelled, but you get on my
> nerves.
>> (she bends down and
>> makes eye contact with
>> JACOB)
> Hello? Listen, I gotta go.

(CONTINUED)

JEZZIE sits on his lap, gives him a big kiss, and
then, unexpectedly, raises two fingers, like horns,
over her head. The gesture catches JACOB's full
attention.

>                    JEZZIE
>                 (continuing)
>         Look, I'm horny. Keep it in mind.
>                 (she kisses his cheek)
>         Love me a little?

>                    JACOB
>                 (speaking with
>                  affection)
>         You are the most unbelievable woman I
>         have ever met. One second you're a
>         screaming banshee and the next you're
>         Florence Nightingale. Who are you?
>         That's what I want to know. Will the
>         real Jezzie Pipkin please stand up.

Suddenly the telephone rings. It startles them.

>                    JEZZIE
>                 (continuing)
>         Oh shit. Tell 'em I've left.

JEZZIE grabs her jacket and shoves her arm in it
upside down. A pocketful of change falls on the floor.
JACOB smiles. JEZZIE curses as she struggles to pick
it up and get the jacket on right. JACOB gets the
phone.

>                    JACOB
>         Hello.

>                    PAUL (V.O.)
>         Jacob Singer?

>                    JACOB
>         Speaking.

>                    PAUL (V.O.)
>         Paul Gruneger!

>                    JACOB
>         Paul Gruneger! Well I'll be
>         goddamned!

JACOB indicates it's for him. JEZZIE throws him a kiss
goodbye and hurries out the door.

>                    JACOB
>                 (continuing)
>         Paul! You son-of-a-bitch, how the
>         hell are you? I haven't seen you in
>         what, five, six, years?

>                    PAUL (V.O.)
>         A long time.

(CONTINUED)

                         JACOB
          Jesus Christ. How've you been? What's
          happening in your life?

                         PAUL (V.O.)
          Nothin' much.

                         JACOB
          Me neither. Nothing too exciting. So
          tell me, to what do I owe the honor?

                         PAUL (V.O.)
          I need to see you, Jake.

                         JACOB
          Shit, Paul. I'd love to see you. But
          I'm kind of laid up here. I've been
          sick.

                         PAUL (V.O.)
          I *need* to see you.


42  INT.    PAUL'S CAR — DAY

     JACOB and PAUL are driving through EAST NEW YORK
     heading toward WILLIAMSBURG. The elevated trains
     rumble above them. JACOB pats PAUL on the back.

                         JACOB
          Jesus, man, you look terrific. You
          must have put on twenty pounds.

                         PAUL
          I work in a bakery.

                         JACOB
          You're lucky. How many vets you know
          are even employed?

                         PAUL
          Count 'em on one hand.

                         JACOB
          It's almost like a conspiracy, huh?

                         PAUL
          No joke. Fuckin' army! That goddamn
          war. I'm still fightin' it.

                         JACOB
          It's not worth it. You'll never win.

                         PAUL
          You tellin' me? How many times can
          you die, huh?

     PAUL looks in his rear view mirror before changing

                                             (CONTINUED)

42 CONTINUED:

lanes. He sees a black car tagging close behind him.
He pulls out. So does the car.

> PAUL
> (continuing)
> Still married, Jake?

> JACOB

Nope.

> PAUL
> You and everybody else. God I hate
> this area. Makes me nervous.

> JACOB
> Why the hell we drivin' here?

> PAUL
> I just need to talk.

> JACOB
> You can't talk in Brownsville?

> PAUL
> I'm not sure where I can talk
> anymore.

> JACOB

What's wrong?

> PAUL
> Let's get a coupla drinks, okay?
> (he looks at his rear
> view mirror)
> Hey, take a look behind us. Do you
> think that car is followin' us?

> JACOB
> (turning to look)
> That black car?

> PAUL
> Pull the mirror down on the sun
> visor.
> (JACOB does)
> Just watch 'em.

> JACOB
> What's goin' on Paul?

> PAUL

I don't know.

> JACOB
> You in trouble?

> PAUL

Yeah.

JACOB notices PAUL's left arm. It is shaking. The

black car passes on the left. Both PAUL and JACOB
stare at it as it speeds by.

## 43 INT. BAR — DAY

JACOB and PAUL are sitting in a dark booth in an
obscure WILLIAMSBURG BAR. It is nearly empty. PAUL is
leaning across the table in a very intimate fashion.

> PAUL
> Somethin's wrong, Jake. I don't know
> what it is but I can't talk to
> anybody about it. I figured I could
> with you. You always used to listen,
> you know?

JACOB nods. PAUL takes a sip of his drink and stares
deliberately into JACOB's eyes.

> PAUL
> (continuing)
> I'm going to Hell!

JACOB's face grows suddenly tense.

> PAUL
> (continuing)
> That's as straight as I can put it.
> And don't tell me that I'm crazy
> 'cause I know I'm not. I'm goin' to
> Hell. They're comin' after me.

> JACOB
> (frightened, but holding
> back)
> Who is?

> PAUL
> They've been followin' me. They're
> comin' outta the walls. I don't trust
> anyone. I'm not even sure I trust
> you. But I gotta talk to someone. I'm
> gonna fly outta my fuckin' mind.

PAUL cannot contain his fear. He jumps up suddenly
and walks away from the booth. JACOB follows him with
his eyes but does not go after him. A YOUNG MAN in the
next booth observes the scene with interest. He looks
vaguely familiar, like we have seen him before.

PAUL stares out the window for a moment and then walks
over to the juke box. He pulls a quarter out of his
pocket and drops it in the slot. His finger pushes a
selection at random. Some '60's rock hit blares out.
JACOB's mind is reeling by the time PAUL sits back
down.

(CONTINUED)

51

                         PAUL
                    (continuing)
          Sorry. Sometimes I think I'm just
          gonna jump outta my skin. They're
          just drivin' me wild.

                         JACOB
          Who, Paul? What exactly ... ?

                         PAUL
          I don't know who they are, or what
          they are. But they're gonna get me
          and I'm scared, Jake. I'm so scared I
          can't do anything. I can't go to my
          sisters. I can't even go home.

                         JACOB
          Why not?

                         PAUL
          They're waitin' for me, that's why.

     PAUL's hand starts to shake. The tremor spreads
     rapidly to his whole body. The booth begins to rattle.

                         PAUL
                    (continuing)
          I can't stop it. I try. Oh God! Help
          me Jake.

     JACOB slides quickly out of his side of the booth and
     moves in toward PAUL. He puts his arm around him and
     holds him tightly, offering comfort as best he can.

     PAUL is obviously terrified and grateful for JACOB's
     gesture. A few PEOPLE at the bar look over in their
     direction.

                         JACOB
          It's okay, Paul. It's okay.

                         PAUL
                    (crying)
          I don't know what to do.

                         JACOB
          Don't do anything.
                    (PAUL begins to relax a
                    bit and the shaking
                    subsides)
          Paul, I know what you're talking
          about.

                         PAUL
          What do you mean?

                         JACOB
          I've seen them too ... the demons!

                                        (CONTINUED)
                         52

> PAUL
> (staring at JACOB)
> You've seen them?

> JACOB
> Everywhere, like a plague.

> PAUL
> God almighty. I thought I was the
> only one.

> JACOB
> Me, too. I had no idea. It's like I
> was coming apart at the seams.

> PAUL
> Oh God. I know. I know.

> JACOB
> What is it Paul? What's happening to
> us?

> PAUL
> They keep telling me I'm already
> dead, that they're gonna tear me
> apart, piece by piece, and throw me
> into the fire.
> > (he fumbles in his coat
> > pocket and pulls out a
> > small Bible and silver
> > cross.
> I carry these everywhere but they
> don't help. Nothing helps. Everyone
> thinks I'm crazy. My mother filed a
> report with the army.

> JACOB
> (stunned)
> The army?

> PAUL
> She said I haven't been the same
> since then. Since that night. There's
> still this big hole in my brain. It's
> so dark in there, Jake. And these
> creatures. It's like they're crawling
> out of my brain. What happened that
> night? Why won't they tell us?

> JACOB
> I don't know. I don't know.

> PAUL
> They're monsters, Jake. We're both
> seein' 'em. There's gotta be a
> connection. Something.

JACOB leans back in the booth, his mind racing. The

(CONTINUED)

43  CONTINUED:

YOUNG MAN in the next booth is watching them with rapt
attention.


**44  INT.   MEN'S ROOM — DAY**

PAUL and JACOB are in the MEN'S ROOM. PAUL flushes the
urinal.

                         PAUL
              I'm afraid to go by myself anymore. I
              keep thinkin' one of 'em's gonna come
              up behind me. Somethin's wrong when a
              guy can't even take a leak by
              himself. I've seen 'em take people
              right off the street. I used to go
              home a different way every night. Now
              I can't even go home.

                         JACOB
              You come home with me.

                         PAUL
              What about your girlfriend. You don't
              think she'll mind?

                         JACOB
              Are you kidding? We've put up more of
              her cousins. You wouldn't believe how
              they breed down there.

PAUL smiles.


**45  EXT.   BAR — DAY**

The TWO MEN leave the bar on a dingy side street. It
is cold outside. Christmas lights seem ludicrous
dangling in the bar's front window. PAUL looks at them
and smiles.

                         PAUL
              Merry Christmas.

PAUL steps into the street and walks to the driver's
side of his car. He pulls out his keys and opens the
door. JACOB looks down on the sidewalk and notices a
dime.

                         JACOB
              Goddamn, this is my lucky day.

He bends down to pick it up. PAUL inserts the key into
the ignition and steps on the gas. He turns the key.

THE CAR EXPLODES. Pieces of metal and flesh fly into
the air. JACOB sprawls out flat on the ground as the
debris hurls above him. He covers his head.

## 46  EXT.    VIETNAM — DAY

CUT TO A HELICOPTER suffering an air bombardment.
Flack is exploding all around it and the shock waves
are rocking the craft violently. JACOB's eyes peer to
the left.

INFANTRY GUNNERS are firing rockets into the JUNGLE
below. A pair of MEDICS are huddled over him. A sudden
gush of arterial bleeding sends a stream of blood
splattering over the inside of the windshield. The
PILOT, unable to see, clears it away with his hands.

JACOB screams over the roar of the chopper. One of the
MEDICS presses his ear close to JACOB to hear.

                    JACOB
          Help me!

                    MEDIC
          We're doing the best we can.

                    JACOB
          Get me out of here!


## 47  EXT.    BAR — DAY

THE YOUNG MAN from the bar grabs JACOB under the arms
and drags him down the sidewalk.

                    YOUNG MAN
          Just hold on.

                    JACOB
          Where am I? Who are you?

The YOUNG MAN yanks JACOB around the corner just as
another explosion consumes the car. The air is filled
with flames and flying glass. The YOUNG MAN pulls
JACOB into the bar.

                    YOUNG MAN
          Just lie still. You're okay. You're
          not hurt.

The CUSTOMERS are in a state of bedlam. Part of the
wall has blown apart and bricks and glass are
everywhere. The cross from around PAUL's neck is
buried in the debris. Sirens are heard in the
distance. A BLACK CAR speeds off down the street.
JACOB looks for the YOUNG MAN who had helped him. He
is gone.

48  EXT.    FUNERAL PROCESSION — DAY

A FUNERAL PROCESSION heads down Ocean Parkway.


49  INT.    JACOB'S CAR — DAY

JACOB and JEZZIE are driving in an old Chevy Nova.
They are dressed up. JACOB's face is bruised and he
has a gauze pad over his ear. They drive in silence.
JACOB appears very sad. Slowly his right hand reaches
across the seat, seeking JEZZIE's. Their fingers
embrace.


50  EXT.    CEMETERY — DAY

The FUNERAL PROCESSION enters the CEMETERY. Cars park
along the length of the narrow road. MEN IN DARK SUITS
emerge from their cars along with WIVES and
GIRLFRIENDS.

They are the SOLDIERS we have seen at the opening of
the film, only they are older now. A small group of
FAMILY MEMBERS are helped to the graveside.

JACOB joins the other VETERANS as pallbearers. They
carry the casket in semi-military formation to the
grave.


51  INT.    PAUL'S LIVING ROOM — DAY

JACOB'S OLD ARMY BUDDIES are sitting together in
Paul's living room, talking. PAUL'S WIFE can be seen
in the BEDROOM. Several WOMEN are comforting her.

JEZZIE is talking to a small group of LADIES in th
DINING ROOM and nibbling off a tray of cold cuts.
PAUL'S SISTER is with her and they seem to be having a
lively, almost intimate, conversation.

JACOB and his BUDDIES are drinking beer. They all have
a tired, defeated look about them.

                    FRANK
          Did anyone see the police report? It
          sounds like a detonation job to me.

                    JERRY
          The paper said it was electrical; a
          freak accident.

                    ROD
          Bullshit. Someone's covering
          somethin'. That was no accident.

                                        (CONTINUED)

                    GEORGE
          Why do you say that?

                    ROD
          Cars don't explode that way. Any
          simpleton knows that.

                    GEORGE
          But the paper ...

                    ROD
          That was set. I'm tellin' you.

                    DOUG
          By who? Why? Paul didn't have an
          enemy in the world.

                    JERRY
          How do you know?

                    DOUG
          Hey, you're talkin' about Paul. Who'd
          want to hurt him?

                    FRANK
          What did he talk about when you guys
          went out? Did he say anything?

                    JACOB
          He was upset. He thought people were
          following him.

                    JERRY
          You're kidding. Who?

                    JACOB
          He didn't know ... Demons.

                    GEORGE
               (obviously struck by the
                word)
          What do you mean, demons?

                    JACOB
          He told me he was going to Hell.

The statement has a surprising impact on the group.
There is immediate silence and eyes averted from one
another.

                    ROD
          What'd he say that for? What made him
          say that? Strange, huh? Strange.

                    GEORGE
          What else did he say, Jake?

                    JACOB
          He was scared. He saw these creatures

                                        (CONTINUED)

> JACOB (CONT.)
> coming out of the woodwork. They were
> tryin' to get him, he said.

> GEORGE
> (his arm shaking)
> How long had that been going on?

> JACOB
> A couple of weeks, I think.

He notices GEORGE's beer can rattling.

> GEORGE
> He say what they looked like?

> JACOB
> No. Not really ...

> GEORGE
> Excuse me a minute. I'll be right
> back.

> ROD
> In one end, out the other, huh
> George?

GEORGE tries to smile as he hurries to the BATHROOM.
His arm is nearly out of control and beer is spilling
on the carpet as he walks.

> ROD
> (continuing)
> Still a spastic, huh? I hope you can
> hold your dick better than you hold
> that can.

No one laughs. There is an uncomfortable silence.


52  EXT.   A BACK ALLEY — DAY

The SIX MEN are walking quietly through an unpaved
alley. It is already gray and getting darker.

> DOUG
> I know what Paul was talking about. I
> don't know how to say this ... but in
> a way it's a relief knowing that
> someone else saw them, too.

> ROD
> You're seeing ... ?

> DOUG
> They're not human, I'll tell you
> that. A car tried to run over me the
> other day. It was aiming straight for

(CONTINUED)

                        DOUG (CONT.)
        me. I saw their faces. They weren't
        from Brooklyn.

                        ROD
        What are you tellin' me? They're from
        the Bronx?

                        DOUG
        It was no joke, Rod.

                        JERRY
        Something weird is going on here.
        What is it about us? Even in Nam it
        was always weird. Are we all crazy or
        something?

                        DOUG
        Yeah, ever since that ...

He hesitates. They all understand.

                        ROD
        What's that have to do with anything?

                        FRANK
        It was bad grass. That's all it was.

                        JERRY
        Grass never did that to me.

                        DOUG
        You know, I've been to three shrinks
        and a hypnotist. Nothing penetrates
        that night. Nothing.

                        ROD
        It's not worth goin' over again and
        again. Whatever happened, happened.
        It's over.

                        JACOB
        ... I've seen them, too.

                        ROD
        Shit!

                        JERRY
        So have I.

                        JACOB
        Look, there's something fucking
        strange going on here. You know
        Paul's not the only one who's died.
        You remember Dr. Carlson over at
        Bellevue? His car blew up, too.

                        ROD
        Dr. Carlson's dead?

                                        (CONTINUED)
                        59

                    JACOB
An explosion, just like Paul's.

                    JERRY
No!

                    FRANK
Jesus!

                    GEORGE
You think they're connected?

                    JACOB
         (he nods)
I think something's fucking connected. I mean, a car tried to run me
over the other day. Doug too, right?
We've got six guys here going fucking
crazy.

                    ROD
Not me, buddy.

                    JACOB
Okay, not you Rod. But the rest of us
are flipping out for some goddamn
reason. They're tryin' to kill us.
Fuck it man, we need to find out
what's going on.

                    DOUG
Do you think it has something to do
with ... the offensive?

                    JACOB
It's got something to do with something. I think we've got to confront
the army. If they're hiding shit from
us, we better find out what it is.

                    ROD
Come on,  Professor. The army's not
gonna give you any answers. You'll be
buttin' your head against a stone
wall.

                    JACOB
Maybe that's the only way to get
through. Besides, six heads'll be
better than one.

                    ROD
Not my head, buddy. Not me. I'm
gettin' a headache just listenin' to
you.

                    JACOB
We should get ourselves a lawyer.

                                    (CONTINUED)

> ROD
> I say you should get a shrink.

> DOUG
> Too late. I've tried. I think you're
> right, Jake. I'm game.

> JERRY
> Me, too.

> ROD
> You guys are fucking paranoid. It was
> bad grass. That's all it was. There's
> no such thing as demons.

53  INT.  **LAW OFFICE — DAY**

JACOB, FRANK, JERRY, GEORGE, DOUG, and ROD are sitting
on plush chairs in the LAW OFFICE of DONALD GEARY.
GEARY, a red-faced man with three chins, is sucking on
an ice cube. He looks at each of the men, and then
spits the cube into an empty glass. It clinks.

> GEARY
> I'm sorry, Mr. Singer, but do you
> have any idea how many people come to
> me with the injustices of the world?
> It'd break your heart.

> JACOB
> This isn't injustice, Mr. Geary. The
> army did something to us and we've
> got to find out what.

> GEARY
> The army. The army. What is it with
> you guys? We're not talking about a
> trip to the library here. This is the
> United States Government for God's
> sake. This is red tape coming out of
> your ass. You know what I mean?

> JACOB
> Exactly. And we need someone to cut
> through it. We hear you're the man.

> GEARY
> Oh yeah? What am I — Perry Mason
> here?

GEARY stands up and grabs a bag of Cheetos from a file
drawer. He chomps down a few and offers the bag to the
others. There are no takers. Thirsty, he downs the ice
cube and cracks it between his teeth.

(CONTINUED)

                              GEARY
                          (continuing)
                    Okay. I'll look into it.

     The MEN are surprised and excited.

                              PAUL
                    Wow! Do you think we have a chance?

                              GEARY
                    What do you want, a fortune teller or
                    a lawyer? ... I'll need sworn
                    depositions from each of you and a
                    list of the other members of the
                    platoon, or their survivors.

                              DOUG
                    Hey, this is great.

                              GEARY
                    I'll tell you, if we find the
                    military is implicated in any way,
                    you could stand to recover quite a
                    lot of money. Not that I can predict
                    anything, but some class action suits
                    of this kind have been awarded fairly
                    generous judgements. That wouldn't be
                    so bad, would it Mr. Singer?

                              JACOB
                    Doctor
                          (GEARY looks at him
                          oddly)
                    Ph.D.

                              GEARY
                    Ah! I thought you were a mailman.

                              JACOB
                    I am.

                              GEARY
                          (confused)
                    Then why aren't you teaching? Why
                    aren't you in a university?

                              JACOB
                    I'm too messed up to teach.

                              GEARY
                          (smiling)
                    Ah! Well then, they're going to have
                    to pay for that, aren't they?

     The MEN all nod in agreement.

## 53  EXT.   OFFICE BUILDING — DAY

JACOB and the others exit the OFFICE BUILDING. They
are jubilant, clasping hands and smacking each other
on the back. We watch as they break up. JACOB heads
for the subway. FRANK and another group hop a cab. As
the cab pulls away we notice that a black car pulls
out behind it. It follows them out of sight.


## 54  INT.   JACOB'S KITCHEN — NIGHT

JACOB and JEZZIE are making wild and unadulterated
love on the kitchen floor. The wastebasket flips over.
JACOB's hand splashes into the dog's bowl. Nothing
impedes their passion. JEZZIE laughs, hollers, and
swoons. Hands grab hold of table legs. Chairs topple.
Feet bang wildly against the stove. It is all mayhem
and ecstasy. And then it ends.

JACOB's face is ecstatic. He can barely talk and
simply basks in JEZZIE's glow.She looks especially
lovely and radiant. They lie exhausted and exhilarated
on the linoleum floor.

> JEZZIE
> So tell me ... am I still an angel?

> JACOB
> (smiling broadly)
> With wings. You transport me, you
> know that? You carry me away.

JEZZIE kisses him softly around his face and gently
probes his ear with her pinky. JACOB loves it.

> JEZZIE
> We're all angels, you know ...
> (she bites his earlobe.
> He winces)
> ... and devils. It's just what you
> choose to see.

> JACOB
> I love you, Jez.

> JEZZIE
> I know.

> JACOB
> Underneath all the bullshit, just
> love.

> JEZZIE
> Remember that.

> JACOB
> You know what? I feel ... exorcised
> ... like the demons are gone.

(CONTINUED)

                              JEZZIE
                How come? The army?

                              JACOB
                In a way. At least now I have some
                idea of what was happening. If we can
                only get them to admit ... to explain
                what they did ... I don't know. Maybe
                it'd clear things up in my head. I'll
                tell you  something, Jez, honestly
                ... I thought they were real.

Silence. Suddenly JEZZIE roars like a monster and
scares JACOB half to death. They laugh and tumble back
to the floor.


55  INT.   JACOB'S APT. — EVENING

JACOB emerges from the bathroom shower and pulls on a
robe. JEZZIE is moving rapidly around the KITCHEN.

                              JEZZIE
                I put a frozen dinner in the oven, a
                Manhandler. It'll be ready at a
                quarter of. I threw a little salad
                together. It's in the fridge. I also
                bought some apple juice, Red Cheek.
                Don't drink it all. Oh, and Jake,
                your lawyer called.

                              JACOB
                He did? When?

                              JEZZIE
                      (grabbing her coat)
                While you were in the shower.

                              JACOB
                Why didn't you call me?

                              JEZZIE
                He didn't give me a chance.
                      (she pauses nervously)
                Look, honey, don't get upset, but
                he's not taking your case.

                              JACOB
                      (stunned)
                What? What do you mean?

                              JEZZIE
                He said you didn't have one.

                              JACOB
                What's he talking about?

                                                    (CONTINUED)

                          JEZZIE
          I don't know. That's all he said. He
          wasn't very friendly. Oh, yeah. He
          said your buddies backed down. They
          chickened out, he said.

                          JACOB
          I don't believe this.

                          JEZZIE
          Baby, I'm sorry. I feel terrible. I'd
          stay and talk but I'm so late. Look,
          don't be upset. We'll talk when I get
          home. See you around midnight.
                    (she kisses him on the
                    cheek.)
          Bye. And don't brood. Watch T.V. or
          something.


56   **JACOB'S APT./FRANK'S APT. — INTERCUT**

     The door slams securely. The locks set. JACOB begins
     instantly rifling through a desk drawer. He comes up
     with a frayed address book and looks up a number. He
     dials.

                          FRANK (V.O.)
          Hello.

                          JACOB
          Frank. It's Jake. Jacob Singer.

     We see FRANK standing at a window fingering the
     venetian blinds. He does not reply. The scene
     intercuts between the two men.

                          JACOB
                    (continuing)
          Listen, I just got a strange call
          from Geary. He said the guys backed
          down. What's he talking about?

                          FRANK
                    (fingering the venetian
                    blinds)
          That's right. We did.

                          JACOB
          What does that mean, Frank? I don't
          get it. Why?

                          FRANK
          It's hard to explain.

                          JACOB
                    (angry)
          Well, try, huh.

                                        (CONTINUED)

                              FRANK
          I don't know if I can. It's just that
          war is war. Things happen.

                              JACOB
          Things happen? What the fuck are you
          talking about? They did something to
          us, Frank. We have to expose this.

                              FRANK
          There's nothing to expose.

                              JACOB
          Jesus Christ! Who's been talking to
          you?
                    (silence)
          What's going on? How can you just
          turn away?
                    (no response)
          What about the others?

                              FRANK
          They're not interested, Jake.

                              JACOB
          Shit! You know it's not half the case
          if I go it alone. We're all suffering
          the same symptoms, Frank. The army is
          to blame. They've done something to
          us. How can you not want to know?

                              FRANK
                    (pausing)
          Maybe it's not the army, Jake.

                              JACOB
          What do you mean?

                              FRANK
          Maybe there's a larger truth.

                              JACOB
          What are you talking about?

                              FRANK
          Maybe the demons are real.

                              JACOB
          Goddamn it. What kind of bullshit is
          that?

                              FRANK
          Listen, Jake. I gotta go.

                              JACOB
          What the hell? What kind of mumbo
          jumbo ... ?

                                        (CONTINUED)

56 CONTINUED:

> FRANK
> I'm hanging up.

> JACOB
> Hey, wait!

> FRANK
> Don't bother to call again, okay?

FRANK hangs up. JACOB stands holding the phone for a
long time, until the high pitched whine from the
receiver reminds him it's off the hook. The sound
frightens him and he slams the receiver down. Quickly
JACOB tears through his address book looking for other
phone numbers. They aren't there.

> JACOB
> Shit!

57  INT.   JACOB'S APT.

JACOB hurries into the BEDROOM and pulls an old shoe
box from the closet. The box is filled with yellowing
army papers, dog tags, and photos of old comrades.
Beneath his discharge papers he finds a sheet
scribbled with the names and addresses of platoon
buddies. JACOB grabs it. Then his eyes fall on the
frayed remains of an old letter. He picks it up and
unfolds it with great care. The letter is written in a
child's handwriting. "DEAR DADDY, I LOVE YOU. PLEASE
COME HOME. JED GOT A FROG. ELI LOST MY KEY. MOM WANTS
YOU TO SEND HER MONEY. LOVE, GABE."

                                              CUT TO:

57A EXT.   BROOKLYN SIDEWALK — DAY

GABE, on a BICYCLE, is rushing down the sidewalk.
JACOB is running alongside him, holding onto the seat.
Plastic streamers trail from the handlebars.GABE is a
bit wobbly, but determined. After a couple of false
starts, JACOB lets go and GABE is riding by himself.
For an instant, GABE looks back at his father with a
huge grin on his face. JACOB is grinning, too. THE
CAMERA HOLDS ON GABE as he pulls away from us and
heads into the distance.

                                         CUT BACK TO:

57B INT.   JACOB'S APT. — NIGHT

JACOB swallows hard as he stands there, holding the
letter. Suddenly his eyes lift off the page and glance
at a full length mirror mounted on the bedroom door.
Something in the mirror, like the image of a child,

                                          (CONTINUED)

seems to move. He looks over. There is nothing there.
Curious, JACOB walks toward the mirror. As his image
appears, he gasps and stops moving. To his horror and
ours, it is his own back that is reflected in the
mirror. The impossibility of the moment startles him.
He lifts his hand. The reflection moves with him.
Frightened but defiant, JACOB moves toward the mirror.
The image in the mirror spins around. It is the
FRIGHTENING VIBRATING FACE he saw at the party with
JEZZIE. An unearthly scream comes from both their
mouths.

> JACOB
>
> NO!!!

## 58 INT. BROOKLYN COURT HOUSE — LATE AFTERNOON

A huge wooden door slams open. JACOB charges through
it.

He is chasing his lawyer, DONALD GEARY, through a
crowded court house corridor. GEARY, sweaty and
unshaven, is cradling a Coke in one hand, a sandwich
and a briefcase in the other. His stomach bounces
wildly as he walks.

> JACOB
> Geary! Mr. Geary! Listen, goddamn it!
> You can't just walk away from this.

GEARY keeps walking. JACOB catches up to him.

> JACOB
> (continuing)
> Who's been talking to you? The army?
> Have they been talking to you, huh?

> GEARY
> Nobody's been talking to nobody. You
> don't have a case, you hear me? It's
> pure and simple. Now leave me alone.
> okay?

JACOB grabs the back of GEARY's jacket and pulls him
up short.

> GEARY
> (continuing)
> Take your hands off me!

JACOB lets go. He stares into GEARY's eyes.

> JACOB
> Listen, will you listen? They're
> trying to get me. They're comin' out
> of the walls. The army's done

(CONTINUED)

                        JACOB (CONT.)
          something to me. I need you.

                        GEARY
          You need ... a doctor.

                        JACOB
          A doctor? And what's he gonna do,
          tell me I'm crazy? They've fucked
          with my head. I've got to prove it.
          You've got to do something.

GEARY gives JACOB a pitiful look.

                        GEARY
          There's nothing I can do.

He turns and walks away. JACOB stands there a moment,
and then rushes after him. GEARY is biting into his
sandwich.

Mayonnaise spills onto his hand. He licks it with his
tongue. JACOB catches up to him.

                        GEARY
          You mind? I'm eating, huh?

                        JACOB
          Something's going on here. You're not
          telling me something. What the hell's
          gotten into you?

                        GEARY
          I'll tell you what's gotten into me.
          I don't know you from Adam, right?
          You come to my office with this
          bizzarro story and demand I look into
          it. Okay. I said I'd check it out and
          I did. Now I don't know what kind of
          fool you take me for, but you have
          used and abused me, and I don't like
          it.

                        JACOB
          Used you?

                        GEARY
          I talked to the Army's Bureau of
          Records. You've never even been to
          Viet Nam.

                        JACOB
          What the hell is that supposed to
          mean?

                        GEARY
          It means that you and your buddies
          are whacko, that you were discharged

                                        (CONTINUED)
                        69

> GEARY (CONT.)
> on psychological grounds after some
> war games in Thailand.

> JACOB
> (stunned)
> War games? Thailand? That's not true!
> How can you believe that? Can't you
> see what they're doing? It's all a
> lie. We were in Da Nang, for God's
> sake. You've got to believe me.

> GEARY
> I don't have to do any such thing.
> I'm eating my lunch, okay?

GEARY takes a swig of his COKE and begins walking
away. JACOB, enraged, charges after him. With a wild
swipe he sends the COKE CAN shooting out of GEARY's
hand. It reverberates down the corridor. GEARY is
stunned.

> JACOB
> You slimy bastard! You goddamn piece
> of shit!

With a powerful thrust, JACOB rips the sandwich from
GEARY's other hand. Tossing it on the floor, he grinds
his heel in it. Tomato and mayonnaise squirt onto
GEARY's shoe. JACOB turns away.

59 CUT TO JACOB walking down the COURT HOUSE CORRIDOR to
the elevators. There is a look of satisfaction on his
face.

60 CUT BACK TO GEARY. He picks up a telephone and dials.
Someone comes on the line. GEARY speaks quietly.

> GEARY
> He's on his way.

61 CUT TO JACOB stepping onto the elevator. The doors
close. The Muzak is playing "Sonny Boy" with Al Jolson
singing. JACOB is surprised to hear it. He presses the
down button for the main floor.

62 The elevator stops at the LOBBY. The doors open
swiftly. SEVERAL SOLDIERS are standing there. They
approach JACOB.

> SOLDIER 1
> Let's go, Singer.

(CONTINUED)

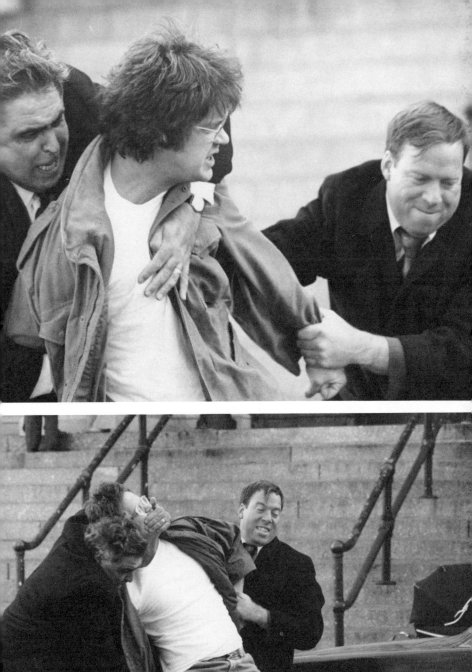

62  CONTINUED:

JACOB is shocked to see them. He tries to get away but
two of the SOLDIERS yank him toward the LOBBY doors.

                    SOLDIER 2
            You're coming with us.


63  INT.    CAR — LATE AFTERNOON.

JACOB is hustled to a waiting car and shoved inside,
in between two officious looking MEN. The doors lock
from the DRIVER's command.

                    ARMY OFFICIAL #1
            Mr. Singer. What an appropriate name
            for a man who can't keep his mouth
            shut.

The car drives off.

                    JACOB
            Who are you? What do you want?

                    ARMY OFFICIAL #2
            We've been watching you for a long
            time. You and your friends. You've
            been exhibiting some very odd
            behavior. Frightening people with
            foolish talk about demons — and
            experiments.

JACOB tries to speak but the other MAN grabs his
mouth.

                    ARMY OFFICIAL #1
            You're in over your head, Mr. Singer.
            Men drown that way. The army was
            another part of your life. Forget it.
            It is dead and buried. Let it lie.

                    ARMY OFFICIAL #2
            I hope we have made our point, Mr.
            Singer.

JACOB stares at the men for a moment and then goes
totally berserk. Letting out a howl, he begins
pounding and thrashing like a madman. He is totally
out of control.

With a wild leap, he grabs for the door handle. The
door flies open. It flaps back and forth, slamming
into parked cars. JACOB tries to jump out, but the men
yank him back in. One of them pulls out a gun. JACOB
sees it and goes crazy. His feet kick in all
directions, slamming the DRIVER's nose into the
steering wheel and shattering the side window.

                                        (CONTINUED)

71

63  CONTINUED:

The car careens around a corner sending the gun flying
to the floor. The men dive for it. It lodges beneath
the seat. In the mayhem, JACOB throws himself out of
the flapping door and sprawls onto the pavement.
People look down at him as the car speeds away.


64  **EXT.    BROOKLYN — LATE AFTERNOON**

JACOB grabs his back. He is in excruciating pain. He
tries to get up, but can't move. He reaches out to
people passing by, but they ignore him and hurry past.

A SALVATION ARMY SANTA has been watching the entire
scene. After a moment's consideration he leaves his
post and ambles over to JACOB. He leans down and
steals his wallet.

                    SANTA
          Merry Christmas.


65  **EXT.    BROOKLYN STREETS — EVENING**

CUT TO THE SOUND OF A SIREN as an AMBULANCE races
through the streets.


66  **INT.    HOSPITAL — EVENING**

AN AMBULANCE CREW rushes JACOB to a HOSPITAL EMERGENCY
ROOM.

                    BEARER
          He's been screaming like a madman.
          You better get something in him.

                    RESIDENT
              (approaching JACOB)
          Hi. I'm Doctor Stewart. Can you tell
          me what happened?

                    JACOB
          My back. I can't move. I need my
          chiropractor.

                    RESIDENT
          Your back? Did you fall?

                    BEARER
          They said he slipped on the ice. May
          have hit his head.

                    ATTENDANT
          Does he have any identification?

                                        (CONTINUED)

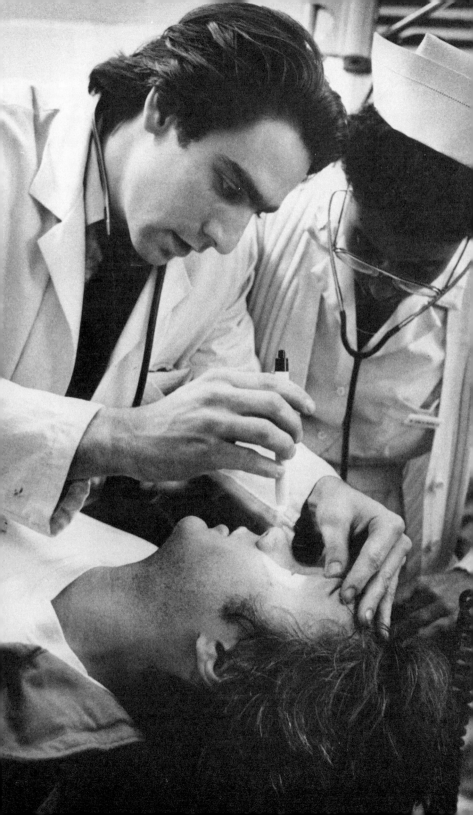

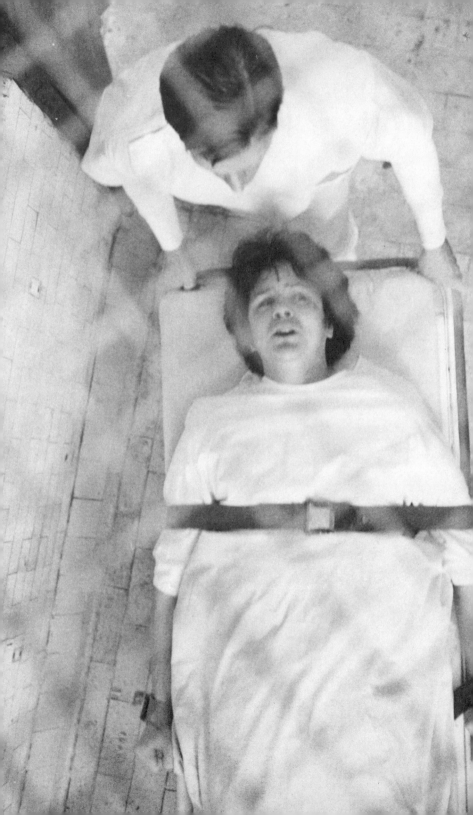

                        BEARER
          No wallet. Nothing.

                        JACOB
          They stole it.

                        RESIDENT
          Who did?

                        JACOB
          I don't know. Santa Claus. I had my
          son's picture in it, Gabe's picture.
          It's the only one I had.

                        RESIDENT
          We better get an orthopedic man in
          here. Is Dr. Davis on call?

                        NURSE
          I'll page him.

                        JACOB
          Call my chiropractor.

                        NURSE
          We're doing everything we can.

                        JACOB
          Louis Schwartz. Nostrand Avenue.

                        RESIDENT
          I'm going to have to move you a bit,
          just to check for injuries. This may
          hurt a little.

                        JACOB
          No. Don't move me.

The RESIDENT ignores him. JACOB screams.

                        RESIDENT
          I don't have to ask if you can feel
          that.

                        JACOB
          Goddamn it. I want Louis.

                        NURSE
          Who's Louis?

                        RESIDENT
          He's out of it. I'm taking him down
          to X-ray.

An ORDERLY pushes the gurney through a pair of sliding
doors. JACOB tries to get up but the pain keeps him
immobilized.

                          73

67 INT.   CORRIDORS — NIGHT

JACOB begins a journey down what appears to be an
endless series of corridors. The wheels of the gurney
turn with a hypnotic regularity. The smooth tile floor
gives way to rough cement. The ORDERLY's feet plod
through pools of blood that coagulate in cracks and
crevices along the way. The surface grows rougher, the
wheels more insistent. Body parts and human bile
splash against the walls as the gurney moves faster.

                    JACOB
          Where are you taking me? Where am I?

                    ORDERLY
          You know where you are.

JACOB, panicked, tries again to get up but to no
effect. He glances to the side and sees mournful
CREATURES being led into dark rooms. No one fights or
struggles. We hear muffled screams from behind closed
doors. Occasionally he glances inside the rooms and
sees mangled bodies in strange contraptions, people in
rusty iron lungs, and hanging from metal cages. Dark
eyes peer out in horror. In one room a baseboard
heater bursts into flame. No one seems concerned. A
door opens. A bicycle with plastic streamers on the
handle bars lies crushed and mangled. One of its
wheels is still spinning. JACOB cries out but it is
not his voice we hear. Rather it is a familiar
unearthly roar. His whole body stiffens. As he rounds
the corner he sees a figure, its head vibrating in
endless terror. It is the same image he has seen
before. JACOB screams.


68 INT.   ROOM — NIGHT

JACOB is wheeled into a tiny ROOM. A number of
"DOCTORS" are waiting. As they draw closer JACOB
notices that something about them is not right. They
bear a subtle resemblance to Bosch-like DEMONS,
creatures of another world. JACOB tries to sit up but
winces in pain. He cannot move. He tries to scream but
no sound comes out.

Chains and pulleys hang from the ceiling. They are
lowered and attached with speed and efficiency to
JACOB's arms and legs. He screams.

                    JACOB
          Oh God!                 .

The "DOCTORS" laugh. There is the sound of a huge door
closing. JACOB is left in semi-darkness. Suddenly a
new group of "DOCTORS" emerges from the shadows. They
are carrying sharp surgical instruments. They surround

                                          (CONTINUED)
                              74

JACOB, their eyes glistening as bright as their
blades. JACOB is panting and sweating in fear. One of
the "DOCTORS" leans over JACOB. He gasps with horror.
It is JEZZIE.

                    JACOB
          JEZZIE?!

She pays no attention to him. He stares at her, THE
CAMERA TILTING DOWN HER BODY. As it gets to her foot
we see it is a decaying mass, swarming with maggots.
The "DOCTORS" laugh. They take great pleasure in his
suffering. Their voices are strange and not human.
Each utterance contains a multitude of contradictory
tones, sincere and compassionate, taunting and mocking
at the same time. The confusion of meanings is a
torment of its own.

                    JACOB
                 (continuing)
          Get me out of here.

                    "DOCTOR"
          Where do you want to go?

                    JACOB
          Take me home.

                    "DOCTOR"
          Home?
                 (they all laugh)
          This is your home. You're dead.

                    JACOB
          Dead? No. I just hurt my back. I'm
          not dead.

                    "DOCTOR"
          What are you then?

                    JACOB
          I'm alive.

                    "DOCTOR"
          Then what are you doing here?

                    JACOB
          I don't know. I don't know.
                 (he struggles like an
                 animal)
          This isn't happening.

                    "DOCTOR"
          What isn't happening?

                    JACOB
          Let me out of here!

                                        (CONTINUED)
                    75

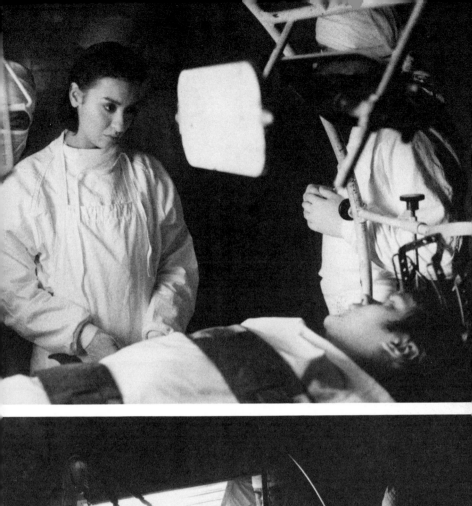
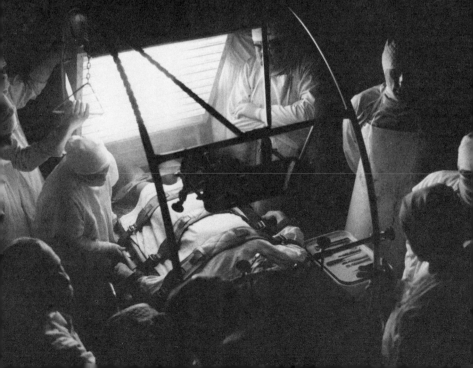

68  CONTINUED:

                         "DOCTOR"
              There is no out of here. You've been
              killed. Don't you remember?

A "DOCTOR" approaches JACOB. As he turns, we notice
with horror that he has no eyes or eye sockets. He
extracts a long needle from his belt and positions it
over JACOB's head. Like a divining rod it locates a
particular point near the crown of his head. With a
powerful thrust the "DOCTOR" shoves the needle into
JACOB's skull and pushes it slowly into his brain.
JACOB howls.


69  EXT.   VIETNAM — NIGHT

CUT RAPIDLY TO VIETNAM and a replay of flashes of the
opening sequence of the film. SOLDIERS with bayonets
are charging over rice paddies in the dark of the
night. ONE OF THE SOLDIERS charges at JACOB with a
long bayonet blade and jams it into his intestines.
JACOB cries out.


70  INT.   ROOM — NIGHT

CUT BACK TO THE "DOCTORS".

                         "DOCTOR"
              Remember?

                         JACOB
              *No! That was years ago. I've lived
              years since then.*

                         "DOCTOR"
              It's all been a dream.

                         JACOB
              No! The army did this to me. They've
              done something to my brain.
                    (he raves like a madman)
              Jezzie! I want my boys! Sarah! I'm
              not dead! I want my family!

The "DOCTORS" laugh and back away, disappearing into
the darkness.


71  INT.   HOSPITAL — NIGHT

Suddenly a fluorescent light flashes overhead. NORMAL
HOSPITAL WALLS materialize instantaneously around him.
A NURSE enters the room followed by SARAH, ELI, and
JED. They approach JACOB who is lying in traction,
suspended over a hospital bed.

                                              (CONTINUED)

                              NURSE
              He's still pretty doped up. I don't
              think he'll be able to talk yet and I
              doubt that he'll recognize you.

                              SARAH
              I just want to see him.

                              JED
                    (eating a Snickers bar)
              Dad. Hi. It's us. We just found out.

                              ELI
              You look terrible. Does that hurt?

                              NURSE
              I'll be outside if you need me.

                              SARAH
              Jake. It's me. We heard what
              happened.

                              JACOB
                    (his voice hoarse,
                    nearly whispering)
              I'm not dead. I am not dead.

                              SARAH
              No. Of course you're not. You've just
              hurt your back. That's all. You're
              going to be fine. It'll just take
              some time.

                              JED
              A month, they said.

                              ELI
                    (trying to joke)
              You just hang in there, Dad.

                              SARAH
                    (smacking him)
              That's not funny.
                    (she reaches over and
                    rubs JACOB's brow)
              What a mess, huh? God I wish there
              was something I could do. I love you,
              Jacob. For whatever that's worth. I
              do.

There is a sudden sound of "DOCTORS" laughing. JACOB
jerks his head painfully, but does not see them.

                              "DOCTOR" (O.S.)
              Dream on!

                              JACOB
                    (yelling at the unseen
                    voice)
              No! Oh God.

                                        (CONTINUED)
                              77

71  CONTINUED:

                          SARAH
          Jacob, what can I do?

                          JACOB
          Save me!

JACOB's plea confuses SARAH. She responds with a kiss.


72  **INT.   HOSPITAL — DAY**

    DAYLIGHT streams through the window in JACOB's ROOM.
    He is still in traction and looks very uncomfortable.
    A new NURSE enters holding a plastic container with a
    straw poking out.

                          NURSE
          Well, don't we look better this
          morning? That was a hard night,
          wasn't it?

                          JACOB
          Where am I?

                          NURSE
          Lennox Hospital.

                          JACOB
          I'm awake?

                          NURSE
          You look awake to me. Here.
               (she holds the straw to
               his lips)
          Drink some of this.

                          JACOB
               (staring at her
               intently)
          Where's Sarah? Where did she go?
               (the NURSE gives him a
               strange look)
          She was here ...

                          NURSE
          No. No. You haven't had any visitors.

                          JACOB
          That's a lie. My family was here.

                          NURSE
          I'm sorry.

                          JACOB
          Last night! They were as real as you
          are!

The NURSE smiles and nods in appeasement.

(CONTINUED)
                          78

                    JACOB
        This is not a dream! This is my life.

                    NURSE
        Of course it is. What else could it
        be?

She giggles nervously. There is a funny glint in her
eyes. JACOB looks away. He doesn't want to see it.


## 73  OMIT


## 73A INT.   HOSPITAL CORRIDOR — EVENING

There is a loud commotion in the HALL. We see LOUIS
SCHWARTZ, JACOB's chiropractor, screaming JACOB's
name.

                    LOUIS
        Jacob! Jacob Singer!

JACOB yells.

                    JACOB (O.S.)
        Louis! I'm here! In here


## 73B INT.   JACOB'S ROOM — DAY

LOUIS storms through JACOB's door followed by several
NURSES and ORDERLIES.

                    JACOB
        LOUIS!

                    NURSE 1
        You can't go in there!

                    ORDERLY
        You're going to have to leave.

LOUIS stares furiously at JACOB stretched out on the
traction apparatus. He begins to yell.

                    LOUIS
        Good God, Jake. What have they done?
            (he examines JACOB and
            screams at the NURSES)
        What is this, the Middle Ages? And
        they call this modern medicine. This
        is barbaric! Barbaric!
            (turning to JACOB)
        It's okay, Jake. It's not serious.
        I'll get you out of here.
            (yelling at the ORDERLY)

                                    (CONTINUED)

73B CONTINUED:

>LOUIS (CONT.)
>What is this, the Inquisition? Why
>don't you just burn him at the stake
>and put him out of his misery?

LOUIS charges over to the traction equipment and
begins working the pulleys that suspend JACOB over the
bed. The NURSES and ORDERLIES become instantly
hysterical and start screaming.

>ORDERLY
>What the hell do you think ... ?

>LOUIS
>Don't you come near me.

>NURSE 2
>You can't do that!

>LOUIS
>What is this, a prison? Stay back.

>NURSE 1
>You can't. Call the police.

One of the ORDERLIES lunges at LOUIS who swings back
at him with one of the pulley chains. It just misses.

>LOUIS
>(to the ORDERLIES)
>You take one step and I'll wrap this
>around your neck.

LOUIS lowers JACOB into a wheelchair while holding the
others at bay.

>LOUIS
>(continuing)
>Hold on, Jake, we're getting out of
>here.

NURSES and ORDERLIES part as he pushes him quickly
from the room.


74  OMIT


75  INT.   CHIROPRACTIC OFFICE — EVENING

LOUIS helps JACOB over to an adjusting table in a room
that, compared with the hospital, is comfortable and
serene. He pushes a lever and the table rises to a
vertical position. JACOB leans against it and rides it
down to a horizontal position. Every moment is agony
for him.

(CONTINUED)

LOUIS

Half an hour from now and you'll be
walking out of here all by yourself.
Mark my words.
          (JACOB barely hears
          them)
Well, you've done it to yourself this
time, haven't you?

JACOB
          (nearly whispering)
Am I dead, Louis?
          (LOUIS leans over to
          hear)
Am I dead?

LOUIS
          (smiling)
From a slipped disc? That'd be a
first.

JACOB

I was in Hell. I've been there. It's
horrible. I don't want to die, Louis.

LOUIS

Well, I'll see what I can do about
it.

JACOB

I've seen it. It's all pain.

LOUIS
          (working on JACOB's
          spine like a master
          mechanic)
You ever read Meister Eckart?
          (JACOB shakes his head
          "no")
How did you ever get your Doctorate
without reading Eckart?
          (LOUIS takes hold of
          JACOB's legs and yanks
          them swiftly.)
Good. Okay, let's turn over gently.
Right side.

JACOB turns to his left. LOUIS shakes his head in
dismay.

LOUIS

The other "right", okay?
          (he helps JACOB turn
          over)
You're a regular basket case, you
know that?
          (he moves JACOB's arm
          over his head)

(CONTINUED)

75  CONTINUED:

                              LOUIS (CONT.)
                    Eckart saw Hell, too.

LOUIS positions JACOB's other arm, bends his legs, and
then pushes down on his thigh. His spine moves with a
cracking sound. JACOB groans.

                              LOUIS
                         (continuing)
                    You know what he said? The only thing
                    that burns in Hell is the part of you
                    that won't let go of your life; your
                    memories, your attachments. They burn
                    'em all away. But they're not punish-
                    ing you, he said. They're freeing
                    your soul. Okay, other side.

He helps JACOB and repositions him. Again he pushes
and the spine cracks.

                              LOUIS
                         (continuing)
                    Wonderful. So the way he sees it, if
                    you're frightened of dying and hold-
                    ing on, you'll see devils tearing
                    your life away. But if you've made
                    your peace then the devils are really
                    angels freeing you from the earth.
                    It's just a matter of how you look at
                    it, that's all. So don't worry, okay?
                    Relax. Wiggle your toes.

JACOB's toes dance as LOUIS gives him a quick,
unexpected jab to the lower vertebrae in his back.

                              LOUIS
                         (continuing)
                    Perfect. We got it.
                         (LOUIS pushes a lever
                         and the table rises back
                         up)
                    Okay. Let's just give it a little
                    try. See if you can stand.

                              JACOB
                    What? By myself?

                              LOUIS
                    You can do it. come on. Easy. Just
                    give it a try.

JACOB steps cautiously away from the table. He moves
hesitantly, with deliberate restraint. LOUIS encourages him like a faith healer coaxing the lame. His first
steps have an aura of the miraculous about them. JACOB
walks slowly, without help. LOUIS smiles impishly. He
looks like a giant cherub.

                                              (CONTINUED)
                                   82

> LOUIS
>
> Hallelujah.

LOUIS puts his arm around him. Then JACOB tries again,
gradually rediscovering his balance and strength. With
each step his confidence returns. LOUIS is pleased.
Then, suddenly, without warning, JACOB turns and heads
toward the door.

> LOUIS
>
> What are you doing?

> JACOB
>
> There's something I've gotta take
> care of, Louis.

> LOUIS
>
> What are you talking about? You can
> barely stand.

> JACOB
>
> I'm walking, aren't I?

> LOUIS
>
> Jake, you need to rest.

> JACOB
>
> Not tonight, Louis. No more rest.

He walks slowly out the door. LOUIS starts to go after
him. JACOB turns around and shakes his head "no." The
look on his face is firm and defiant. LOUIS stands
back and lets him go.

> JACOB
>
> I love you, Louis.

76 EXT.    U.S. ARMY RECRUITING HEADQUARTERS — NIGHT

CUT TO A SIREN blaring and a fire engine racing
through the streets of lower MANHATTAN. A CROWD is
forming. Banks of lights and television cameras amass
in the cold night air. Police cars and mobile units
rush to the scene.

CUT TO JACOB. In one hand he is holding a brightly lit
torch. In the other he is holding a container of
gasoline and pouring it on the steps of the U.S. ARMY
RECRUITING HEADQUARTERS. The volatile liquid splashes
against his pants and shoes and runs down the
pavement. A five gallon container lies emptying
nearby. Gasoline belches from it insistently and pours
onto the street. Bystanders back away as the gasoline
snakes toward them.

Television cameras and microphones are pointing in
JACOB's direction, but at a safe distance. He is

(CONTINUED)

yelling at them, his teeth chattering from the cold.

> JACOB
> Listen to me. There were four
> companies in our battalion. Five
> hundred men. Seven of us were left
> when it was over. Seven! Four
> companies engaged in an enemy
> offensive that not one of us who
> survived can remember fighting.

> BYSTANDERS
> Use the torch!

> ONLOOKER
> Shut up! Let him talk!

POLICE AMBULANCES are arriving at the scene. FIREMEN
ready hoses at nearby hydrants. T.V. CAMERAS are
rolling.

> JACOB
> (shouting)
> You don't forget a battle where 500
> men were killed. They did something
> to us. I want to know the truth, the
> goddamn truth. We have a right to
> know.
> (he yells toward the
> cameras)
> Are you getting all this? I want this
> on national T.V. I want the whole
> country, the whole world to know.

He holds up the torch. A loudspeaker blares through
the crowd.

> VOICE
> Throw that torch away, young man.
> Give yourself up. You're under
> arrest.

> JACOB
> For what? For seeking the truth?

> VOICE
> Please come quietly.

> JACOB
> You come near me and I'll blow us all
> up.

> VOICE
> We're not going to hurt you.

> ONLOOKER
> Give him a chance to talk!

(CONTINUED)

                         JACOB
          The army will deny it. They've
          falsified my records. They've lied to
          my lawyer, threatened my buddies. But
          they can't threaten me.

                         BYSTANDER
          You tell 'em!

                         BYSTANDER
          Use the torch.

                         VOICE
          Okay, let's clear the area. Everyone
          out.

Suddenly a lighted match flies in JACOB's direction.
JACOB is enraged. He brandishes the torch at the
crowd.

                         JACOB
          What the fuck do you think you're
          doing?

Another match hurls toward him and dies in mid-air.
PEOPLE on the fringe of the crowd begin to run. JACOB
does not move.

                         VOICE
          Clear the area. This is an order!

                         JACOB
          What is wrong with you?

We hear laughter from PEOPLE in the crowd. As JACOB
looks out into some of their eyes he sees demons
looking back. One of them throws another match.
Crazed, JACOB runs toward them. PEOPLE jump back.

Suddenly JACOB freezes. Standing on the sidelines, he
sees one of the ARMY OFFICIALS who trapped him in the
car. He is reaching for a gun. JACOB, stunned, yells
at the top of his lungs.

                         JACOB
          NO!

With a defiant roar, he hurls the torch straight up
into the air. We see it from high above the crowd
spinning higher and higher. All eyes stare upward
watching it in a kind of wonder. Then, reaching its
apex, just below the camera, it begins its descent.
The eyes of the crowd turn to fear. SOMEONE yells.

                         ONLOOKER
          He'll burn us all!

Screams fill the air as PEOPLE scramble to escape the
potential conflagration. Only JACOB remains

                                        (CONTINUED)

motionless, standing silently, almost heroically, in the middle of it all.

Suddenly the torch hits the ground and a pool of gasoline ignites with a blinding flare that sends flames shooting in all directions. PEOPLE panic. T.V. REPORTERS and CAMERAMEN run for their lives. The ARMY OFFICIALS run, too. The flames travel toward the Army Headquarters and rush along the curb. Water hoses are trying to douse them as they spread. JACOB, surprisingly untouched by the fire, walks slowly through the frightened crowds, as if in a daze. Viewed through the flames the scene momentarily resembles a vision of Hell.

77  **INT.   JACOB'S APT. — NIGHT**

JACOB, stark naked and covered with goose bumps, runs his hands under a shower spray. The water is freezing and taking forever to warm up. Anxious, he dashes past his gasoline drenched clothes, grabs a suitcase from the BEDROOM closet, and stuffs it with clothes. Then he hurries back to the shower, tests it, and jumps in.

Lather covers JACOB's hair and hangs over his tightly closed eyes. His entire body is covered in suds. He is washing as quickly as he can. Suddenly he hears a noise as someone enters the BATHROOM. He tenses.

>                    JACOB
>           Who's there? Who is it?

JACOB struggles to rinse the soap from his eyes. They are burning. There is a shadow behind the curtain.

>                    JACOB
>                 (continuing)
>           Goddamn it! Who's there?

JACOB rubs his eyes, fighting to see. Suddenly the shower curtain is thrown back. JACOB backs against the wall. A hand reaches in and pulls his nipple, pinching hard.

>                    JEZZIE
>           It's just me.

>                    JACOB
>           Jezzie?

>                    JEZZIE
>           Who else were you expecting?

>                    JACOB
>           Let go!

>                    JEZZIE
>           Where were you, Jake? Where've you

(CONTINUED)

>                    JEZZIE (CONT.)
> been? Why haven't you called?

>                    JACOB
> Stay away from me, Jez.

>                    JEZZIE
> I want to know. You tell me!

>                    JACOB
> You wanna know? Turn on the T.V.
> Watch the fucking News!

He pushes her away, and jumps out of the shower.

CUT TO JACOB dressing and piling the last of his
clothes into his suitcase. JEZZIE, in a robe, is
watching him.

>                    JEZZIE
> Why are you doing this to me? You
> can't just go away like that.

>                    JACOB
> I can do anything I want.

She stares at him with confusion. THE PHONE RINGS.

>                    JACOB
> Don't!

>                    JEZZIE
> It might be for me.

>                    JACOB
> I'm not here. You haven't seen me.

>                    JEZZIE
>              (picking up the
>              receiver)
> Hello ... No. He's not here. I
> haven't seen him all night ... I
> don't know when ... What? Tell him
> what?
>              (JACOB looks up)
> Vietnam? ... What experiments?

JACOB lunges for the phone.

>                    JACOB
> Hello. This is Jacob Singer.
>              (he listens with growing
>              fascination)
> God almighty! ... Yes. Yes. Right .
> Where would you like to meet?
>              (he listens)
> How will I know you?
> (JACOB seems uncomfortable)
> Okay. I'll be there.

(CONTINUED)

He hangs up the phone and stands silently for a moment.

> JEZZIE
>
> Who was that?

> JACOB
>
> A chemist. Part of a chemical warfare unit out of Saigon. He said he knows me and that I'll know him when I see him.

> JEZZIE
>
> How?

> JACOB
>
> I have no idea.
>> (he thinks)
>
> I was right. There were experiments. I knew it. I knew it. My God.

> JEZZIE
>
> How do you know he's telling the truth?

JACOB stares at JEZZIE for several moments but does not respond. The 11:00 NEWS is coming on. JACOB's image can be seen on the screen. We hear the NEWSCASTER speaking.

> NEWSCASTER
>
> Leading the news tonight, a bizarre demonstration on the steps of the U.S. Army Recruiting Headquarters, in downtown Manhattan. Jacob Singer, an alleged Vietnam vet ...

> JACOB
>
> Alleged? Alleged?

> NEWSCASTER
>
> ... challenged the United States Army to admit conducting secret experiments involving hundreds of American soldiers during the Vietnam war.

JEZZIE stares at the T.V., dumbfounded. JACOB takes his suitcase and hurries to the front door. He opens it a crack and peers into the hallway. JEZZIE runs after him.

> JEZZIE
>> (almost threatening)
>
> Don't leave me, Jake.


78  INT.    BUILDING CORRIDOR — NIGHT

JACOB gazes at JEZZIE for a moment and then hurries

(CONTINUED)

78 CONTINUED:

down the HALL. He stops at the stairwell and looks back.
JEZZIE is still standing there. She is very angry. JACOB
just stares at her for a moment and then disappears down
the stairwell.


79 EXT.   WESTSIDE HIGHWAY — NIGHT

     JACOB is standing near the WESTSIDE HIGHWAY. GROUPS OF
     MEN in black leather jackets are cruising the area and
     look at JACOB with curiosity. One MAN in particular
     cruises by several times and then approaches him.

                    MICHAEL
          Jacob? Hi. I'm Michael Newman.
          Friends call me Mike.

     JACOB is startled when he sees him. He is the same
     YOUNG MAN who has appeared throughout the film,
     assisting JACOB in moments of crisis.

                    MICHAEL
               (continuing)
          Surprised, huh? I told you you'd know
          me. I've been tracking you for a long
          time. I just wish I'd spoken to you
          before tonight.

                    JACOB
          I don't get it. Who are you? Why have
          you been following me?

                    MICHAEL
          Observation, mainly. Clinical study.
          You were one of the survivors.

     A POLICE CAR passes them on the street. MICHAEL grabs
     JACOB's shoulder and turns him away nervously.

                    MICHAEL
               (continuing)
          Come on, we're not safe around here.


80 HUDSON RIVER PIER — NIGHT

     JACOB AND MICHAEL are sitting on a deserted WEST SIDE
     PIER that juts into the Hudson River. JACOB is wide-
     eyed as he listens to MICHAEL's story.

                    MICHAEL
          So first I'm arrested, right? Best
          LSD I ever made, right down the
          drain. I figure this is it, twenty
          years in the joint, if I'm lucky.
          That was '68.

                                        (CONTINUED)

                         JACOB
Long time ago.

                         MICHAEL
                    (nodding his head)
Next thing I know I'm on Rikers
Island. Ever been there?
                    (JACOB shakes his head)
Suddenly they take me from my cell to
the visitors room with those bank
teller windows, you know. Four army
colonels, medals up their asses, are
standing on the other side. They tell
me if I'll come to Vietnam for two
years, no action, mind you, just work
in a lab, they'll drop all the
charges and wipe the record clean.
Well, I'd only been in jail for
thirteen hours and I already knew
that Nam couldn't be any worse.

                         JACOB
Shows how much you knew.

                         MICHAEL
No shit. They had me by the balls.
Next thing I know I'm in Saigon ...
in a secret lab synthesizing mind-
altering drugs. Not the street stuff
mind you. They had us isolating
special properties. The dark side,
you know? They wanted a drug that
increased aggressive tendencies.

                         JACOB
Yeah, sure. We were losing the war.

                         MICHAEL
Right. They were worried. They
figured you guys were too soft. They
wanted something to stir you up, tap
into your anger, you know? And we did
it. The most powerful thing I ever
saw. Even a bad trip, and I had my
share, never compared to the fury of
the Ladder.

                         JACOB
The Ladder?

                         MICHAEL
That's what they called it. A fast
trip right down the ladder.
                    (he makes a downward
                    dive with his hand)
Right to the primal fear, the base
anger. I'm tellin' you, it was

                                        (CONTINUED)

                         MICHAEL (CONT.)
          powerful stuff. But I don't need to
          tell you. You know.

JACOB can barely catch his breath, the information he
is receiving is so powerful to his mind.

                         MICHAEL
                    (continuing)
          We did experiments on jungle monkeys.
          They bashed each other's heads in,
          gouged out their eyes, chewed off
          their tails. The brass loved it. Then
          they made us try it on Charlie.
                    (he pauses)
          They took these POW's, just kids
          really, and put 'em in a courtyard.
          We fed 'em huge doses of the stuff.
                    (he stops for a moment;
                    a tear rolls down his
                    cheek)
          They were worse than the monkeys. I
          never knew men could do such things.
          The whole thing still blows me away.

MICHAEL stands up and begins walking in circles around
the PIER. JACOB, astounded, gets up and walks beside
him.

                         MICHAEL
                    (continuing)
          Anyway, this big offensive was coming
          up. Everyone knew it; Time Magazine,
          Huntley-Brinkley. And the brass was
          scared 'cause they knew we couldn't
          win. Morale was down. It was gettin'
          ugly in the States. Hell, you
          remember.

                         JACOB
          Like it was yesterday.

                         MICHAEL
          A couple days later they decided to
          use the Ladder, on one test
          battalion. Yours. Just in an
          infinitessimal dose in the food
          supply, to prove its effectiveness in
          the field. They were sure your unit
          would have the highest kill ratio in
          the whole goddamn offensive. And you
          did, too. But not the way they
          thought.

JACOB is beginning to shake. MICHAEL pulls a container
of pills out of his jacket pocket.

                                        (CONTINUED)

> MICHAEL
> (continuing)
> Hey, want something to calm you down?
> Made 'em myself.

JACOB shakes his head no.

> JACOB
> None of us can remember that night. I
> get flashes of it but they don't make
> sense. We saw shrinks for years. But
> nothing they did could ever touch it.
> What happened? Was there ever an
> offensive?

> MICHAEL
> A couple of days later. It was
> fierce. You guys never saw it.

> JACOB
> But there was an attack. I can still
> see them coming. There was a fight,
> wasn't there?

> MICHAEL
> Yeah. But not with the Cong.

> JACOB
> Who then?

He hesitates, obviously uncomfortable. His eyes grow
puffy. He looks at the river for a moment and then
turns to JACOB.

> MICHAEL
> You killed each other.

JACOB's mouth drops open. The words hit him like a
truck.


**80A EXT.   VIETNAM — NIGHT**

Gunfire explodes in the darkening sky. We are in
Vietnam. JACOB is at the bottom of a trench fighting
with FRANK. Chaos surrounds them. Men are screaming.
The ENEMY is storming at them from the rear. ROD
raises his bayonet and jams it into the belly of his
ATTACKER. It is only after a series of jabs that he
sees that it's another American he's killed. ROD's
eyes go blank with confusion and terror.

> ROD
> Oh my God! WHAT'S HAPPENING?

JACOB looks up from the trench and sees a continuing
wave of AMERICAN SOLDIERS bearing down on them.
FRANK jumps up, knocking JACOB to the ground and

(CONTINUED)

slamming his rifle into JACOB's back. As he spins around
JACOB sees another SOLDIER charging at him. His bayonet is
aimed at JACOB's stomach. For the first time JACOB
remembers the face of his attacker. He is a YOUNG MAN,
about 19 years old, clean cut, wearing glasses. The two
men stare at one another in terrible confusion. It seems
   like a moment out of time. And then the SOLDIER
   lurches forward and rams his bayonet deep into JACOB's
   abdomen.

CUT TO MICHAEL BACK ON THE PIER. JACOB is ashen-faced.

                    MICHAEL
          It was brother against brother. No
          discrimination. You tore each other
          to pieces. I knew it would happen. I
          warned them. I WARNED THEM. But I was
          just a hippie chemist, right? Jesus!
          And I helped 'em make the stuff ... I
          talked to the guys who bagged the
          bodies. They're in worse shape than
          you, believe me. They saw what was
          left. It's a blessing you don't
          remember. Of course the brass covered
          the whole thing up right away. Blamed
          it all on a surprise attack.
                    (he pauses)
          I needed to find you. The Ladder was
          my baby.

Tears start flowing down MICHAEL's face. He wipes them
with his sleeve. It takes him a moment to regain his
composure. JACOB is shivering. MICHAEL takes off his
jacket, drapes it over JACOB, and leads him to the
wooden planks overhanging the water. They sit and gaze
at the JERSEY SHORE.


**80B** CUT TO A WIDE SHOT OF MICHAEL AND JACOB in pre-dawn
light.

                    MICHAEL
          I always suspected the effects might
          come back. That's why I had to follow
          you. I had a hell of a time getting
          hold of your records.

                    JACOB
          If you knew, why didn't you say
          anything?

                    MICHAEL
          The truth can kill, my friend. Five
          hundred men died out there. This
          isn't a story they'd ever want out.
          When Paul's car blew up I realized

                                        (CONTINUED)

80B CONTINUED:

>                    MICHAEL (CONT.)
>           the scope of the thing. I knew they
>           meant business.
>
>                    JACOB
>           So why tell me now?
>
>                    MICHAEL
>           Because I can get rid of the demons.
>           I can block the Ladder. I have an
>           antidote. We can kill them off,
>           chemically speaking. They'll all
>           disappear. It's chemistry, my friend.
>           I know. I created it. Come with me. I
>           can help.


81  INT.    HOTEL — DAWN

JACOB and MICHAEL enter a sleazy HOTEL near the docks,
obviously frequented by a gay clientele. JACOB is
uncomfortable as they check in. MICHAEL, however,
seems to know the ropes. They go to a small room.

>                    JACOB
>           You come here often?
>
>                    MICHAEL
>           Sometimes. When it's convenient.
>
>                    JACOB
>           How do I know this isn't just some
>           kind of, you know, seduction or
>           something?
>
>                    MICHAEL
>           Hey, I'm not the problem. You've got
>           bigger problems than me.

MICHAEL reaches into his pocket and casually extracts
a vial.

>                    MICHAEL
>                (continuing)
>           I came up with the formula back in
>           Nam but I never got a chance to use
>           it.
>
>                    JACOB
>           Never?
>
>                    MICHAEL
>           I'd hoped I'd never have to. Just
>           open your mouth and stick out your
>           tongue.
>
>                    JACOB
>           What is it?

(CONTINUED)

94

                         MICHAEL
          Don't worry. Take it. It'll free your
          head. Come on.

                         JACOB
                (fearful)
          I don't know.

                         MICHAEL
          "Yea though I walk through the valley
          of the shadow of death I shall fear
          no evil," but no one ever said I
          wouldn't be shittin' in my pants
          every step of the way, huh?
                (JACOB smiles, his mouth
                open)
          Stick out your tongue.
                (JACOB obeys as an
                eyedropper deposits a
                drop of liquid on the
                back of his tongue)
          That'a boy. Now why don't you just
          lie down and relax.

                         JACOB
          One drop?

                         MICHAEL
          It's strong stuff.

JACOB stretches out on the bed. He stares up at the
ceiling and examines its pock-marked lunar look. Long
cracks and shallow craters erode the surface. It is an
alien terrain.

                         JACOB
          I think I'm falling asleep.

                         MICHAEL
          Pleasant dreams.

The words send a jolt through JACOB's body. He tries
to get up but can't. He's frightened.

                         JACOB
          I can't move.

                         MICHAEL
          Just relax.

                         JACOB
          What's happening? Help me.

The ceiling begins to rumble. Cracks split wide open.
Huge crevasses tear through the plaster. JACOB's world
is crumbling. He stares in horror as DEMONIC FORMS
attempt to surge through the rupture above him.
Piercing eyes and sharp teeth glimmer in the darkness.

                                        (CONTINUED)

Hooved feet and pointed claws clamor to break through.

                         JACOB
                    (continuing)
          HELP ME!

Instantly MICHAEL appears standing over him. He is
holding the vial with the antidote. He draws an
eyedropper full of the fluid and holds it over JACOB's
mouth.

                         MICHAEL
          Take it!

JACOB fights him, but MICHAEL forces the entire
contents of the eyedropper down his throat. JACOB
gags. He tries to spit it out, but can't.

Suddenly the ceiling erupts in violent clashes as
whole chunks break off and collide like continental
plates. The collisions wreak havoc on the DEMONS,
chopping and dismembering them. Body parts fall from
the ceiling like a Devil's rain. Horrible screams echo
from the other side.

                         MICHAEL
                    (continuing)
          Don't fight it. It's your own mind.
          It's your own fears.

Flashes of light and dark storm over JACOB's head,
thundering like a war in the heavens. It is a scene of
raw power and growing catastrophe. It builds in fury
and rage until suddenly the ceiling explodes. JACOB's
eyes stare into the formlessness expanding around him.
All space is becoming a dark liquid void.

Gradually the liquid grows bluer, clearer. There is an
undulating sense to the imagery, a feeling of
womb-like comfort. Strange lights appear and sparkle
before us like sunlight on the ocean. JACOB is rushing
upward, toward the surface.

With the delirious sound of water giving way to air,
JACOB breaks through. To his amazement, he finds
himself floating out-stretched on shimmering sunlit
water. Above him are clouds of such wondrous beauty
that they cannot possibly be of the earth. Pillars of
golden light reach down from the heavens creating a
cathedral of light. It is a vision of heaven, a vast,
almost mythic paradise. JACOB is awed.

A sudden movement catches his attention. He looks over
and sees MICHAEL standing before him. Only MICHAEL
looks different. His face seems to radiate an inner
light, a transcendental beauty. JACOB is nearly
blinded by his presence and must shield his eyes to
look at him.

                                        (CONTINUED)

>                    MICHAEL
>           So, how you doin'?

The casualness of the words catches JACOB by surprise.
He sits up. To his shock and amazement, he finds that
he is back in THE HOTEL ROOM. MICHAEL is standing at
the foot of the bed. JACOB is totally disoriented. His
eyes move slowly around the room, taking everything
in. He doesn't speak.

>                    MICHAEL
>                  (continuing)
>           It was better than you expected, huh?

JACOB just stares at him for a while and then suddenly
begins to laugh. It is a huge laugh, full of energy
and life.

>                    MICHAEL
>                  (continuing)
>           And no more demons. I told you they'd
>           be gone.

>                    JACOB
>           I don't believe this. It's a miracle,
>           Michael. A miracle.

>                    MICHAEL
>           Better living through chemistry,
>           that's my motto.


## 82  EXT.    GREENWICH VILLAGE — DAY

JACOB and MICHAEL are walking through the STREETS OF
GREENWICH VILLAGE. It is early MORNING and the
sidewalks are bustling with PEOPLE. JACOB stares into
their faces and beams when they smile back. MICHAEL
enjoys JACOB's happiness.


## 83  EXT.    WASHINGTON SQUARE — DAY

JACOB and MICHAEL walk through WASHINGTON SQUARE PARK.

>                    JACOB
>           It was paradise, Michael. You showed
>           it to me. You were there.

>                    MICHAEL
>           Well that's good to know.

>                    JACOB
>           Mike, it was real. It was glorious.

>                    MICHAEL
>           Glorious. I'm not surprised. I fed

>                                      (CONTINUED)

97

                              MICHAEL (CONT.)
               you enough of that stuff to send a
               horse to heaven. I'm just glad you
               came back.

                              JACOB
               I would have stayed there if I could.

                              MICHAEL
               I'm sure. You've got nothing but
               troubles waitin' for you here.

He points to two POLICEMEN on the far side of the
SQUARE.

                              MICHAEL
                      (taking JACOB's arm)
               Come on.


**84  EXT.   GRAMERCY PARK HOTEL — DAY**

The TWO MEN head up to GRAMERCY PARK and stop in front
of the GRAMERCY PARK HOTEL. Reaching into his wallet,
MICHAEL pulls out a huge stack of credit cards and
hands one to JACOB.

                              MICHAEL
               Here. I've got every credit card ever
               printed. Take this. Stay here till
               you can arrange to get away. It's on
               me.

                              JACOB
               No. I couldn't.

                              MICHAEL
               What? You want the Plaza? Don't be
               foolish. Here. Take this, too.
                      (he pulls out a business
                      card)
               This is my place on Prince Street.
               It's got my phone, everything. Call
               if you need me ... but you won't.
               Everything's gonna work out. You just
               get outta town as fast as you can.
               The New York police can be effective
               when they want to be.

                              JACOB
               I don't know what to say.

                              MICHAEL
               Save the words ... Just send back my
               credit card.

MICHAEL laughs, hugs JACOB, and walks away.

85 INT. HOTEL ROOM — DAY

    JACOB is in a lovely HOTEL ROOM overlooking GRAMERCY
    SQUARE. He is sprawled out happily on the bed when
    there is a knock at the door. He jumps up and opens
    it. JEZZIE is standing there. She looks at JACOB
    quizzically. He smiles and takes her in his arms,
    swinging her into the room.

                    JEZZIE
        What are you doing here? Are you all
        right? How do you expect to pay for
        this?
            (JACOB smiles)
        Everyone's looking for you, Jake. I
        dodged people all over the place,
        reporters, police. I don't know what
        you're gonna do.

                    JACOB
        I'm gonna make love to you. That's
        what I'm gonna do.

                    JEZZIE
        Are you out of your mind?

                    JACOB
        Yep. Finally. I love you, Jez.

                    JEZZIE
        God, I can't keep up with all your
        changes.

                    JACOB
        Me neither.

                    JEZZIE
        What's gotten into you?

    JACOB grins.

    CUT TO JACOB and JEZZIE lying in bed gently caressing
    one another. For all his ardor JACOB is exhausted from
    the events of the preceding day. While stroking
    JEZZIE's hair he begins to fall asleep. JEZZIE crawls
    on top of him and shoves her hands down his pants.
    JACOB smiles.

    DISSOLVE TO JACOB and JEZZIE making love.

                                 TIME CUT:


86 DISSOLVE TO JACOB and JEZZIE lying in front of the
    T.V. watching a romantic movie. JEZZIE snuggles up to
    JACOB.

                            (CONTINUED)

> JEZZIE
> It's amazing, you know, that a drug
> could change things like that,
> destroy a life and then give it back.
> It's hard to believe that the world
> could be so hellish one day and like
> heaven the next.

> JACOB
> I tell you, it was so wonderful. I
> felt like a little boy. I saw
> Paradise, Jezzie.

> JEZZIE
> It's so hard to believe.

There is a knock at the door. JACOB throws on a
bathrobe. JEZZIE jumps under the sheets.

> JACOB
> Who's there?

> BELLBOY (V.O.)
> It's your dinner, sir.

JEZZIE's eyes brighten. JACOB opens the door. A
BELLBOY wheels in a table set for dinner. He sets it
in the corner of the room. JEZZIE jumps out of bed,
runs to the table, sniffs at the food, and squeals
excitedly.

> JEZZIE
> This is one of my dreams, Jake. Ever
> since I was a little girl. I never
> thought it would happen.

> JACOB
> Stick with me, kid.

JEZZIE smiles.

> TIME CUT:

87 DISSOLVE to JACOB and JEZZIE sitting next to a large
window overlooking GRAMERCY PARK. They are sipping
champagne.

> JEZZIE
> I want to go with you, Jake. Wherever
> you go.

> JACOB
> It's not practical, Jez. It'll be
> hard enough alone.

> JEZZIE
> I can waitress. I'm good.

> (CONTINUED)

100

> JACOB
> No. Things are too hot. Later. I'll
> send for you.

> JEZZIE
> Bullshit!

> JACOB
> I promise.

> JEZZIE
> Please.

> JACOB
> No. I'm a marked man, Jez. I'm the
> only one left. I don't want to expose
> you to that. It's not right for you
> or me. Be reasonable.

> JEZZIE
> Reasonable? Reasonable? Jake ...
> You're gettin' me angry.

> JACOB
> I love you when you're angry.

> JEZZIE
> Oh yeah?
>       (her eyes twinkle
>       suggestively)
> Try leavin' without me.

JACOB laughs. JEZZIE doesn't. Unexpectedly she grabs
JACOB and pushes him onto the bed. In seconds they are
all over each other, their clothes flying in all
directions. They seem as happy as could be.


**88  OMIT**


**89  INT.   GRAND CENTRAL STATION — DAY**

JACOB enters GRAND CENTRAL STATION. He checks out all
the PEOPLE around him. Not a DEMON in sight. Hurrying
to the TICKET WINDOW he gets in line. The TICKET
SELLER looks up.

> JACOB
> Chicago. One way. For tomorrow.

> SELLER
> How many?

> JACOB
> One.

(CONTINUED)

89  CONTINUED:

                 That'll be $119.75.

JACOB pulls out MICHAEL's credit card. The SELLER
rings it up. While he is waiting JACOB notices a
POLICEMAN looking at him. The stare unsettles him. The
SELLER hands JACOB his ticket. He takes it and hurries
into the CROWD. Looking back he notices the POLICEMAN
is following him.


90  **INT. MEN'S ROOM — DAY**

JACOB enters the MEN'S ROOM. He hurries into one of
the stalls, drops his pants, and sits. He eyes the
graffiti on the walls and then notices a wad of tissue
stuffed into a hole between him and the next stall. It
is moving. Suddenly the tissue falls to the floor.
JACOB glances at the hole curiously and leans forward
to examine it. He is shocked to see an eye staring
back at him.

                          JACOB
                 Goddamn it!
                          (he covers it with his
                          hand. A pencil jabs his
                          palm. He yells)
                 Fucking pervert.

Two lips form around the hole. A tongue wags
obscenely.

                          VOICE
                 Dream on!

                          JACOB
                      (shocked)
                 What?!

The mouth is gone. JACOB hears the stall door fly open
and feet running from the room. He jumps up and grabs
his pants. He dashes out of the MEN'S ROOM. He hears
footsteps and chases after them.


91  **INT.   GRAND CENTRAL STATION — DAY**

JACOB bursts into the MAIN TERMINAL. He sees someone
rushing toward the main doors and speeds after him.
HOMELESS PEOPLE, huddling along the corridors, watch
as they run past. Escaping to the street, the MAN
disappears in the holiday throngs. JACOB, crazed,
stands gasping for breath. His fists dig into his coat
pocket. Suddenly he feels something and seems
surprised when MICHAEL's CARD emerges in his hand.

92  OMIT


93  INT. SOHO LOFT BUILDING — EVENING

JACOB runs up the stairs in a SOHO LOFT BUILDING. It
is a dingy, industrial staircase, poorly lit. He
reaches a door with MICHAEL's name painted on it in
large black letters. He knocks loudly. There is no
answer. He pounds on it. Another door opens on the
floor above. A head sticks out.

                    MAN
          You lookin' for Mike?

                    JACOB
               (panting hard)
          Where is he?

                    MAN
          Don't know. Hasn't picked his mail up
          in days. It's not like him.

JACOB has a frenzied look in his eyes. He searches
around the staircase and sees a pile of lumber stacked
in a corner. He grabs a two-by-four and lunges at the
door.

                    MAN
          What the hell are you doing?

JACOB doesn't answer. He smashes wildly at the door
until the lock flies open.


94  INT.   MICHAEL'S LOFT — EVENING

JACOB charges into the dark space groping for a light.
He finds it. The LOFT is a disaster area. Nothing is
standing. JACOB runs from room to room. In the back he
discovers a large private chemistry lab. Glass vials
and bottles are shattered on the floor.

JACOB rifles through the cabinets. A few bottles are
intact but their labels mean nothing to him.

He reaches for one cabinet and notices a reddish
liquid oozing out from the bottom. He opens it.
MICHAEL's severed head stares him in the face. It is
smiling.

A scream rings out as the MAN from upstairs sees what
JACOB has seen. JACOB jumps back, trips, and falls
over MICHAEL's headless body. It is lying sprawled
across the floor.

                    MAN
          Oh my God!

                                    (CONTINUED)

94  CONTINUED:

JACOB stumbles to pull himself up. He is in a state of
unrelieved panic. He runs past the MAN and spills out
the door. He takes two and three stairs at a time,
nearly flying to the street.

## 95  EXT.  SOHO STREETS — NIGHT

JACOB rushes into the icy air and runs wildly down the
sidewalk as fast as his legs will move. With unexpected violence he charges into the side of a building.
Over and over again he hurls himself against it. He
grabs for the bricks. His fingers insert themselves
into the crevices. It is a though he is trying to
merge with the wall.

Suddenly JACOB turns and dashes into the street. A
taxi is speeding toward him, its lights the only sign
of life and warmth in the dark night. JACOB steps into
its path. It is hard to tell if he is trying to stop
the cab or waiting to be hit. The taxi screeches to a
halt. JACOB stares at it a moment and then steps to
get in. The DRIVER tries to pull off but JACOB yanks
at the door and drags himself inside.

## 96  INT.  TAXI — NIGHT

Rain is beginning to fall. It streaks the windows.

> JACOB
> (barely audible)
> I'm going to Brooklyn.

> DRIVER
> Sorry, Mac. Not with me you're not. I
> get lost in Brooklyn.

> JACOB
> I know the way.

JACOB reaches into his pants pocket, pulls out a
twenty dollar bill, and hands it to the DRIVER. He
takes it.

> JACOB
> (continuing)
> Look, this is all the money I've got
> in the world. Take me home and it's
> yours.

> DRIVER
> ... Where's your home?

CUT TO THE TAXI heading down WEST BROADWAY,
approaching the BROOKLYN BRIDGE, crossing the EAST
RIVER, and driving through dark BROOKLYN STREETS.

(CONTINUED)

104

JACOB's face passes in and out of dense shadows. Every time he is bathed in light his image seems to alter. Something in him is falling away.

## 97 EXT.   SARAH'S APARTMENT BUILDING — NIGHT

JACOB gets out of the TAXI and approaches the LOBBY of SARAH'S APARTMENT BUILDING. JACOB is greeted by the DOORMAN.

> DOORMAN
> Dr. Singer. It's been a long time.

> JACOB
> (greeting him warmly)
> Hello, Sam.

> DOORMAN
> (noticing JACOB's
> battered condition)
> Are you all right?

> JACOB
> I'm okay.

> DOORMAN
> Do you want some help? I can call upstairs.

> JACOB
> No, don't. But thanks.

## 98 INT.   HALLWAY — NIGHT

JACOB stoops in front of the APARTMENT door and reaches his hand underneath a section of the hallway carpet. It comes back with a key. He inserts it into the lock and gently opens the door. He calls out.

> JACOB
> Hello. It's me.

## 99 INT. SARAH'S APARTMENT — NIGHT

Some lights are on. The APARTMENT looks comfortable and cozy.

> JACOB
> Hello? Is anyone home? Jed? Eli?
> Daddy's here.

There is still no answer. JACOB is surprised. He peers into the dark LIVING ROOM and then walks to the KITCHEN. No one is around. A photo of JACOB, SARAH,

(CONTINUED)

AND THEIR BOYS is sitting on the counter. He picks it up and carries it with him through the apartment. He walks into his old BEDROOM and then the BOYS' ROOM. The beds are still unmade. There is no one home. He sees his image in the BATHROOM mirror and turns away in disgust. He walks back to the LIVING ROOM. He is about to switch the lights on when he hears footsteps coming down the hall. He calls out.

> JACOB
> Sarah, is that you? I hope you don't mind. I needed to come home.

JACOB is startled to see JEZZIE enter the room. She does not seem her usual self. She appears larger, more imposing.

> JEZZIE
> Hello, Jake. I knew you'd come here in the end.

JACOB is nervous.

> JACOB
> What're you ... ? Where's Sarah? Where are the boys?

> JEZZIE
> Sit down, Jake.

> JACOB
> Where are they?

> JEZZIE
> Sit down.

> JACOB
> No! What's going on? Where's my family?

> JEZZIE
> It's over, Jake. It's all over.

> JACOB
> Where have they gone?

> JEZZIE
> Wake up. Stop playing with yourself. It's finished.

JEZZIE stares at JACOB with a frightening, powerful glare. The edge of her coat rustles and flutters as she moves toward him. It is an innocent sound at first, but after a moment it transforms into something else, an obsessive flapping noise, the sound of a wing.

JACOB's body feels the first waves of an inner tremor. His legs are shaking.

(CONTINUED)

106

> JACOB
>
> What's going on?

> JEZZIE
>
> Your capacity for self delusion is
> remarkable, Dr. Singer.

JEZZIE begins walking around the dark living room as
she talks to him. Something about her walk is very
unnatural. JACOB eyes her fearfully.

In the darkness JEZZIE's movements become increasingly
strange and elusive. We see her pass before a shadow
and disappear within it, only to reappear, seconds later, in a doorway on the other side of the room. JACOB
spins around, confused. Suddenly JEZZIE is inches from
his face, although it seems like there has been no time
for her to get there. Her movements are totally impossible, defying all logic, all physical laws.

> JEZZIE
> (continuing)
> What's wrong, Jake?
> (she mocks him)
> Forget to take your antidote?

> JACOB
>
> Who are you? What are you doing to me?

> JEZZIE
>
> You have quite a mind, Jake. I loved
> your friends. That chemist — the
> Ladder. What an imagination you have!

JACOB freezes.

> JEZZIE
> (continuing)
> And your vision of paradise ...
> fantastic! You're a real dreamer, you
> know that? Only it's time to wake up.

JEZZIE has dissapeared in the darkness of the room.
Only the sounds of flapping wings remain. They grow
louder and more menacing, whooshing past him with no
visible source.

> JEZZIE
> (continuing)
> Your mind is crumbling, Jake. No more
> "army." No more conspiracies. You're
> dying, Dr. Singer. It's over.

JACOB, frightened, turns toward the door as if to
hurry out. "JEZZIE" laughs.

> JEZZIE
> (continuing)
> Where's to run, Jacob? Where's to go?

(CONTINUED)

100 CONTINUED:

JACOB pauses a moment and then turns to confront the
terror behind him.

> JACOB
>
> WHO ARE YOU?

> JEZZIE
>
> How many times have you asked me
> that? How many times?

> JACOB
>
> TELL ME, DAMN YOU!

> JEZZIE
> (with consummate power)
> YOU KNOW WHO I AM.

JEZZIE appears from the shadows. Her coat collar
obscures her and it seems for a moment that she has no
face. Then, to JACOB's horror, she turns around. He is
staring at the vibrating creature he has seen so often
before. Glimpsed almost in abstraction it is a living
terror, dark and undefinable. Its face is a black and
impenetrable void in constant vibration. Its voice is
an unspeakable demonic cry, the essence of fear and
suffering. JACOB pulls away from it, overwhelmed by
confusion. He is rooted in fear.

A sudden wind howls through the room, great gales
blowing JACOB's hair straight up. It is like a
hurricane pushing him into the wall. He can barely
stand. He struggles to pull himself away. The flapping
sound returns, charging at him from all directions. It
is as if the darkness itself is swooping down, trying
to envelop him.

> JACOB
> (whispering to himself)
> This isn't happening.

New terrible sounds arise, chain saws slashing through
the air, knives, and sabers ripping through space with
unrelenting anger. Guns fire and explode past his
head. It is as though all the sounds of destruction
are closing in on him. JACOB yells but his own voice
is lost in the melée. Terrified, he looks heavenward,
as if crying for help.

Suddenly, from the noise, a calm voice rises,
speaking, as if from a distance. It is LOUIS. JACOB is
shocked to hear him. He stands motionless.

> LOUIS (V.O.)
> If you're frightened of dying you'll
> see devils tearing you apart. If
> you've made your peace then they're
> angels freeing you from the world.

(CONTINUED)

108

The voice fades. JACOB just stands there, not sure
what to do. And then the sounds return. Only now they
are more terrifying than ever. Hideously loud, they
become a cacophony of sounds, voices of parents,
friends, lovers, the sounds of battle, fighting, and
dying.

JACOB looks up and sees the creature in the center of
the room. All the sounds seem to emanate from it. The
more JACOB stares at it the louder they become. After
a moment, JACOB takes a huge breath. We sense a great
resolve forming inside him. Then, slowly, courageous-
ly, he begins moving toward it.

New and more terrifying noises assault JACOB,
attempting to drive him back, but he will not be
stopped. He continues walking toward the creature.

In the hallway a standing lamp slams sparking to the
floor. It rolls back and forth like a living thing,
with a maddening hypnotic regularity. Doors slam open
and closed, unlatching, snapping , shutting, with
deafening force. The room itself seems like an organic
presence. It is alive, angry, threatening.

The CREATURE sits in the midst of the insanity like
the source of madness itself. It writhes, contorts,
and vibrates with unstoppable fury. JACOB, terrified,
but unrelenting, continues to approach it.

AS THE CAMERA DRAWS CLOSER TO THE CREATURE'S HEAD the
density of its featureless form overwhelms the screen.
It is like staring into emptiness itself, the ultimate
darkness.

With superhuman effort JACOB grabs hold of the
creature. It is like grabbing hold of a live wire. His
body begins shaking uncontrollably like a man being
electrocuted. He is flying in all directions but does
not let go. His fingers claw at the creature's head.
JACOB struggles defiantly with the monster.

Suddenly a terrible voice emerges from within it.

                    CREATURE
          WHO DO YOU THINK YOU'RE FIGHTING!

JACOB does not respond. It cries out again.

                    CREATURE
          WHO THE HELL DO YOU THINK YOU'RE
          FIGHTING?

Deep inside the darkness JACOB begins to make out the
presence of a form, something writhing and tortured
lurking before us. It looks briefly like an animal
until we realize it is the image of a human face. It
is covered by a dark suffocating film, like a mask.

                                        (CONTINUED)

JACOB digs into it with all his might and pulls it off.

CUT TO:

DEAD SILENCE as JACOB SEES HIS OWN FACE staring back at him from beneath the mask. It is JACOB SINGER as we first saw him on the battlefield in Vietnam. Only now his image is pale and lifeless. It takes JACOB a moment to realize that he is dead. The recognition is one of terrible confusion and pain. JACOB stares at himself for a long time as a huge cry wells up inside him. It bursts forth with devastating sadness.

At that instant the whole of space seems to explode in a flash of cataclysmic power. Hundreds of images from JACOB's life flash before us, his birth, his childhood, his adulthood. The demons, the room, JEZZIE, LOUIS, MICHAEL, SARAH, all seem to assail us in a rush of blinding intensity.

We are flying over a landscape of memories, zooming across a constantly changing field of images. Some of the images move, some of the people in them speak. They are not particularly significant moments, in some ways they are quite banal, but something about them is infused with life and joy. Even the painful moments resonate with vital force. Some of the moments we recognize from the time we've spent with JACOB. Some we have not seen before. There is no order to them, no logic to why they have been recalled.

A newborn baby takes its first breath and screams. SARAH pulls clothes off a clothes line on a rainy day. JACOB's FATHER stands in the Florida surf as sea foam laps gently at his legs. PAUL, FRANK, and JACOB play cards on the edge of a rice paddy. GABE rides his bike into the path of an oncoming car. A child puts her ear next to a bowl of cereal, listening to it talk. A young girl standing in a doorway, lifts up her blouse to show her new breasts. JACOB and SARAH slice a wedding cake that topples to the floor. JEZZIE looks at JACOB and asks "Love me a little?"

And then it is over. Total silence overwhelms the screen, a wonderful soothing calm. JACOB's eyes open and he is shocked to find himself sitting on the floor in SARAH's apartment. He is all alone. The first rays of early morning sunlight are filtering through the window. Something about the apartment seems transfigured, magical. JACOB sits motionless, stunned to be back there.

The faint sound of music can be heard coming from the hallway. It is warm and familiar, the tinkling of a music box. JACOB listens to it for a few moments and then something registers inside him. Curious, he gets

(CONTINUED)

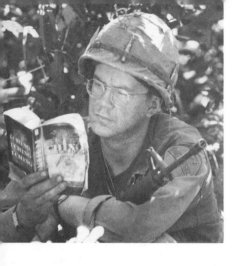

up and approaches the corridor.

> JACOB

> Hello?

There is no response. Suddenly the music stops. JACOB freezes for a moment. He sees someone standing in the shadows at the other end.

> JACOB
> (continuing)
> Who is it? Who's there?

Tentatively JACOB moves forward. As he draws closer he begins to see the outline of a child. Then, all of a sudden, he realizes who it is. His eyes well up as he stands there, the full impact of the moment register- ing inside him. It's his son, GABE. He is carrying the same musical lunch box we have seen before. The young boy smiles warmly at his father. It is the smile of an angel. JACOB swallows hard.

> JACOB
> (continuing)
> Gabe? Gabe!

JACOB runs to his son. Unable to hold back the tears, he embraces him in a rush of love and emotion.

> JACOB
> (continuing)
> Gabe. Oh God. I don't believe ...

They hug one another over and over. JACOB, overcome, sits down on the stairs. After a moment GABE puts his arm around his father's shoulder in a gesture of sur- prising maturity and compassion. We sense for an in- stant that their roles have reversed. GABE reaches for JACOB's hand and gently encourages him to stand up.

With a sweet tug GABE leads his father up the steps.

Sunlight streams down from the top of the stairs, hitting the first landing. GABE is bathed in its warm glow. As JACOB reaches the landing, he too is sur- rounded by the comforting light.

GABE hurries up the last set of stairs. JACOB turns to follow but is stunned by the brilliance of the light pouring in from above. Squinting, he cannot see his son. Then suddenly GABE steps back out of the light and takes his father's hand once more. His eyes sparkle with excitement.

> GABE
> Come on Dad ... You know what we've
> got? a sandbox just like the
> Williston's, only it's bigger and the

(CONTINUED)

>           GABE (CONT.)
> sand's all white. You won't believe
> it.

JACOB smiles at his son. GABE smiles at him. It is a
moment of total euphoria. THE CAMERA HOLDS as they
continue up the stairs.

>           GABE
>         (continuing)
> And my parakeet. Remember, the one
> grandma let out of the cage? He's
> okay. And he's talking now. He knows
> my name.

GABE's voice slowly trails off as he and his father
disappear in the intensity of the light. THE CAMERA
holds on the image. For a brief but stunning moment
there appears to be a huge ethereal staircase shimmering before us. It rises up into infinite dimensions.
Then the brilliance of its blinding light overwhelms
the screen.

Suddenly the brightness condenses into a smaller light
source. It holds for a second and then flashes off. An
overhead surgical lamp remains stubbornly in view.


**101 INT.    VIETNAM FIELD HOSPITAL — DAY**

A DOCTOR leans his head in front of the lamp and
removes his mask. His expression is somber. He shakes
his head. His words are simple and final.

>           DOCTOR
> He's gone.

CUT TO JACOB SINGER lying on an operating table in a
large ARMY FIELD TENT in VIETNAM. The DOCTOR steps
away. A NURSE rudely pulls a green sheet up over his
head. The DOCTOR turns to one of the aides and throws
up his hands in defeat.

AN ORDERLY wheels JACOB's body past rows of other
DOCTORS and NURSES fighting to save lives. A YOUNG
VIETNAMESE BOY pulls back a screen door to let them
out of the tent. It is a bright, fresh morning. The
sun is rising.


                    THE END

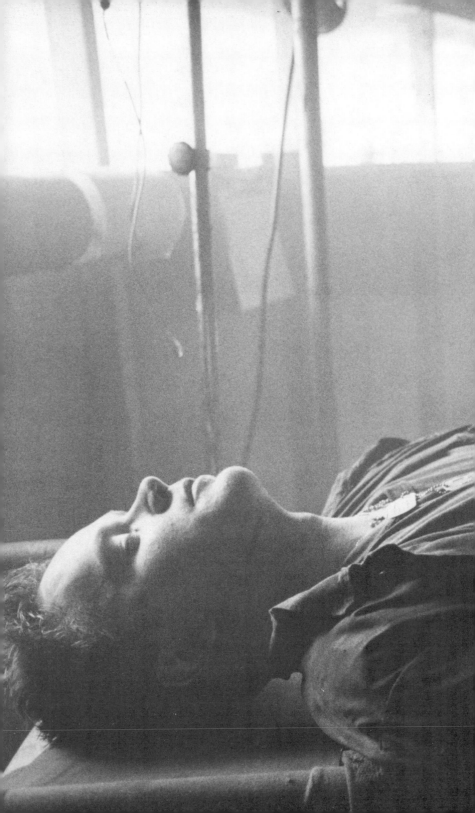

# Scenes
# Deleted
# Prior to
# Production

# ADDENDUM 1
## PROFESSOR STERN

The Professor Stern sequence survived nearly all the early changes in the script. Neither Adrian nor I wanted to alter or eliminate it, although we both knew that it was a long scene, and almost totally expositional. This is the kind of material that rarely makes it into the final cut of a film: all about character, with little impact on the advancement of the action, when a film is long or top-heavy it is almost always the first to go.

Adrian and I were very attached to this sequence. Professor Stern established Jacob as a philosopher, a Ph.D., and this was a key pillar in the formation of his character. It was the first serious introduction of Jacob's fear of demons and placed the entire subject of demonology into a cultural and historical framework. The sequence established the brilliance of Jacob's mind, his background in Existentialism, and the reason for his becoming a postman. The scene also explained Jacob's problem as a spiritual matter, and not necessarily as a sign of insanity. And lastly, the introduction of Stern in the classroom allowed for a brief expression of four mystical doctrines central to the thesis of the movie. Obviously these are all significant elements. In the larger framework of the film, however, they were expendable. Several of the character ideas were layered into the first chiropractor scene with Louis and the others were dropped.

I have to take full responsibility for cutting the scene. As much as I loved it and felt it added tremendously to the film, I knew that it was doomed and felt that I should be the one to lower the axe myself. Of course, in the end, Adrian agreed with me. The movie was long and something had to go. It was a painful decision but making movies is a daring and often painful process. One can only hope that what survives the cutting process will have its own integrity and that the movie will work on its own terms. This process is carried on long beyond the writing phase. The editing of a movie involves hundreds of cuts that have nothing to do with the script. The final cutting is done with celluloid with the writer nowhere around.

**INT.   CITY COLLEGE LECTURE HALL - DAY**

CUT TO a huge amphitheatre-style LECTURE HALL at CITY COLLEGE. It is almost empty. No more than FORTY STUDENTS are scattered near the front of nearly three hundred seats. All are listening to PROFESSOR EMANUEL STERN who is nearing the end of his lecture.

115

                    STERN
          Thus at the core of today's discus-
          sion we find four fundamental doc-
          trines. First, that the world of
          matter and individual consciousness
          are both manifestations of one Divine
          Reality.

One of the STUDENTS seems about to fall asleep and
keeps nodding his head.

                    STERN
          Even you, Mr. Palmer, are part of it,
          as amazing as that may seem.

MR. PALMER sits up quickly in his seat as other STU-
DENTS smile.

                    STERN
          Second, human beings are capable not
          only of knowing about this Divine Re-
          ality by inference but can realize
          its existence by direct intuition,
          superior even to reason.

A door opens in the upper reaches of the lecture hall.
JACOB enters and walks quietly down the stairs to
within hearing range of the professor.

                    STERN
          Third, man possesses a double nature,
          an ego and an eternal self, what we
          call "spirit" or soul."

JACOB takes a seat at one of the desks. There is a
pencil lying on it which he fingers distractedly.

                    STERN
          Fourth, and most important, man's
          life on earth has only one end and
          purpose, to learn to let go of the
          separate ego and to identify with the
          Divine spark within.

MR. PALMER is nodding off again.

                    STERN
          Almost impossible to believe, isn't
          it Mr. Palmer, that somewhere in that
          unconscious head of yours lies the
          source of all consciousness?

                    PALMER
          Yes, Sir. Very hard.

                    STERN
               (nodding his head)
          Well now, having reached this

                    STERN (CONT.)
        apotheosis there seems little, if
        anything, left to say. So rather than
        try, you are dismissed.

The STUDENTS seem surprised but not unhappy with the
sudden dismissal. They quickly gather their books and
begin the long climb to the exits. Only JACOB remains
seated.

                         JACOB
        Hello Prof.

PROFESSOR STERN looks up and stares at JACOB for several seconds before recognizing him.

                         STERN
        My oh my. Doctor Singer. Isn't this a
        happy surprise?

JACOB comes down the aisle and clasps hands with his
old PROFESSOR.

                         STERN
                (looking at JACOB's uni-
                form)
        Are you in the service?

                         JACOB
        The postal service. I'm a mailman.

                         STERN
                (surprised but non-
                judgemental)
        Ah. Neither snow nor sleet, nor dark
        of night ... I always admired that.

                         JACOB
                (smiling)
        It's good to see you.

                         STERN
        Likewise.


**EXT.    CITY COLLEGE - DAY**

JACOB AND PROFESSOR STERN walk down the city streets
that constitute the CAMPUS of CITY COLLEGE.

                         STERN
        And how is your wife? Sarah, no?

                         JACOB
                (shrugging his shoul-
                ders)
        I haven't seen her in months.

                         117

                    STERN
              (understanding)
Ah!

                    JACOB
I'm with another woman now. We're
both with the post office, Midtown,
34th Street branch.

                    STERN
Hmm. I don't suppose there are too
many philosophers in the post office?

                    JACOB
Oh, you'd be surprised. They just don't
have their doctorates, that's all.

                    STERN
              (he smiles)
Last I heard you were offered a position in the West somewhere. Tucson
was it?

                    JACOB
Oh, that goes way back. They had a
hiring freeze, one of those last minute things. Bad timing for me though.
Middle of the war. The draft.
              (STERN nods his head.
              They walk a moment in
              silence)
I'll tell you Prof, after Viet Nam
... I didn't want to think anymore. I
decided my brain was just too small
an organ to comprehend this chaos.

                    STERN
              (looking at JACOB with
              affection)
Jacob, if it was any other brain but
yours, I might agree.
              (he pauses)
Tell me, does your lady friend know
what a brilliant thinker, what a sub-
lime intellect she's living with?

                    JACOB
              (smiling coyly)
I doubt it's my mind that interests
her. I tell you Prof, she's a fiery
lady.

                    STERN
              (with a fatherly
              demeanor)
Well, try not to get burned. You have
a great mind, Jacob. Don't let anyone
tempt you away from it.

## INT.   OFF CAMPUS COFFEE SHOP - DAY

JACOB and PROFESSOR STERN are sitting at a quiet table
in a nearly empty coffee shop. They are both fixing
cups of tea, not speaking. Suddenly JACOB looks at
STERN.

                    JACOB
          I've got a problem, Prof. More Augus-
          tine than Kierkegard, if you know
          what I mean.
                    (STERN looks at him
                    questioningly)
          I need to know about ... demons.

                    STERN
                    (surprised)
          Demons, Jacob? Why demons? Are you
          writing ... ?

                    JACOB
          No.
                    (he pauses a moment)
          I see them.

                    STERN
          See them?
                    (he smiles uncomforta-
                    bly)
          What do you mean? Physically?

                    JACOB
                    (hesitantly)
          Yes.

STERN pauses. He looks at JACOB. The intensity of his
gaze is unsettling and JACOB reaches for his tea. The
cup rattles.

                    STERN
          I know very little about demons, Ja-
          cob, fleshy ones anyway. I know them
          as literary figures, biblical ones
          ... Dante, Milton ... but Jacob,
                    (he pauses)
          this is the 20th Century. We don't
          see demons now.

                    JACOB
          I see them, Prof. Everywhere. They're
          invading my life.

A look of concern fills STERN's eyes.

                    JACOB
                    (continuing)
          Christ, I know how it sounds.

119

                    STERN
        Have you considered a doctor? A psy-
        chiatrist?

                    JACOB
        Yes.
                (suddenly uneasy)
                JACOB (CONT.)
        I don't want them. I'm not looking
        for analysis or drugs. It's too easy
        to dismiss as some kind of psychosis.
                (he pauses uncomforta-
                bly)
        It's more than that. I can feel it. I
        need you Prof. You're the only one I
        can talk to.

                    STERN
        I don't know what to say.

                    JACOB
        I need your insight, your intuition.

        STERN sips his tea slowly. He is thinking.

                    STERN
        Demons? I don't know what to tell
        you. It sounds like a spiritual mat-
        ter to me. The problem, Jacob, is
        that you have no context for it.
        You're a renegade Existentialist suf-
        fering demons a hundred years after
        Freud. How the hell am I supposed to
        make it fit?

                    JACOB
        I'm afraid, Prof. Nothing makes
        sense.
                (he pauses)
        Please help me.

                    STERN
                (trying to be delicate)
        Jacob, I don't believe in demons, not
        in the empirical sense. I don't be-
        lieve in devils fighting for our
        souls. I don't believe in eternal
        damnation. I don't believe in other-
        worldly creatures tormenting us. We
        don't need them. We do a good enough
        job on ourselves.

                    JACOB
                (disturbed)
        But I see them.

                    STERN
        Look. I don't pretend to know what's

                    120

                    STERN (CONT.)
      going on inside your head. For all I
      know it's pathological and they
      should be pumping Valium into your
      veins by the quart. But if you're not
      willing to accept the help of sci-
      ence; and believe me, I admire you
      for that: then you'll have to do bat-
      tle on your own. What can I say? It's
      a lonely pilgrimage through our times
      even for the strongest souls. But to
      be pursued by ... demons no less ...
      There are no guides, Jacob.
                    (he muses)
      You wanna know what I'd do if I sud-
      denly started seeing demons? I'd hail
      the first taxi that came along, shoot
      over to Bellevue and beg them for
      shock treatment. I'm no saint.

                    JACOB
      Hell, you think I am?

                    STERN
      I've never understood you, you know
      that? You were by far the best pupil
      I've ever had, bar none. Intellectu-
      ally, you were the most original, the
      most imaginative. Who knows, maybe
      you've been "elected" to see demons.
      Maybe you're in touch with ... some-
      thing. Nothing would surprise me
      about you Jacob. Nothing.

JACOB gazes at his old friend and mentor, frustration
blazing in his eyes. They are both surprised to see
tears form and run down his cheek. JACOB reaches for a
napkin and dries them quickly. STERN, uncomfortable in
the face of emotion, turns away.

## ADDENDUM 2
## THE PARTY AT DELLA'S

The original transformation of the dancers into demons at Della's party was more satisfying in the original script than in the final
version. Adrian and I worked on this section for nearly a year but ultimately it was the story board drawings rather than my attempt at a
written scene that gave the dance its final coherence. Still, the original description was a central moment in sucking the reader into the
script and it feels appropriate to preserve it here.

Suddenly a strange and terrifying spectacle unfolds
before him. The DANCERS undergo a shocking transforma-

tion, a full three-dimensional alteration of their
physical forms. Clothes fuse to their bodies like new
skin. Horns and tails emerge and grow like exotic gen-
italia, exciting a frenzy among the DANCERS. New ap-
pendages appear unfolding from their flesh. Dorsal
fins protrude from their backs. Armored scales run in
scallops down their legs. Tails entwine sensuously.
Long tongues lick at the undersides of reptilian bel-
lies. The metamorphosis holds a biological fascination. Bones and flesh mold into new forms of life,
creatures of another world.

CUT TO JACOB's face as it registers terror and disbelief. He stares at the DANCERS. They are perverse,
corrupt aspects of their normal selves. He is mesmerized by JEZZIE. Her flesh has grown hard and wrinkled
and has the markings of a snake. Her tongue, long and
curled, darts in and out of her mouth repeatedly. Her
eyes are thin and domineering. They lock JACOB in
their gaze. He wants to stop, to run, but JEZZIE won't
release him.

JACOB grabs his eyes as though trying to pull the vision from them but it won't go away. The music throbs.
His actions become spastic, almost delirious. His hys-
teria attracts the attention of the other DANCERS.

A circle forms around JACOB and JEZZIE as their frenzy
transcends the boundaries of dance and erupts into an
almost orgiastic display. JACOB is out of control. His
fury becomes a kind of exorcism, a desperate attempt
to free himself from his body and his mind.

CUT TO JACOB as his eyes pass beyond pain. The dark
walls of the APARTMENT fade away.


**EXT.   VIETNAM - NIGHT**

Strange faces in infantry helmets appear in the darkness, outlined by a bright moon that is emerging from
behind a large cloud. The faces are looking down and
voices are speaking.

                    VOICE
          He's burning up.

                    VOICE
          Total delirium.

                    VOICE
          He'll never make it.

                    VOICE
          That's some gash. His guts keep
          spilling out.

                    VOICE
          Push 'em back.

                    122

                    JACOB (V.O.)
                 (crying weakly)
          Help me!

His eyes focus on the moon. Rings of light emanate
from it filling the sky with their sparkling brilliance. The rings draw us forward with a quickening
intensity that grows into exhilarating speed. The rush
causes them to flash stroboscopically and produce a
dazzling, almost sensual, surge of color. The display
is spectacular and compelling. A voice can be heard in
the distance.

                    VOICE
          I think we're losing him.

Suddenly the flickering rings begin to define a tangi-
ble image, a kind of CELESTIAL STAIRCASE, rising up
into infinite dimensions. As we speed toward it, it
grows increasingly majestic. The image is so awesome
and other-worldly that it is difficult to grasp what
is being seen.

Music can be heard in the distance. It too is celestial in its beauty. Then, unexpectedly, it grows hard
and insistent, like a heartbeat. Heavy breathing accompanies the sound. The image of the STAIRCASE shatters and disappears, replaced by intense flashes of
red and blue light. The music grows louder and reaches
a thundering crescendo. Then silence.


## ADDENDUM 3
## JACOB'S LIVING ROOM

In the original version of the script there was a sub-theme sug-
gesting that the world was approaching Armageddon. It was essentially a red herring to imply that the demons Jacob was seeing might
in fact be a real Biblical presence invading the streets of New York. I
felt that a dying man might fantasize that not he but the world itself
was coming to an end. It was an interesting concept that ultimately
got in the way of the central story and so I dropped all references to
it. One of the last of these scenes to be cut was a television commen-
tary that played just before Jacob receives his call from Paul. Reading
it over I am not sorry that it is gone but I am still fascinated by the
ideas it represents.


INT.   JACOB'S LIVING ROOM - DAY

CUT TO APPLAUSE from a real television game show as
JACOB switches channels on the LIVING ROOM T.V. He
stops on an interview program, turns up the sound, and

                        123

runs to the BATHROOM. The CAMERA stays on the
television. JACOB can be heard urinating in the
distance.

MAC HAYES, a young, virile, and smug REPORTER is
speaking.

                    HAYES
          The Reverend Norman Murphy, leader of
          one of the largest groups supporting
          the Armageddon Committee, told our
          cameras that we are no longer dealing
          in decades but years.

THE REVEREND fills the T.V. screen.

                    MURPHY
          The battleground is being readied.
          Our planet is the battlefield. Our
          souls are the prize. All the signs
          point to the inevitable confrontation
          between the forces of good and evil.
          People must choose sides. There is no
          draft evasion in *this* war. All are
          called. All must take up weapons. Are
          you prepared? That's the question we
          ask.

The toilet flushes and JACOB walks back into the
LIVING ROOM and turns down the sound.

                    HAYES
          Do you find people scoffing at you,
          Reverend? After all, there have been
          doomsayers for thousands of years and
          we're still here.

                    MURPHY
          People are less apt to laugh these
          days. The prophecies are too close
          for comfort. I mean, all you have to
          do is watch the news.

                    HAYES
          There are some who claim that your
          pessimism is defeatist and what the
          world needs now is hope, a positive
          thrust.

                    MURPHY
          I think the time for hope has passed.
          The seeds have been planted. We shall
          reap what we've sown.
                    (he pauses)
          Pessimists, no. I think we are
          perceived as the only realists
          around.

HAYES
Other movement leaders agree. In an
interview ...

Suddenly the telephone rings. It startles JACOB. He
jumps. It rings again. He reaches down, turns off the
T.V., and picks up the phone. His eyes continue to
stare at the blank screen as he talks.

# ADDENDUM 4
# JACOB'S BEDROOM

Jacob's joyous lovemaking with Jezzie following his first meeting with his lawyer was originally an hallucinogenic experience in which a mystical staircase seemed to appear in the shadows of her face. This staircase had a powerful symbolic presence in the early drafts of the film and I felt it was essential to associate it with Jezzie. The suggestions of Jezzie's demonic and angelic aspects were a key thematic element in the final resolution of the movie.

It should be noted that there was also an image of this staircase in the dance at Della's apartment during Jacob's wild visions. By layering it into the script I hoped to maintain a sense that Jacob was not only seeing demonic forms but that heaven-like images occasionally arose as well. It was increasingly obvious however that Adrian would not be using the staircase in its mythical or Biblical form and so we stopped foreshadowing it throughout the script.

### INT.    JACOB'S BEDROOM - NIGHT

THE BEDROOM is dark. JACOB and JEZZIE are making love.
A half-smoked joint is smouldering in an ashtray by
the bed. JEZZIE is poised on top of JACOB and his eyes
are focused on her face.

A hurricane lamp casts a warm glow over their bodies.
Its flickering plays games with JACOB's eyes and for a
moment JEZZIE seems to disappear. JACOB reaches out
for her breasts and his hands seem to vanish into the
shadows dancing across her. With sudden, hallucinogenic impact, JACOB feels himself drawn into a starry
universe opening from inside her.

THE CAMERA plunges through her image into a galaxy of
stars and rushes toward one that is twinkling
brightly. Pulsations of its light whiten the screen.
Out of the whiteness appears a momentary flash of the
CELESTIAL STAIRCASE, accompanied by sounds of sexual
climax.

The STAIRCASE sparkles for an instant and then it's

gone. The sparkle becomes a glimmer in JEZZIE's eye as
her face fills the screen. She looks especially lovely
and radiant. Her image moves with the lamplight.

JACOB's face is ecstatic. He can barely talk and
simply basks in JEZZIE's glow. Slowly, she leans
forward and whispers in his ear.

                    JEZZIE
          So tell me ... am I still an angel?

                    JACOB
               (smiling broadly)
          With wings.
               (he strokes her hair)
          You transport me, you know that? You
          carry me away.


# ADDENDUM 5
# DEMON IN THE WALL

One of my favorite scenes to be eliminated from the script had
Jacob sitting in his living room staring at the wall. The scene occurred just after Jacob talks to Frank and is told that his buddies are
not going to pursue their case against the Army. We decided instead
to use this section to reintroduce Gabe and the vibroman figure that
became so central to Adrian's final version of the story.


**INT.    JACOB'S APARTMENT - DAY**

JACOB is sitting in a comfortable chair in his living
room. He is reading. The room is dark, lit only by a
reading light. The walls are mostly in shadow. The
light, however, falls on one section of the wall, a
portion that has been lined in fake wood paneling.

JACOB's eyes suddenly lift off the page and roam over
the wood grain on the wall. All of a sudden he notices
something strange, an image in the grain. He stares at
it. The more he stares the more precise its
definition. The image of a DEMON appears in the wall.

JACOB sits up quickly and stares at the wall. It is
impossible to get the DEMON's image out of the grain.
It seems etched, even imbedded, in the paneling.

JACOB looks away and returns to his book. He is
reading about archetypes and the primordial mind. But
the book does not hold his attention. He is obsessed
with the wall. Its molecules seem suddenly active, the
wood grain subtly animate. Layers begin to appear in
the surface of the wall as the grain patterns slowly
define a rocky, barren landscape.

The DEMON is growing solid. Cries and screams rise up
in the distance. Flames and a red glow emanate from
the space extending rapidly into the wall. The image
of Hell erupts before him.

JACOB stands up. He can see bodies suffering beyond
the wall, masses of PEOPLE wailing and enduring the
torments of a fiery world. The DEMON's arm slowly
extends from the plane of the wall and reaches into
the room. He is huge, covered in flames and skulls, a
living horror. He grabs hold of JACOB and pulls him
toward the wall. JACOB tries to back away but he
cannot. His face is white with fear. The DEMON draws
JACOB toward the inferno.

                    JACOB
              (yelling at the top of
              his lungs)
          NO!

Suddenly JEZZIE appears, the light from the BEDROOM
flooding the paneled wall. The DEMON vanishes
instantly.

                    JEZZIE

     Jake, are you all ... ?

She stops dead in her tracks.

CUT TO JACOB pressed up against the wall, defying
gravity and logic, as though about to merge with the
solid surface. His body holds there for a moment and
then collapses to the floor. JEZZIE goes to him.

                    JEZZIE
     Jake? Jake?

He doesn't answer. He looks at JEZZIE with a blank
stare. His body begins shaking.


**INT.   JACOB'S BEDROOM - NIGHT**

JACOB is lying on the bed, curled up in a fetal pose.
JEZZIE is stroking his hair and trying to calm him.

                    JEZZIE
          It's going to be all right, Jake.
          It's going to be all right. Don't be
          afraid.I've got you now.

                    JACOB
          Hold me, Jezzie. Hold me.

JEZZIE wraps herself around his shivering body and
warms him with her own. The image seems tender and
comforting until we notice JEZZIE's tongue darting

nervously in and out. It looks strangely like a
snake's.

## ADDENDUM 6
## THE HOSPITAL

The original version of the hospital scene was more in keeping
with my sense of archetypal imagery. The fires of Hell were more lit-
eral, the doorway to the inferno was right through the wall. Adrian's
version is infinitely more interesting and visually stunning. Still, I
wanted to show the introduction to the scene in its original form.

The RESIDENT injects the serum into JACOB's veins
while two ORDERLIES hold him still. JACOB barely
struggles. His eyes fixate on the EMERGENCY ROOM WALL.
It is white and sterile. Within moments it begins to
emit a reddish glow. JACOB watches with astonishment
as the wall's two dimensional surface separates into
three dimensional planes. The solid surface gives way
to a DARK CHAMBER that was not there before.

Out of the transmuted space CREATURES begin to form.,
Bosch-like DEMONS with horns and tails, undeniably of
another world. Slowly several of them emerge from the
wall and approach JACOB. They look like parodies of
doctors and nurses, wearing traditional hospital
gowns. Without a word they wheel him through the space
where the wall had been. JACOB tries to scream but no
sound comes out.


INT.   HELL - NIGHT

The DARK CHAMBER is filled with mournful CREATURES
being led by DEMONS through a series of CORRIDORS. No
one fights or struggles. JACOB's stretcher is moved
through the darkness. He tries to sit up but is forced
back down. He is obviously drugged.

JACOB is wheeled into a tiny CHAMBER. A number of
DEMONS are waiting for him. Chains and pulleys hang
from the ceiling. They are lowered and attached with
speed and efficiency to JACOB's arms and legs. The
devices are manipulated smoothly and JACOB is lifted
off the stretcher. The chains retract, stretching him
spread eagle in the air. He screams loudly.

                         JACOB
            Oh God!

The DEMONS laugh. There is the sound of a huge door
closing. JACOB is left in darkness. The darkness is
hallucinogenic. Fires appear beyond the boundaries of

the wall; images of Dante's Inferno, souls of the dead
in endless torment. JACOB is but one of countless
beings sharing a vastness of torment. His own screams
for help are lost in the magnitude of voices crying.

Suddenly, out of the menacing shadows, a contingent of
DEMONS emerges. They are carrying sharp surgical
instruments. They surround JACOB, their eyes
glistening as bright as their blades. JACOB is panting
and sweating with fear. For an instant one of the
DEMONS looks like JEZZIE. JACOB calls out to her.

> JACOB
> Jezzie! Help me!

The DEMONS laugh as she changes form. They take great
pleasure in his suffering. Their voices are strange
and not human. Each utterance contains a multitude of
contradictory tones, sincere and compassionate,
taunting and mocking at the same time. The confusion
of meanings is a torment of its own.

# ADDENDUM 7
## JACOB'S BEDROOM

For a long time there was a scene after Jacob comes back from
being healed by Louis, before he decides to go to the army headquarters. It was a powerful scene, even though it was in some ways a recapitulation of earlier scenes in the film. There is no new information
given here but it does crystallize Jacob's paranoid terror of Jezzie in a
very satisfying way.

### INT. JACOB'S BEDROOM

JACOB is lying on the floor of his BEDROOM doing exercises for his back. He has several days' growth of beard
and does not look well. His mind is drifting and only the
occasional pain in his back reminds him of what he is doing. JEZZIE can be heard vacuuming the carpet in the
LIVING ROOM. Suddenly the door swings open. The wail of
the vacuum cleaner causes JACOB to tense. His eyes drift
down from the ceiling. JEZZIE vacuums around him and
seems insensitive to his presence.

JEZZIE shoves the vacuum cleaner under the bed and
hits something. JACOB tightens. She looks and is
shocked to discover a can of gasoline and boxes of
kitchen matches. It takes her a second to understand
the implications of what she has found. JACOB is ready
when she begins yelling.

> JEZZIE
> You're completely off your rocker,

                    JEZZIE (CONT.)
     you know that? You'd think you fell
     on your head instead of your back.
     What are you planning to do, burn
     down the apartment along with your
     demons?

She begins to remove the gasoline can.

                    JACOB
               (yelling)
     Don't you touch it.
               (he glares at her)

JEZZIE lets go of the can and grabs the vacuum. She
moves it furiously across the carpet. Suddenly JACOB
sees her tongue darting in and out, unconsciously. She
looks strange, not human. JACOB freezes. He yells out.

                    JACOB
     Who are you?

The sound of the vacuum cleaner drowns out his voice.
He yells again. JEZZIE sees him and turns off the
machine. His voice booms out.

                    JACOB
               (continuing)
     Who the hell are you?

JEZZIE ignores the question and turns the vacuum
cleaner back on. JACOB rolls over and pulls out the
plug.

                    JACOB
     Why won't you answer me?

                    JEZZIE
               (angry)
     Cause you know goddamn well who I am.

                    JACOB
     I don't know you.

                    JEZZIE
     You've lived with me for two years.

                    JACOB
     That doesn't mean shit. Where do you
     come from, huh? And I don't mean
     Indiana.

                    JEZZIE
     What do you want me to say? My
     mother's tummy?

                    JACOB
     You know goddamn well what I mean.

                    JEZZIE
You're out of your fucking mind. I'm
not gonna stand around here gettin'
interrogated by you.

                    JACOB
Well leave then. Go to Hell.

                    JEZZIE
          (furious)
You son-of-a-bitch. Who do you think
you are? I don't deserve this. Who
takes care of you day and night? Who
cleans the floor and washes your
goddamn underwear? Well, I've had it.
You flip out on your own, you
ungrateful bastard. I'm done holding
your hand. I don't want anything to
do with you, you hear? Nothing!

She storms out of the room, kicking the vacuum cleaner
as she goes. JACOB can see flashes of her through the
open crack of the bedroom door. Occasional curses and
epithets hurl through the opening along with a flood
of tears.

JACOB catches glimpses of her as she grabs her coat
from the hall closet and as she pulls her money out of
the desk drawer. He can see the lamp as she shoves it
to the floor and hears it shatter as she stomps on it
with her foot. There is a blur as she heads to the
front door and a deafening bang as she leaves.

JACOB's eyes drift up to the ceiling. They hardly
blink. He stares at the plaster, chipped and cracked,
above him. Suddenly the cracks begin to move. JACOB
jumps up. A DEMON is materializing over his head. JA-
COB yells and grabs hold of the extension pole for the
vacuum cleaner. With a furious cry he begins jamming
it at the ceiling. Rather than blot out the evolving
image his attack helps to define it. JACOB slams hard-
er. Plaster and wood lath cover the floor. The DEMON
is gone. Panting hard, JACOB reaches for matches and
the gasoline can. He stops and stares at them with
great intensity.


## ADDENDUM 8
## THE ANTIDOTE SEQUENCE

As Michael gives Jacob the antidote, Jacob experiences a hellish
episode that transforms into a heavenly vision. This heavenly vision
became a very difficult section for Adrian. My original version took
Jacob to a setting much like the Garden of Eden, a kind of paradise in

which Michael appears transformed into an angelic being. This section was a prelude to the end of the movie where Eden is revealed as a kind of doorway to the ethereal staircase leading to Heaven and Michael is seen once more as an angelic presence helping to guide and liberate Jacob from his worldly form.

Because Adrian did not buy into this interpretation it was necessary to eliminate the Edenesque aspects of the sequence and the more overt aspects of Michael's angelic form. Adrian also felt it was wrong to show Heaven twice in the movie. I argued that Eden was a doorway to Heaven and not Heaven itself. I believed that the final reveal of the celestial staircase at the end of the movie, the real image of Jacob's Ladder, would be a spectacular culmination to the visual power of the antidote sequence. Adrian, however, did not agree, and so the scene became a much simpler image. Following is the original version of that scene.

The ceiling begins to rumble. Cracks split wide open. Huge crevasses tear through the plaster. JACOB's world is crumbling. He stares in horror as DEMONIC FORMS attempt to surge through the rupture above him. Piercing eyes and sharp teeth glimmer in the darkness. Hooved feet and pointed claws clamor to break through.

                    JACOB
              (continuing)
         HELP ME!

Instantly MICHAEL appears standing over him. He is holding the vial with the antidote. He draws an eye-dropper full of the fluid and holds it over JACOB's mouth.

                    MICHAEL
         Take it!

JACOB fights him but MICHAEL forces the entire contents of the eyedropper down his throat. JACOB gags. He tries to spit it out, but can't.

Suddenly the ceiling erupts in violent clashes as whole chunks break off and collide with one another like continental plates. The collisions wreak havoc on the DEMONS, chopping and dismembering them. Body parts fall from the ceiling like a Devil's rain. Horrible screams echo from the other side.

Flashes of light and dark storm over JACOB's head, thundering like a war in the heavens. It is a scene of raw power and growing catastrophe. It builds in fury and rage until suddenly the ceiling explodes.

Matter atomizes instantly. Trillions of particles hurl
chaotically in all directions. The walls shatter into
a dazzling brightness. For a moment there is a sense
of intense forward movement, a rush toward oblivion.
And then, suddenly, it stops. There is absolute quiet
and stillness.

JACOB's eyes stare into the formlessness sparkling
around him. All space has become a shining void. Gradually faint pastel colors appear like colored molecules, dancing and spinning, redirecting space into
new formations. They weave patterns of intricate complexity and stunning beauty.

As the colors grow brighter and more vivid their abstraction gives way to solid form. A GARDEN SCENE
emerges. It is a GARDEN OF LIGHT, a vast, almost mythic, Rousseau paradise. It radiates an intense shimmering light.

JACOB's eyes are captivated by the vision before him.
A sudden movement catches his attention. He looks up
and notices MICHAEL still standing beside him. MI-
CHAEL, however, is rapidly changing form. It is a
full, plastic, three-dimensional metamorphosis. His
very flesh seems to expand and glow with its own inner
light. His face shines and radiates an almost transcendental beauty.

JACOB is nearly blinded by MICHAEL's presence and must
shield his eyes to look at him. MICHAEL smiles an extraordinary and joyous smile that radiates such intense luminosity that JACOB has to squint to see it.

Suddenly MICHAEL steps off the ground. He rises into
the air and floats above JACOB. JACOB can barely
breathe as he watches him. MICHAEL rises into a sky
filled with orbs and blazing lights. The lights shine
on JACOB'S head. He effervesces and shimmers in their
glow.

One of the orbs sends a burst of light exploding over
JACOB. So intense is the light that JACOB grabs his
eyes. As he opens them again he sees that the GARDEN
is fading back into pure light. MICHAEL, too, is fading.

Another burst of light and the GARDEN is reabsorbed by
the void. Only the brightness remains. It is many seconds before we realize that the HOTEL ROOM is coming
together, reconstructed by the light. In moments it is
fully formed. Sunlight is pouring through the window.
MICHAEL is sleeping lightly in a chair. He hears JACOB
stir and sits up.

JACOB is sitting on the bed. He does not seem to know
where he is. His eyes are filled with awe. They move

slowly around the room, taking everything in. He
doesn't speak. MICHAEL gets up and sits beside him. He
respects his silence.

## ADDENDUM 9
## HOTEL ROOM

In the original version of the script Jacob has left the bus station
in a panic and instead of going to Michael's loft he returned to Jezzie
in the hotel room. It was a powerful scene in which Jezzie is
glimpsed in a momentary flash of demonic regalia, a final confirma-
tion of Jacob's fears. It is this glimpse that sends Jacob on a mad dash
to find Michael and get the antidote.

We all agreed that this scene was expendable. As much as we
liked it, no new ground was covered. Still, it had a powerful impact
in the original reading of the script and so it is included here.

INT.    HOTEL ROOM - DAY

JACOB enters the HOTEL ROOM. JEZZIE is already there
watching the evening news. She is still in her postal
uniform, lying on the bed. She taps the mattress, inviting JACOB to lie next to her. A WOMAN is crying to
a REPORTER on the T.V.

                    WOMAN
          It's been four days. No word. It's
          not like him. He's never done any-
          thing like this before. It's like he
          just disappeared from the face of the
          earth.

                    REPORTER
          The Bureau of Missing Persons is con-
          founded by the continuing surge of
          reports ...

JACOB snaps off the T.V.

                    JEZZIE
          What'd you do that for? It's an in-
          teresting story. All these people are
          still disappearing. Right off the
          street.
                  (staring at JACOB)
          Hey, what's wrong? Are you all right?

                    JACOB
          I'm okay. I just don't want to lis-
          ten.

                    JEZZIE
          You look upset.

134

                    JACOB
          (angry)
I'm not upset.

                    JEZZIE
Jake, what is it?

                    JACOB
I'm tired.

                    JEZZIE
You look terrible. What happened?
          (he turns away. She
          stares at him for a mo-
          ment, concerned)
Jake ... is it the antidote?

                    JACOB
Goddamn it. Why do you say that?

                    JEZZIE
Look at yourself. You look like
you've seen a ghost.

                    JACOB
Shit! Can't I just have a bad day?

                    JEZZIE
You can have anything you want.

                    JACOB
Then don't bug me.

                    JEZZIE
I'm not bugging you. Come and lie
down. I'll give you a massage.
          (she taps the mattress
          again and JACOB joins
          her. She unbuttons his
          shirt)
Where'd you go today?

                    JACOB
          (evasively)
Mid-town mostly.

                    JEZZIE
Oh yeah? What was happenin' there?

                    JACOB
          (looking away from her)
I picked up my ticket.
          (he pauses)
I'm leaving in the morning, Jez.

                    JEZZIE
          (tensing)
Oh?
          (acting innocent)
Where you going?

                    JACOB
              (nervously)
West.

                    JEZZIE
              (growing angry)
Where West? New Jersey?

                    JACOB
Don't be funny.

                    JEZZIE
I always liked the West, west of Illinois anyway. But you gotta give me
time to pack.

                    JACOB
Stop it, Jez. Don't do that.

                    JEZZIE
Do what? I haven't done a thing.

                    JACOB
Don't play games with me. There's
nothing more to say.

There is a quiet rage building in JEZZIE's eyes as she
continues to stroke JACOB's chest. He tries to relax
and give himself over to the movement of her hand. Silently she leans over and begins licking his stomach.
JACOB's eyes close. His stomach hardens. He reaches
back and adjusts the pillow beneath his head. Slowly,
JEZZIE works her way back up to his chest. Her tongue
darts in and out suggestively. Her eyes are burning
with anger. Her mouth poises itself over his nipple.
She toys with it for a few seconds and then chomps
down hard. The bite draws blood.

JACOB screams. His eyes shoot open. For the flash of
an instant he sees a DEMON hovering over him, a hide-
ous horned creature licking his blood. JACOB flies off
the bed as the creature hurls to the floor. JACOB is
ready to pounce on it when he sees that it is JEZZIE
lying at his feet. His head begins reeling. He backs
away from the bed, not taking his eyes off JEZZIE for
a second. He backs to the closet and grabs his coat.

                    JEZZIE
          Jake. What are you doing? Look, I'm
          sorry, I didn't mean to bite. Let me
          get you a towel.

JACOB grabs his wallet and his glasses. He backs toward the door.

                    JEZZIE
          Jake, don't. You can't leave. You're
          not seeing things clearly. The drug's
          wearing off.

                      136

She stands up and begins to approach him. JACOB lifts up a desk chair and holds it in front of him. Blood is running down his chest.

> JEZZIE
> Jake, don't leave me!

JACOB throws the chair at the floor, opens the door, and hurries into the HALLWAY. JEZZIE scurries around the chair and runs to the door. She yells after him, but he is already gone.

# ADDENDUM 10
# THE END OF THE MOVIE

As has been explained throughout the introduction, the ending of the film was debated for well over a year. Following is the ending as it was originally written.

### INT.   HALLWAY - NIGHT

JACOB stoops in front of the APARTMENT door and reaches his hand underneath a section of the hallway carpet. It comes back with a key. He inserts it into the lock and gently opens the door.

> JACOB
> (calling out)
> Hello. It's me.

### INT.   SARAH'S APARTMENT - NIGHT

The lights are on and the APARTMENT looks comfortable and cozy.

> JACOB
> Hello? Is anyone home? Jed? Eli? Daddy's here.

There is still no answer. JACOB is surprised. He walks into the LIVING ROOM and then the KITCHEN. No one is around. He walks into his old BEDROOM and then the BOYS' ROOM. He is surprised to hear footsteps coming down the hall. He turns around and calls out.

> JACOB
> Sarah, is that you? I hope you don't mind. I needed to come home.

JACOB is startled to see JEZZIE enter the room. She does not seem to be her usual self. She seems larger, more imposing.

                         JEZZIE
          Hello, Jake. I knew you'd come here
          in the end.

JACOB is nervous.

                         JACOB
          Where's Sarah? Where are the boys?

                         JEZZIE
          Sit down, Jake.

                         JACOB
          Where are they?

                         JEZZIE
          Sit down!

                         JACOB
          No! What's going on? Where's my
          family?

                         JEZZIE
          It's over, Jake. It's all over.

                         JACOB
          Where have they gone?

                         JEZZIE
          Wake up! Stop playing with yourself.
          It's finished.

JEZZIE stares at JACOB with a frightening, powerful
glare. Her lips snarl. Her tongue begins darting in
and out, only now it is not a nervous habit but a conscious act. JACOB's body feels the first waves of an
inner tremor. His legs are shaking.

                         JACOB
          What's going on?

JEZZIE smiles at him. Her tongue wags and suddenly
shoots from her mouth beyond human extension. JACOB
recoils.

                         JACOB
                  (whispering to himself)
          This isn't happening.

                         JEZZIE
          Your capacity for self delusion is
          remarkable, Dr. Singer.

JEZZIE's head begins to tighten and squeeze, as though
she is suffering from cramps. JACOB watches in horror
as her skull gives birth to pointed horns.

                         JACOB
          Oh God!

                         138

                         JEZZIE
              What's wrong, Jake?
                   (she mocks him)
              Forget to take your antidote?

                         JACOB
                   (screaming)
              Goddamn you!

                         JEZZIE
                   (smiling and then
                   laughing)
              I loved your chemist, Jake. The
              height of fantasy. And your vision of
              paradise.
                   (she laughs with a hu-
                   miliating tone)
              A most romantic creation. You're
              quite a dreamer, Jake. Only it's time
              to wake up.

JACOB's eyes are locked on JEZZIE. His mouth is wide
open. His body is shaking badly. He tries to back away
from her but his legs barely move.

                         JEZZIE
              There is nowhere to run, Jacob.
              You're home.

Suddenly the pictures on the wall crash to the floor.
Plaster from the ceiling breaks off in huge chunks and
slams to the carpet. Light bulbs and lamps explode.
JACOB runs to the door. He pulls it open and screams.
He is on the edge of a fiery abyss. JEZZIE laughs with
a new intensity of demonic force. JACOB spins around.

                         JACOB
              WHO ARE YOU?

                         JEZZIE
              How many times have you asked me
              that? How many times?

                         JACOB
              TELL ME, DAMN YOU!

                         JEZZIE
                   (with consummate power)
              You know who I am.

Suddenly JEZZIE reaches for her tongue and pulls at it
with all her might. It is an act of total, unrelieved
grotesqueness. With each yank the horror grows as JEZ-
ZIE literally pulls herself inside out before JACOB's
eyes.

The emerging creature is JEZZIE transfigured, a demonic presence beyond anything we have seen before. It is

                            139

black and covered with a thick oozing slime. Its head, still recognizable as JEZZIE, is rodent-like, with piercing green eyes and terrible horns protruding from its brow. Its powerful arms have long spiked claws. Its feet are cloven hooves. Extending from its back is a long, thick, muscular tail that whips around the room with devastating force. It throws furniture crashing through the air.

A sudden cracking sound emerges from the DEMON's back. Dark forms penetrate the air. JACOB is breathless as huge wings unfold and spread out to the living room walls. The sound of their flapping is deafening. The walls shatter from their blows. As they crumble darkness appears on the other side. There are no other rooms. The VOID envelopes them. The INFERNO emerges in all directions. The DEMON roars.

> DEMON
> (with JEZZIE's voice)
> Still love me, Jake?
> (it laughs and reaches
> out to him)
> COME!

CUT TO JACOB's face. He has gone beyond fear. An intensity of rage is building in him that we have not witnessed before. His whole image seems transformed by it. He glows like a volcano before it erupts.

Suddenly he explodes. The full fury of the ladder detonates inside him. He yells at the DEMON with all his might.

> JACOB
> NO!!!!!

With a power and energy of devastating force he attacks the DEMON. JACOB is battling for his very soul and tears at the DEMON with an animalistic fury that takes it by surprise. Its giant wings flap furiously, lifting them both up off the floor. JACOB keeps fighting. He claws, bites, and rips at the wings, decimating their delicate fabric.

The DEMON, shocked, and trying to gain control, crashes up through the last fragments of the ceiling. JACOB does not let go. They burst into the fiery darkness. The room crumbles beneath them and disappears into the void.

The abyss opens beneath them. JACOB continues his attack. His legs are locked around the DEMON's waist. His hands dig into her eyes. The DEMON shrieks and surges downward with awesome velocity.

The CREATURE charges into a rocky slope, smashing JACOB into its cliffs. JACOB claws at her wings, shred-

ding as much of them as he can reach. The DEMON takes
a huge chunk out of JACOB's arm. JACOB screams, grabs
a rock, and shatters the DEMON's teeth. The DEMON
falls to the ground. JACOB holds on.

All of a sudden the CREATURE begins to shrink. JACOB
is shocked and struggles to contain it. As it dwindles
in size it reorders its shape. Within seconds a powerful INSECT is cupped in his hands. JACOB tries to
crush it but it stings with such force that JACOB's
entire body recoils. The stinging persists. JACOB
hurls himself to the ground on top of his arms to hold
the CREATURE down. So massive is the INSECT's attack,
however, that JACOB's whole body heaves off the ground
with each sting. Then the attacks subside. JACOB waits
for the next blow.

Suddenly JACOB's body shoots straight up. His hands
fly apart as a new life form erupts between them. He
holds on tightly as flesh and blood mold and expand
between his fingers. The new body takes rapid shape.
It is a CHILD. JACOB grasps it with all his might as
it completes its identity. He is horrified when he
sees it. It is his son.

                    ELI
          Daddy!

                    JACOB
          Oh God!

                    ELI
          You're hurting me.

                    JACOB
               (yelling)
          Stop!!!!

                    ELI
          Daddy. Let go.

                    JACOB
          What do you want from me?

                    ELI
          LET GO!

JACOB does not let up. In an instant his SON explodes
into a gelatinous form, constantly undulating and
changing shape. Within its translucent mass a new body
is forming. JACOB stares at it with growing terror. It
is himself. A terrible perplexity fills JACOB's eyes
as he struggles to dig in and destroy his own image.
He recoils as his own voice calls out to him.

                    VOICE
          Who the Hell do you think you're
          fighting?

                    141

The words shock him and for the first time, he lets
go.

Instantly the image disappears and the jelly-like mass
dissolves into an oily liquid rapidly encircling his
feet. JACOB looks down at the shallow pool spreading
out beneath him. Its surface reflects a smoky, unearthly light.

JACOB gazes into the darkness. He is all alone. The
quiet overwhelms him. The only sound is his own
breath. He looks around, in all directions, but can
see nothing. The CAMERA holds on him as he stands
waiting for the next assault, but nothing comes. He is
left only with his anticipation and with himself. He
stares at the terrible darkness.

A subtle phosphorescence begins to glow in the liquid
beneath JACOB's feet. He steps away from it, but it
follows his movement.Suddenly, as if by spontaneous
combustion, it bursts into flames. JACOB screams and
tries to run but the flames move with him, lapping at
his legs. He cannot escape them. As far and as fast as
he runs the fire is with him. He yells and cries and
screams as the fire eats at his lower limbs. He falls
and jumps back up again, his hands charred. His eyes
grow wild.

                    JACOB
        Oh God, help me.

Instantly the flames roar and engulf him. It is total
conflagration. JACOB's skin blisters and turns black.
His flesh crackles. Writhing in pain he runs through
the flames but can find no freedom from his suffering.

All at once JACOB stops running. He throws his hands
up into the burning air and stands motionless, in absolute agony. It is a gesture of total submission and
surrender to forces beyond himself. His flesh bubbles
and chars but something is suddenly quiet inside him.

Through the flames JACOB'S dark form can be seen as it
slowly sits down, like a Buddhist monk, in the midst
of the holocaust. He appears a figure of sudden nobil-
ity as the flames annihilate him.

Gradually the fire dies. JACOB's body, his flesh like
a charred and brittle shell, sits motionless, beyond
pain. An orange glow from the embers of his body slowly fades, leaving him in the final darkness.

The SCREEN stays dark for as long as possible. Then,
slowly, an eerie light appears in an unfamiliar sky.
It backlights JACOB, revealing his silhouette. The
CAMERA dollies slowly toward him. It approaches the
burned and unrecognizable remains of JACOB's face. It
is the face of death. The CAMERA holds on the image.

Suddenly, with shocking impact, JACOB'S eyes move.
Within the crumbling shell of a body something is
still alive, still conscious. The eyes survey the
darkness and the first stirrings of a new light.

It is dawn. JACOB's dark remains are suffused by a
preternatural glow. Slowly, huge orbs begin to appear
on the horizon. JACOB's eyes open to the growing light
as they seek out the familiar in the still dark landscape. Gradually the orbs begin their ascent like a
thousand suns rising at the same time. JACOB's eyes
widen as his new world stands revealed. He is sitting
in the GARDEN OF LIGHT, the Rousseau paradise he has
visited once before.

A sudden burst of light fills the sky directly overhead. The vegetation around him is instantly illuminated with its soft glow. Like a gentle breeze MICHAEL
descends from the light and stands radiant before JA-
COB. He smiles and the air itself seems to brighten.
MICHAEL quietly approaches JACOB's body.

                    MICHAEL
          I am with you, Jacob.

JACOB stares at him through dark eyes with a mixture
of awe and disbelief.

                    MICHAEL
               (speaking with a gentle
               compassion)
          It's all right now. It's over. You've
          won. You're here.
               (JACOB stares at him
               questioningly. MICHAEL
               reaches out his hands)
          Trust me.

Softly MICHAEL places his hands on top of JACOB's head
and begins to peel at the charred flesh. Layer by
layer he strips it away. Then, with an unexpected gesture, he rips away a whole section with one quick
pull. A BLAZE OF LIGHT bursts through the gaping hole
in JACOB's head and beams into the air around them. It
is an astounding sight.

                    MICHAEL
          Come on. Don't make me do it all.
               (his eyes sparkle)
          Stand up.
               (JACOB's eyes are burst-
               ing with wonder)
          You can do it.

Slowly JACOB begins to stir. He moves feebly at first,
like an old man. His black flesh creaks and cracks and
through each sudden fissure another beam of light

                    143

blasts out with laserlike intensity.

                    MICHAEL
          Stop hobbling. Your flesh can't hold
          you any more.

JACOB nods in response and takes a huge, gigantic
breath. His lungs expand and suddenly all the old
flesh bursts from his body as a radiant being of light
breaks through beneath it. JACOB stands transfigured,
filled with his own luminosity. His face is like a
child's as he stares in amazement at his own hands,
glowing with light.

MICHAEL directs JACOB's vision to the sunrise. It is
majestic, almost Biblical in its grandeur. Great rays
of light penetrate vast cloud formations and descend
into the GARDEN. Slowly the clouds, as if orchestrated
by some higher power, begin to part. A massive light
complex emerges from behind them. JACOB watches, awe-
struck, as the CELESTIAL STAIRWAY stands revealed. It
reaches down from unknown heights, radiating an infinite power and grace. It touches down far in the distance, hovering over many acres of the GARDEN. JACOB's
eyes are filled with its splendor. MICHAEL looks at
him and nods.

                    MICHAEL
          Go on, Jacob. It has come for you.

JACOB cannot speak. His eyes are fixed on the STAIRWAY
dazzling him from afar. He can see ANGELIC FORMS moving up and down it. Suddenly, as if transported by
light itself, he feels himself floating up into the
air. He looks down upon EDEN sparkling below him. His
mouth is wide open as he soars above it.

The light pulsating from the STAIRWAY is brilliant and
thrilling. JACOB's own inner light intensifies as he
approaches it. The STAIRWAY grows increasingly wondrous as we draw nearer. It pulls JACOB toward it.

STREAMS OF ANGELS enter the STAIRWAY like  a fast
flowing river. It carries them instantly within its
current up beyond the visible reaches of the glitter-
ing sky. Billowing clouds glow in a parade of colors
and the starry heavens seem to part as the STAIRWAY
reaches beyond all known dimensions.

JACOB stares at the light that is about to absorb him.
It is a moment of total euphoria. He surges into the
stream as the brilliant light of the STAIRWAY overwhelms the screen.

Slowly the brightness of the screen condenses into a
smaller light source. An overhead surgical lamp remains stubbornly in view.

## INT.   VIETNAM FIELD HOSPITAL - DAY

A DOCTOR leans his head in front of the lamp and removes his mask. His expression is somber. He shakes
his head. His words are simple and final.

> DOCTOR
>
> He's gone.

CUT TO JACOB SINGER lying on an operating table in a
large ARMY FIELD TENT in VIET NAM. The DOCTOR steps
away. A NURSE rudely pulls a green sheet up over his
head. The DOCTOR turns to one of the aides and throws
up his hands in defeat.

TWO ORDERLIES wheel JACOB's body past rows of other
DOCTORS and NURSES fighting to save lives. A YOUNG
VIETNAMESE BOY pulls back a screen door to let them
out of the tent. It is a bright, fresh morning. The
sun is rising.


THE END

Date: August 18, 1989
To: All concerned
From: Adrian
Re: Time of JACOB'S LADDER

JACOB'S LADDER is, ostensibly, set in 1975, in Brooklyn, three years after the end of Vietnam war. We flash back to Jacob Singer being wounded during the war in 1972.

At the end of the movie the audience discovers that what we thought was flashback was in fact — the reality — that Jacob Singer died in the Vietnam war and the movie we have just seen was in his head while he was dying.

So, we have something of a problem. In that, while we are watching the movie it should feel like 1975, New York, after the war's end. But when we get the kicker at the end of the movie, and find out that Jacob died in Vietnam in 1972, we should not be able to point to anything that we have just seen as being at odds with 1972.

For example: If the New York Knicks won the championship in 1975 we should not mention it because Jacob would not be able to know. But a general reference to the Knicks applies because the Knicks existed in both 1972 and 1975.

# Jacob's
# Chronicle

I began writing *Jacob's Ladder* in the fall of 1980. I had just moved to DeKalb, Illinois with my wife, Blanche, and two sons, Joshua, eight years, and Ari, one month old. We were leaving Bloomington, Indiana where Blanche had received her doctorate degree in Art Education. Northern Illinois University, in DeKalb, was to be the site of her first professorial position. While her salary was not huge, we felt it would be enough to support us while I wrote. Little did I know.

Two years previously I had sold my first screenplay, originally titled *The George Dunlap Tape*. It would later become the basis for a motion picture called *Brainstorm*, an MGM production directed by Douglass Trumbull and starring Christopher Walken, Natalie Wood, Louise Fletcher, and Cliff Robertson. This was the first time I had ever received money for writing anything, and it seemed substantial at the time, about $65,000. I even took photographs of the check just to prove to myself that I was a real writer. It was a good thing I took those photos. Once we paid off our debts, purchased a car, modest home, and some furniture, there was nothing left. Blanche's teaching position was a godsend.

For the first year in DeKalb I led a writer's dream life. I had my own office in the house and many hours available just to write. The only interruption was the baby, whom I fed, diapered, and took for strolls in the neighborhood. These moments were wonderful diversions, and nourished rather than depleted my creative energies. It was a blissful period. It was during this time that I began *Jacob's Ladder*.

I nearly failed the only screenwriting course I ever took at New York University. The professor had a theory of screenwriting that involved a concept called "triangularity." I never understood what that meant. It had something to do with the three points of conflict required for a scene to work effectively and somehow came into play even when there were only two people on the screen. I hated that class and despaired that I would never be a writer if understanding triangularity was the measure of success. I have always been weak in the left brain, or whichever side controls logical thought. Structures and stratagems are a continual mystery to me. Plotting a script in logical fashion has almost always proved mind-boggling. I work

149

mostly from intuition and my best work occurs when I trust it to lead me.

*Jacob's Ladder* began as an act of faith. I really had no idea where it would go or even what it was going to be about. I only knew that something was stirring deep inside me that wanted to get out and that this script would be the vehicle for its release.

It began as a dream: A subway late at night; I am traveling through the bowels of New York City. There are very few people on the train. A terrible loneliness grips me. The train pulls into the station and I get off. The platform is deserted. I walk to the nearest exit, and discover the gate is locked. A feeling of terrible despair begins to pulse through me as I hike to the other end of the platform. To my horror, that exit is chained, too. I am totally trapped and overwhelmed by a sense of doom. I know with perfect certainty that I will never see daylight again. My only hope is to jump onto the tracks and enter the tunnel, the darkness. The only direction from there is down. I know the next stop on my journey is hell.

At that instant I woke up, in a sweat, panting. The singular thought in my head at that moment was "What a great idea for the opening of a movie." And so *Jacob's Ladder* was born.

The more I examined the dream, the more the movie emerged. This would not be the story of a man going to hell, but of a man already there. It would be the story of a man who had already died, but did not know it. All his life experiences—wife, mistress, children, career—would be, in truth, a feverish fantasy. The horror of the movie would be in the revelation that hope is hell's final torment, that life is a dream that ends over and over with the final truth, that life was never real, that we are all creatures trapped in eternal suffering and damnation.

The only problem that I had with this idea was that I did not believe it. It was profoundly at odds with my own religious and spiritual background. Although Jewish by birth, I had spent many years delving into the mystical and philosophical teaching of Eastern religions. I had traveled for nearly two years in the Orient, visiting many spiritual centers, including a Tibetan monastery, where I lived for about three months. Many of these religions propound a vision of heaven and hell, but these realms are projected as states of mind or states of being rather than actual locales. According to these religions, souls luxuriating in heaven and those trapped in hell are both caught in the same illusion. Even life on Earth is seen as part of that illusion.

For the Eastern mystics, life in all its manifestations, heavenly, worldly, and hellish, is really an experience of Mind. The goal of existence is to get beyond the mind, to free oneself of all manifestations, and to see the truth, the void, the clear shining light of reality. It is said that the effort leading to Enlightenment is not an easy process. It can take many incarnations, many lifetimes. But ultimately it is believed that all human beings will awake to the entrapment of these illusions; that they will step off the endless wheel of life and death, and find Nirvana, peace, the cessation of all suffering. The trick for me was, how do I write a movie about all this?

I had almost no idea how to proceed. Most Westerners of Judeo-Christian faith are not particularly interested in their own mystical religious traditions, let alone those of Eastern faiths, and I knew for a fact that not many Hollywood films ever explored the subject. Still, for some absurd and inexplicable reason, I felt there was a commercial movie here.

The story treatment for *Jacob* came out of my head almost as if I were dreaming it again. It had the richness of dream, the surreal power of nocturnal imagery. I hardly knew where it was coming from, but sensed I was tapping into something very deep inside me. I had completed several pages when Blanche came into my office and started reading them. Her face grew pale. After finishing a few paragraphs, she turned to me and asked: "What are you writing this for?" I didn't know. Nothing I had written in the past was so dark, so primal, so disturbing.

The treatment seemed to create itself, the story emerging in three days of heated writing. When I conferred upon the main character the biblical name Jacob, the title, *Jacob's Ladder*, seemed ordained, and I knew at that instant that I had a movie. The metaphor of Jacob's ladder, the biblical resonance, all seemed to enlarge and direct the flow of the story. It was thrilling to watch it come into being, its complications and convolutions ready-made. And even though the actual script would go through many changes and transformations, the heart and soul of the film seemed to rise fully formed in these early pages.

As I drew toward a conclusion, the only problem was that I did not know how to end the film. Rather than force the issue, I developed three possible directions for the ending to go: the horror ending with Jacob left in hell, the Hollywood ending with Jacob fighting his way to heaven, or the unsaleable ending in which Jacob rises above both and discovers a transcendent existence beyond duality in which heaven and hell do not, and never did, exist.

Obviously, I was drawn to the third interpretation but decided, for the time being, to put the entire decision aside. I knew one day I would figure out what to do. Little did I know that a decade later I would be playing with that decision through the production and editing of the film.

I finished the treatment (without the ending) in September 1980 and sent a copy of it to my wonderful friend and agent, Cindy Derway, the only agent I know who left Hollywood behind in order to pursue a doctoral thesis in Ecclesiastical Medieval Philosophy.

Cindy was a gift to me from my lawyer of 25 years, Charlie Shays. He actually coaxed her out of retirement, saying that he thought we would be good for one another. She had read my script, *The George Dunlap Tape* (A.K.A. *Brainstorm*) which, at that time, was a more metaphysical script than the movie that resulted from it. She was very excited to find a writer of mutual sensitivity, and we became fast friends.

Because Cindy had retired from Hollywood and was living in New York, her connections to the film world were not what they had been. Her ability to get me a development deal with the studio paying me to write *Jacob's Ladder* was not very strong. She had one good friend in New York with independent money, however, and approached him with my treatment for *Jacob*. He did not bite.

At this time I was beginning to realize that the dream of living on my wife's university salary was not as practical a reality as I had hoped. Without a second income, our savings dwindled rapidly. I naively proposed to Cindy that her friend could pay me a stipend and that I would give him title to anything I produced in the next year. Again he did not bite. I was left to fend for myself, a proposition I have never enjoyed. The result was that I decided to write *Jacob's Ladder*, fast.

Writing *Jacob* was a stunning experience. In truth it felt more like I was reading it, transcribing it. I never knew from moment to moment what would happen next and often found myself, like a reader, panting with fear at what would be around the corner.

My family learned not to disturb me during this period. If anyone should come into my office as I was writing, even if they knocked softly, I would literally jump out of my chair. I couldn't control myself. I was in a constant state of fear whenever I sat down to write. It became a joke for everyone but me. Writing at night was the worst. Every sound, every shadow was magnified. It was hard to tell if Jacob's hallucinations were mine or his. I couldn't wait to finish it.

About halfway through the script I experienced a major obstacle —I could not figure out how Jacob had died. Since I was beginning the film with Jacob already on a subway train, rushing through the proverbial "tunnel of light," I secretly hoped I could somehow evade this issue. But it would not go away.

For a long time I had quietly imagined Jacob being pushed off a subway platform by someone, but I never really knew who would have done it or why. I knew it had something to do with the military, but I wasn't sure what. It didn't feel right. I began to question the whole nature of what I was writing. All I knew was that Jacob was in hell, that he had died, and that near the end of the story, the film would reveal that fact. But suddenly I realized that I needed to know more about Jacob. His death had to be a major consequence of his life.

The film was beginning to feel shallow, stagnant. I felt trapped. Something was missing. The dramatic thrust of Jacob confronting demons who told him he was dead and then revealing that yes, in fact, he was dead, was somehow superficial and unsatisfying. For nearly three days I stopped working. I felt the script was a disaster in the making and I grew terribly depressed. I didn't want to proceed.

I had come to this point in many scripts, that moment of total devastation, where you realize that what you are writing is absolute garbage, that you have strayed from your path, and that you are deluded to think you were ever a writer in the first place. I have never known despair as total as this, as consuming, or as predictable. How a writer overcomes this obstacle is in many ways what determines his success or failure. It is a time of battle, of sacrifice, of killing your babies as some writer once said. It is a terrible and ultimately liberating struggle, if you get through it. It weds you to your material in a blood ceremony that makes it yours. It becomes your life.

Suddenly it hit me. Jacob is not dead. He is dying. The journey we are taking is not a hellish vision, but the struggle for Jacob's soul, the confrontation between the forces of light and the dark within him. It is the last moment of every human being, the final battle.

So many thoughts rushed into me I could barely breathe. It was a kind of euphoria, a massive rush of insight and creative completion. I was so excited, I jumped up and began pacing the house, walking in powerful circles around the living room, around the dining table. I couldn't stop.

Blanche, watching me, could barely believe the energy, the excitement I was feeling. I started talking and couldn't stop, detailing all the new ways the script would change. I told her about a film I had seen as a college student, Robert Enrico's *Occurrence at Owl Creek*

*Bridge*, based on the Civil War short story by Ambrose Bierce. A Confederate soldier is about to be hung from the pilings of a bridge. As the plank is kicked out from beneath his feet and he begins to fall, we wait for the rope to fracture his neck. Instead, the rope breaks and he falls free into the water below. Eluding the gunshots of his captors, he swims downstream and escapes into the woods. With fervent energy, he makes his way back to a farmhouse where his wife waits for his miraculous return. They see each other and rush joyfully into one another's arms. Just as they embrace, the soldier's head jerks back strangely and we cut to the rope over the bridge as it snaps taut. He is dead. It is an amazing moment when we realize that we have just experienced the last millisecond of a man's life. Anyone who has ever seen *Owl Creek* will never forget it.

I realized that I was writing a feature length version of that remarkable piece, a movie about the last moments, or hours, of a dying man wildly imagining his life as it is being taken away from him. I understood the philosophical relevance of my film to *The Tibetan Book of the Dead,* which details the progress of the soul through the various dreams and illusions it experiences during death. Suddenly the entire film found its spiritual relevance and grew from a horror film into a work of potential power and significance.

A new and potent structure for the film was emerging. Starting with a battle in Vietnam, the film would follow Jacob from the moment he is stabbed until the instant he is pronounced dead by medics. It would chart his progression from the battlefield to the field hospital in a series of "flashbacks" strategically placed throughout the film and then, in the epiphany of the film's final moments, reveal that the flashbacks were, in fact, real time, and that the life he was leading throughout the film was in truth, an illusion, the product of his mind.

I knew that if I didn't pull it off, it would be a terrible cheat for which the audience would never forgive me. But I was willing to take that risk. I felt that I finally understood my movie. I was ready to begin again.

I started to rewrite, introducing the Vietnam sequences, coaxing them out of the visual and emotional nuances of the script. The flashlight, for instance, that discovers Jacob crawling in the bush, becomes sunlight piercing the venetian blinds of his bedroom window. A chiropractic adjustment sends his mind reeling back into Vietnam. The script sprang to life and I finished it, working day and night, within a month.

Finished it, perhaps, isn't quite accurate. Once again, the ending eluded me, particularly the complex role of Jezzie. I did not know how to resolve her character, the combination of the angelic and demonic, especially for a Western audience that has not transcended the principal of duality, of good and evil. This became a constant concern and primary struggle with every succeeding draft of the film.

I sent the script to Cindy in January of 1981. Blanche had already read it and loved it. On a Saturday morning, around 11:00, I got a call from Cindy. She was nearly breathless. She said she had read only half of the script but couldn't wait to tell me how brilliant it was. Her excitement was contagious and lasted until her next phone call later in the day, when she had to admit that the last half of the script disappointed her. She felt it needed a lot of work.

With Cindy as a catalyst, I began two more drafts of the script. The process lasted five months and involved a lot of trimming and strengthening of the subsidiary characters. Louis become more central to the film, and Professor Stern, who did not survive the script cuts made just before production, developed a pivotal presence. It was Cindy's idea, for example, to have Louis rescue Jacob from the hospital, and she gave Professor Stern a more authentic professorial voice. The ending went through many, mostly unsuccessful, revisions.

I began to let friends and relatives read the script. The experience is always one of total vulnerability. Never in life are you more naked, more exposed. At this moment people have enormous power over you. How they exercise that power is something you will remember for the rest of your life. Brutal reactions can close you down for months. Criticism merged with gentility is appreciated forever. In the end, however, it is the true reaction, the honest response, that is appreciated most. It is one of the few ways a writer has to review, reconsider, and re-imagine his work. Unfortunately, a strange thing happens when I first show my script to someone. If they tell me they love it, I tend to read it again and love it, too. When they hate it, however, I usually hate it as well. Objectivity is hard for a writer. It requires an heroic act of detachment repeated over and over. The responses to Jacob were wonderful. But this time I was not pleased. And Cindy also felt it needed another pass.

In the summer of 1981, I did battle once more with the script. Pulling out my blue pencil, I cut many of my favorite scenes and much of the dialogue that explained my philosophical ideas. I realized the film was flawed if it couldn't communicate in strictly visual terms.

The cuts were instructive for me, almost humbling. It seemed the more I cut, the better and more cohesive the script became. I discovered, as I do with every script, the power of cinematic shorthand. It is always amazing how much can be said with so little. What I refer to as the synaptic effect occurs. Thoughts seem to form of their own volition as facts leap from one neuron to another. It's as if you don't actually have to state an idea. It emerges on its own as two images are cut together to form a third image or idea that is not on the screen. This is Eisenstein's concept of "montage." Good writing and good filmmaking are most exciting when they evoke images and ideas rather than spelling them out. Cutting seems to help that process. By eliminating the connective tissue, it forces the readers, the viewers, to form that tissue themselves. Their brains become participants in the creation of the work.

On August 10, I sent the third draft of the script to Cindy. I was very pleased with it, almost smug. I had convinced myself that the first person to read the script would finish it, wait about two minutes (enough time to catch his breath and marvel at what he had read), and then pick up the phone, call Cindy, and make a deal to buy the script on the spot. Right! Wishful thinking!

One would like to think that experience is a good teacher and that I would have learned a lesson from *Brainstorm*. That screenplay was completed in 1973 and did not get purchased until six years later. And even then, it took three more years to get made. In truth, scripts rarely sell quickly, and the fact that any film gets made at all is a kind of miracle.

The odds are against screenwriters from the start. Studios, and studio executives, have too much at stake. For them to make a film, or recommend one for production, puts them at enormous risk. Their desire to minimize that risk is great. Therefore, they are much happier saying no to a project than saying yes. Yes puts them in the line of fire.

When studio executives read a script, one of their first thoughts will be, would I put twenty million dollars into making this movie? If what you have put on paper does not elicit that twenty million dollar response, the likelihood of your movie getting made is nil. And it's not just one person you have to excite. You have to excite an entire line of production executives. If they like your movie a little, or just some of the elements, it is likely they will simply say no. Or, in the parlance of Hollywood, "pass." But no matter what they say, even if they are interested, the decision to move forward will not usually come quickly or easily. On rare occasions a studio will buy a script overnight, but the fact that you read about these deals in the newspapers testifies to their rarity, not their common occurrence.

There is a common arrogance among most writers handing in a finished script. I have seen it over and over again in myself and among my friends. One always tends to feel that one's latest draft is the best thing he has ever written and that he will only allow Steven Spielberg, Stanley Kubrick, or Martin Scorsese to direct it. He also decides on the lowest sale price he will accept for his work. Mine was $750,000. How quickly the scales shift.

Luckily, Cindy's response to *Jacob* was immediate. She was very excited by the draft and felt it was time to send it out. This was a difficult moment for her since now she would have to call in favors from her Hollywood days and make phone calls to cronies she had not spoken to in years. But she was excited by the script, emboldened by it, and ready to begin. Charlie Shays printed fifty scripts for us and the long arduous process began.

Cindy evolved a strategy of submissions. The first script went to Thom Mount, then president of Universal Pictures. I knew after a day passed that my fantasy of a deal two minutes after he read the script had not materialized. He did call Cindy two days later, however, to say he loved the script, loved the writing, but that it was not for his studio. Those words became a constant refrain as the script began to make its way through the studios. People loved it but wouldn't make it. Most said it was too expensive, or too downbeat for the current climate.

For a full year I received letters from Cindy detailing the major executives and directors who loved the script: Sidney Lumet, Ulu Grossbard, David Putnam, Michael Apted and lots of names I'd never heard of. But nothing ever came of them. At times discussions would open up with directors, only to fall away at the last moment. It was a strange twilight zone period in my life, with fame, fortune, and success just over the next horizon.

Life in DeKalb had begun to grow sour as the romance of small town America wore desperately thin. There was no energy in the place, no vitality. Even the corn was having trouble growing. An exciting evening was going to K-Mart. I was claustrophobic. We would go to Chicago every three or four months for an infusion of culture and quality, but it was not enough.

Only the fact that *Brainstorm* was finally getting made by MGM kept me excited. Unfortunately, even that was a mixed blessing since the draft that I loved, the version co-written by my friend Phil Messina, was now being rewritten into oblivion. Not only were Phil and I not involved in the rewrites, we weren't even invited to watch the filming. Unwilling to have a movie in production without somehow being part of it, I borrowed money and flew out to Hollywood in the fall of 1981 for a week. It was both an exciting and humiliating experience. It was thrilling to see my private images translated into moving pictures, to watch armies of people working on huge sets that were first constructed in my mind. On the other hand, it was very painful when I understood there was no real reason to be there.

The writer on a production is the proverbial fifth wheel. Next to janitors, you are the lowliest person on the set. Your work has been usurped by others. Your characters are no longer yours. They belong to the actors, the costume designers, the makeup people, the hair stylists. The primary pleasure for a writer is hearing your own words being read (assuming they are still your words). Of course, writers feel that they could still make valuable contributions to the entire production. They probably know the material better than anybody. But many directors believe writers are too possessive and that their presence complicates an already complicated process. Therefore, it is rare for a writer to be on the set for any great length of time. The writer becomes like any other visitor, just another transient guest. It is a strange and discomforting experience.

My stay in *Brainstorm*, however, was relatively pleasurable. Natalie Wood was particularly gracious and I was grateful for the opportunity to spend time with her. I flew home on the Wednesday before Thanksgiving, excited, despite my reservations, that I actually had a film in production, and a foothold in Hollywood.

Thanksgiving was particularly happy that year. A lot of family came in for the holiday and we had a huge Thanksgiving feast. There was a lot of excitement about the movie and it was wonderful to have so much love and nourishment. Then, the next day, the bottom dropped out.

I got the news early from my sister Marci who called from Atlanta. Natalie Wood was dead. I was in a state of shock for days. The phone kept ringing as reporters from all around the country tracked me down. I foolishly speculated that there was a strange connection between Natalie's death and the subject of the film itself. Unwilling to elaborate, afraid to give away the plot of the film, that was all I would say. The next thing I knew, the newspapers and tabloids were full of quotes from me detailing a bizarre connection between the film and Natalie's drowning.

Doug Trumbull called and asked me to please keep my mouth shut, we had enough trouble as it was. He explained that MGM was considering using Natalie's death as a pretext for abandoning the film. Doug and I both knew that Natalie had finished nearly all of her scenes and that the film could be completed without her. But MGM was not willing to hear this. For months it appeared that *Brainstorm* was over.

This was a very difficult period for me and my family. We had run out of *Brainstorm* money and I was forced to find a job. It is always humbling looking for work, especially when you have only two marketable skills, writing and typing. I had worked as a museum curator, Head of the Film Department at the Whitney Museum in New York ten years before. But there were no museums in DeKalb. I had made documentaries and industrial films, but that was not a major industry in a town of 12,000. I went to Chicago, 75 miles away, looking for employment, but the few existing film companies were fully staffed. Then I decided there might be one thing I could do closer to home. Perhaps I could teach.

I approached the university in DeKalb and bravely and graciously offered to instruct a class in screenwriting. I dropped a few anecdotes about *Brainstorm* and *Jacob's Ladder*, thinking that they did not get many "Hollywood" writers out this way. Unfortunately, that did not impress them one bit. This was, I realized, a town where people were proud of the fact that they hadn't been to a movie since *Ben Hur* in 1957.

Several days later I got a call saying that they did need someone to teach four sections of Public Speaking 101, a required course for all university students, which means it was a class no one wanted to take. I told them I'd have to think about it. An hour later I said yes.

My teaching days were the low point of my life in DeKalb. Preparing the classes took so much time that I could not write. My students' only interests were getting married or going to business school. I was appalled. I told them all to drop out of school, to have some meaningful affairs, and to travel for a while before committing to anything as serious as marriage or an MBA. To the best of my knowledge, no one listened.

Occasionally during that period, I'd get an encouraging call from Cindy saying that some producer or director had a copy of the script and that we'd hear from them soon. And we usually did. But the answers were always the same. We loved it. Wonderful writing. Not interested.

At the same time I was getting reports from Hollywood on the progress of *Brainstorm*. Legal battles were brewing. Lloyds of London had been convinced that the film could be completed and MGM did not want want to accept their finding. They wanted the insurance money. Doug Trumbull locked himself in the vault with the film's negative so no one could touch it. It was all very bizarre from two thousand miles away.

During that time, the most exciting possibility to emerge for *Jacob's Ladder* came from the director who had long been my dream candidate, Ridley Scott, who had made *Alien* and was now finishing *Blade Runner*. I had seen some of the uncut special effects footage for that film and it was among the most wondrous and magical cinematic imagery I had ever seen. Marvin Minoff, my first agent and an old friend living in Hollywood, contacted Ridley for me.

Ridley loved the script and for about a month, it actually looked like we would make *Jacob* together. The idea was to shoot it right after he completed his next film, *Legend*. Then *Legend* ran into scheduling problems and he decided that he could not commit to *Jacob*. It was a terrible blow. In a sense, it represented the last serious Hollywood possibility for making the film.

Although occasional young directors, producers, and even actors would express interest in the project, nothing ever again emerged that seemed real enough to get it off the ground. I gradually resigned myself to the fact that *Jacob's Ladder* would join the pile of unproduced screenplays on my bookshelf.

Steven Rubello, a writer for *American Film* magazine, had read *Jacob's Ladder* and wanted to include it in an article called "The Ten Best Unproduced Screenplays in Hollywood." That seemed to me a dubious distinction, but then again I was pleased to have it acknowledged at all. I was surprised, when the article came out, to discover that the ten scripts were not simply Steve Rubello's choices, but that they had been picked by top Hollywood executives and culled from thousands of selections. I had no idea so many people had read my script. The article was exceedingly complimentary and made me feel for a moment that maybe I really could write.

Soon afterward I was approached by Kyle Counts, a writer for a film magazine called *Cinefantastique*, asking if he could do a story on *Jacob's Ladder*, the film Hollywood dared not to make. I was hesitant at first, but after meeting with Kyle I felt he was an honest and compassionate reporter who could document the story of *Jacob* and perhaps get some in-depth attention in the Hollywood community. When I finally moved to L.A., I was amazed to find many executives knew who I was, because of these two articles. I was also amazed to discover that *Jacob* had become a kind of cult script. It actually did seem to serve as a challenge to Hollywood, a cinematic dare.

As the school year came to a close, I decided to use the summer to write another script, *Secrets of the Astral Plane,* a fantasy about a young man having out-of-body experiences. I wrote a treatment first and sent it to Cindy. She introduced me to Bob Sherman, who had produced, among other films, *Convoy* and *Missouri Breaks.* Bob loved my idea for *Astral Plane* and arranged a meeting for me pitch it to the president of Warner Brothers. It was, I am told, one of the longest pitches in the history of Hollywood, well over an hour. I did not get the assignment. Disappointed, I went back to DeKalb and spent the next six months writing the script on my own.

During the fall of 1982, Lloyds of London convinced MGM to complete *Brainstorm.* It was cheaper for Lloyds to finish the film than to scrap it. The crew began wearing T-shirts that read "BRAIN-STORM, A LLOYDS OF LONDON PRODUCTION!"

The following spring, I got a phone call from the Writers Guild. They were going to arbitrate the writing credits for *Brainstorm* and it was possible that I could end up with no credit for the film at all. I found that unbelievable. While I knew that none of my dialogue had survived the final drafts of the script, the original story and concepts for the film were clearly mine. Still, I had heard horror stories about major Hollywood writers who had lost all credit on their films during an arbitration. I was told that unless I volunteered to accept a "Story by" credit and give "Screenplay" credit to my friend Phil Messina and another writer whom I had never met, I might end up with nothing to show for eight years of work.

This was a terrible dilemma for me. After much agonizing, I decided to simply accept the "Story by" credit with the view that the film was still my creation, even if the screenplay was no longer my personal work. It was a painful experience. In fact, almost everything to do with *Brainstorm* had been painful.

Years later I learned that this kind of suffering was a common experience for Hollywood screenwriters, one that burns its way into the chromosomes and makes it impossible to forget. To this day it affects every decision I make about marketing my screenplays. I would never again sell a screenplay without being involved in the production of that work. I also knew that I would do everything in my power to get the opportunity to direct my own material. The chance to direct, however, does not come easily. For most writers, it is necessary to sacrifice one or more of your babies on another direc-tor's altar in order to gain that chance. It is a bizarre process.

Someone once told me that directing is actually the last draft of a screenplay. I strongly believe this. That is why, if you are not directing your screenplay, you had better feel very close to the director who is. You must have enormous trust in the person who is completing your work. Unfortunately, getting a film produced is usually so difficult that finding any director, any producer, seems like a blessing. Often writers are quick to compromise their work just to see their scripts on the screen. It is a tragic dilemma.

In July of 1983, Joel Freedman, *Brainstorm*'s producer, called me to say he had spoken to an MGM executive and that she had confessed to him that *Brainstorm* was one of the best films she had ever seen, ever, and that it had changed her life. I was astounded. Could I have been wrong all this time? Was Doug actually making a great film?

Borrowing money again, I flew out to Los Angeles the next week to see what they were talking about. The screening was true to the long line of horrific *Brainstorm* experiences. I hated it. It was, in many ways, everything I feared it would become. Many of my ideas were there, but the story barely touched the depths that had once been on the page. Phil Messina joined me in trying to convince Doug to make some last minute changes. He was not interested.

Deeply depressed, I spent the next several months in DeKalb despairing about my career. It seemed over before it had started. But then something interesting happened. Print ads for *Brainstorm* appeared in the trade press. I saw my name on them. Some early reviews came in. They were glowing. *US* magazine's reviewer was ecstatic, calling the film a breakthrough work in the same league with *Star Wars*.

For a brief period I began to doubt my own sensibilities. Maybe the film wasn't as unredeemable as I thought it was. Perhaps it wasn't what I wanted it to be but it played well for other people. Who was I to judge? That euphoria did not last long. While at a screening in New York I spoke with an old colleague, Howard Kissell, a film critic for *Women's Wear Daily*. His first words to me were, "So Bruce, I see you were involved with that unspeakable abomination, *Brainstorm*." I don't think I caught my breath for a week.

*Brainstorm* opened in September, 1983, to mixed reviews and modest revenues. America seemed divided right down the middle. Literally. Audiences and press west of the Mississippi received *Brainstorm* with praise and the box office was more than respectable. East of the Mississippi, however, it was a disaster. Make of it what you will. In five weeks, eight years of profound personal and creative turmoil were over. *Brainstorm* was dead. It was later resurrected in the burgeoning video market and became what people politely call a "cult" film.

Professionally, very little good came out of *Brainstorm*. Agents and producers never talked to me about it. It was a failed film, politely to be avoided in genteel conversation. Everyone in Hollywood has these films, often long lists of them. When people at parties or on airplanes ask what you do, you hesitate to even acknowledge them as yours. They are like children who have died. You cannot discuss them in a casual way. Few people understand. Not that you don't grieve for them the rest of your life. They just aren't part of your public expression.

But there was one very powerful, life changing event that emerged from the *Brainstorm* experience. When Blanche and I came to Los Angeles for the Hollywood premiere, we spent an afternoon with an old friend, director Brian de Palma. It was a casual get together, full of reminiscences.

Brian and I had been classmates at NYU in 1963. I was his assistant director on *Hi Mom* in 1969 and we made another film together that year, a two screen interpretation of an off-off Broadway play, *Dionysus In '69*. (Brian, Robert Fiore, and I were all credited as "Filmmakers"). In later years, Brian kept telling me I was growing too old to get into the movie business, that you had to be youthful, in your twenties, to withstand the rigors of a Hollywood career. But during this visit Brian altered his position and said something that changed my life. He said that if I wanted a Hollywood career, I would have to move to Los Angeles.

Now that was not the first time someone had said that to me. In truth, the idea had been lurking in the back of my mind since I was a child. I just wanted to pretend it wasn't there. I had been to Los Angeles when I was young and knew instantly that I did not belong there. I was a New Yorker. I knew I was a New Yorker the instant I realized that I'd been born in the wrong city, Detroit. All my young years were involved in planning a way to escape from Michigan and move to the East Coast. New York University became that escape. I moved there in 1963 and never looked back. I loved New York. When Brian said Los Angeles, everything inside me shuddered.

I knew it was not Los Angeles the place that terrified me. It was "Hollywood," the ultimate testing ground, Make-It-or-Break-It U.S.A., which had kept me at a safe distance all these years. If I failed to make a career there, my deepest dreams would be shattered. But this time when Brian told me I had to move to L.A., a dynamic factor came into play: Blanche.

Returning to DeKalb the following day, Blanche told her boss at

Northern Illinois University she was leaving at the end of the school year. That same afternoon she put our house on the market. I was amazed, not to mention terrified and thrilled. Without Blanche's determination, I would never have done it. This, she said, was a do-or-die moment in our lives. She understood how deeply I wanted my career and she was willing to sacrifice everything for a chance to make it happen. It was a huge leap of faith.

Cindy did not feel she could represent me effectively in Hollywood. With her blessing and the help of Bob Sherman, I began the search for a different agent. It took several months to find new representation. Being an out of town writer didn't help. Hollywood agents need to build a client, to make him visible. Still I found someone who was willing to take me on. What he was not willing to do was answer my phone calls. It was not a good relationship.

During this time I finished *Astral Plane*. With only a modicum of help from my agent, it had a brief run around Hollywood. Unfortunately, it quickly joined *Jacob* on the top of my bookshelf. It was simply too big, too expensive, and too unwieldy a production. After *Astral*, I wrote some more industrial films and sent treatments for new screenplays to my agent. On those rare occasions when he did get back to me he would simply announce that my recent ideas and treatments were not commercial enough. My favorite of those treatments, a film called *Ghost*, especially upset him. Hollywood does not make ghost movies, he told me.

The same day we sold our house in DeKalb, my agent called to announce that he no longer wanted to represent me. My work, he said, was "too metaphysical." I was stunned. I told him that we had just sold our house. I reminded him we were coming to Los Angeles in two weeks to find a new home and he was supposed to be setting up meetings for me to pitch a new script idea. With a quiet voice, my agent announced that he had never set up any meetings. Then he wished me well and hung up. I was devastated. I told Blanche the bottom had fallen out of our plans and was amazed when she did not seem at all disturbed. "It's the best thing that could have happened," she said. "Now you'll find a great agent who really understands your work and everything will be fine."

Of course she was right. Two weeks later we were in Los Angeles and I met with several high powered representatives, all of whom had read *Jacob's Ladder* and all of whom offered to represent me. But one of them stood out, Geoffrey Sanford of the Sanford-Beckett Agency.

Like Cindy, Geoffrey too was studying philosophy, at UCLA,

and, like Cindy, he was deeply intelligent and caring. He was also the only agent who did not flinch when I told him I could last for only four months in L.A. without work. After that, my family and I would be living on the beach, and he knew I did not mean Malibu. We would be broke. He was confident he could have me working shortly after I arrived and was willing to take me on knowing that he had the weight of an entire family's survival on his shoulders. I felt blessed to find him.

But Geoffrey was not the only blessing of that trip. Blanche had recently completed a two-week evaluation study for the J. Paul Getty Center for Education in the Arts, and was invited to deliver a paper on her findings while we were in L.A. Minutes after her delivery, she was offered the possibility of a full time job, based in L.A. It had been Blanche's dream to work for the Getty, which was rapidly becoming a major force in the world of art education, her speciality. But she never expected such a sudden, almost miraculous offer. She accepted on the spot.

The following morning we had to find a house to live in. True to the remarkable nature of our trip, we fell in love with the very first house we saw, a beautiful home on an acre of land with palm trees and a swimming pool. The owners seemed to like us and were willing to rent at a price we could afford with an option to buy. We have since purchased the house and have recently tripled its size. The Hollywood dream.

We moved to L.A. on June 30, 1984, and within four days Geoffrey, true to his word, had me writing a screenplay for a major film company and making more money than I had ever earned in my entire life.

I've now written and rewritten six feature screenplays since our move to Los Angeles, each a major chapter in my life, each full of its own history and drama.

The first screenplay was *Little Brother* for Embassy Pictures, the story of a young boy who discovers that his computer is programming him. In a sense, *Little Brother* was never finished. I went through three supervising executives and then the demise of the company before a final draft of the script was ever completed. It is not unusual in Hollywood to change executives during the writing of a script. The problem is that each executive has a different approach to the material and it is not uncommon to completely rewrite a script for each new management. I found this incredibly debilitating, as would most writers.

The real gift to come out of this period was meeting Lindsay

Doran. She was my first creative executive on *Little Brother* and the best story editor I have ever known. Her sense of what makes a screenplay work was astounding to me. With script conferences that could last as long as six hours, she was like a teacher. I would have paid to study with someone like her. But here I was being paid.

I always felt that a screenwriter has to have all the answers in Hollywood, but I learned through Lindsay that creative executives can have a wonderful, collaborative involvement in the development of a script. It does not have to be an adversarial relationship. Rather, it mimics the role of a book editor in the creation of a published work. The interaction provides insights, challenges ideas, and helps solve creative problems. It can be a highly constructive process.

Of course, it can also be equally destructive. Some executives have laid claim to their position in highly unusual ways. Perhaps they were the studio president's personal trainer or his gardener. I've had my share. Their script comments are about as valid and meaningful as your grandmother's.

Lindsay, I came to realize, is an angel in my life. It was she who first recommended *Jacob's Ladder* to Steve Rubello for the article on the ten best unproduced screenplays in Hollywood. And she did other things for me without ever saying a word. Contrary to type, this executive felt I was not being paid enough for writing *Little Brother*. One day, I got a call from Geoffrey. He was amazed. He had just been told that Embassy Pictures was *giving* me an additional $15,000. I could feel an angel working behind the scenes. I don't have to emphasize that such largesse does not occur regularly in Hollywood.

A few months later Lindsay called me. "I have good news and bad news," she said. "The bad news is that I am leaving and that I won't be able to finish *Little Brother* with you. The good news is that I am going off to become a vice president at Paramount Pictures and that I will hire you to write movies there and you will make a lot more money than you're making here." I laughed. But it all came true. And it was eventually through Lindsay that *Ghost* and then *Jacob's Ladder* came to be made, fortunately, or unfortunately, at the exact same time. But that was all a few years later. A few other projects and hurdles had to be overcome first.

I wrote a television "Movie of the Week" for ABC, produced by Marvin Minoff. It was called *Student Affairs* and never got made. It was my first and last experience in television writing. I am not sure if one experience in television is enough to allow one to generalize about the differences between movies and TV, but suffice it to say that the president's chauffeur would have been preferable to the story executives Marvin and I had to deal with. I have never witnessed such arrogance or pomposity.

The movie I was writing was about a student prostitution ring, which the network president told us had to be contrasted with women who sleep with their professors for grades. Not one of your more exalted subjects. I was writing it because my son Ari had broken his leg and needed prolonged and expensive medical care. I did not pretend to the network that I was Anton Chekhov or Eugene O'Neill. In truth, I did not think talents of their magnitude would be required, given the subject matter.

The script never measured up to their expectations. It is hard to be kind to these people. There is a Kafkaesque quality to their demands for brilliance when they dictate plots and confrontations that are banal and obvious. It is an endless Catch 22. The only way out of such absurdities is to stay out. I returned to film.

I wish I could say that I was being offered lots of jobs, but that was not the case. Instead, I spent a couple of months pitching my original script ideas to various studios and production companies without much success.

Pitching is an art. You sit facing an executive who has just listened to fifteen or more pitches that day and countless numbers that week. You must tell him a story idea in three minutes that will make him jump up and offer to put his job on the line, to risk his mortgage, his car payments, his kids' tuition, in order to champion what he has just heard. As you can imagine, this does not happen all too often. At this phase in my career, it did not happen at all. People listened politely, even enthusiastically, but no one was willing to gamble his livelihood on my ideas.

All the same, it was great practice. I learned how to tell a story and I learned what elements were not working. Watching people respond to your storytelling is a great barometer, the only one you will have until you see your film on the screen. Every time you see someone fidget, or their eyes begin to glaze, you have a story problem. Each pitch is an opportunity to rework your tale.

I like to compare pitching to the experience I had as a child in kindergarten where my teacher would tell stories and we listened wide-eyed with our mouths open. If you can get exhausted and often jaded executives to become five years old again, if you can enchant and enthrall them, you have achieved something monumental. If you can excite their desire for money and their primal urge for success, you may even have a deal.

167

One day Bob Sherman called about a book he wanted me to adapt. At that point I almost didn't care what the book was about. I wanted the work. But when I read *Friend*, the story of a young genius who uses his skills at robotics to save his girlfriend from death by implanting a robot's brain in her head, I felt that this was not a project for me. I had not come to Hollywood to write films on that level. I called Bob and politely turned him down.

The next morning I was meditating, as I do every morning and have for many years. I was feeling particularly smug and self satisfied, pleased that I had turned down this movie and maintained my integrity. Suddenly I heard a voice in my head.

"Schmuck!" it said. "There is more integrity in providing for your family than in turning down jobs." It instructed me to get up, go to the telephone, and call Bob Sherman to see if I could still get the job.

It was 7:30 in the morning. Hesitantly, I stood up from my cross-legged position, hobbled over to the phone and called Bob. I told him I had some new ideas about the film and felt I could do a good job, if it was still available. He said other writers were already being considered by Warner Brothers but he wanted me to do it. He would see what he could work out.

For the next few hours I considered how I could make this material into something worthy and ended up envisioning the film as a real and affecting love story. When Bob called back and said I had the job, I was delighted.

Wes Craven, fresh from *Nightmare on Elm Street*, was hired to direct. Craven was anxious to be liberated from the horror film genre and was delighted that I had focused on the human elements in the piece. Now he would have an opportunity to inspire and explore emotions apart from fear. Lucy Fisher, vice president at Warner Brothers, called to say she loved the script, that it had made her cry. "What script?" I asked. I was amazed.

Ultimately, in the end, the film was a failure. Audiences did not want a sensitive human drama from Wes Craven. They wanted blood. After test audiences rebelled against his more human portrayal, the studio instructed us to add six scenes of escalating carnage. The title of the film was changed from *Friend* to *Deadly Friend*, and most people associated with it were embarrassed by what it had become.

Despite the final product, *Deadly Friend* was one of the happiest writing experiences of my career. Ari, five years old at the time, was like a mascot on the set. And Joshua befriended every actor and crew member. In the end, the film bought us our house, paid for Joshua's

Bar Mitzvah, and connected me with Joe Dante, a director I greatly admired. Through Joe, I was able to launch my next project.

The film was a continuing gift to me. During the writers' strike, when I had not seen any income for five months and our bank account was down to $400, I received a residual from *Deadly Friend*. It came out of the blue on the same day Blanche was wondering how we were going to pay our mortgage. Opening the envelope I saw a check for $3,400. Blanche smiled and told me to look again. I had missed a zero. The check was for $34,000—a gift from heaven. How can you not be grateful for an experience like that?

As *Deadly Friend* was coming to an end, the pitching season began again. I was particularly interested in my idea for *Ghost*, a supernatural thriller told from the perspective of the ghost. After three years of rehearsal I had gotten the pitch down to a work of art and was ready to shop it around. In one week I pitched it to four producers and each of them wanted to do it. Lisa Weinstein, a producer at Paramount, was especially sympathetic. She cried when I told her the story and I could feel her connection with it. I felt deeply that she was the person to produce this film. Together we took it to the studio. Dawn Steel, president of production, loved it and we had a deal. Lindsay Doran, my angel from Embassy, became our executive. It was a magical confluence of creative energies.

As I began writing the script, I completed the deal for my next film, *Way Station*, with Joe Dante at Warner Bros. I could not believe I had deals for two pictures, back to back.

I completed several drafts of *Ghost* before we showed it to the studio. Lisa and Lindsay were confident that people would like it, but none of us were prepared for the avalanche of excitement that greeted the script. Dawn Steel called me up personally to say she would drive me to the premiere. We began a search for a director immediately. I figured we would be in production in just a few months. I had once again forgotten that it could take years to get a film made, even one a studio wanted to make.

Making submissions to directors is a very time-consuming process. The protocol is to send a script to one director at a time and then wait for his or her response. If that director is in Australia and not presently looking at scripts, you might have to court his agent for weeks to convince him to intercede. If the director is just finishing another film, you have to wait until there is a break in production for him to read your script. If that director has twelve offers on the table, you have to wait for a decision to see if you are even in the running. This can be a grueling experience.

While this was going on, I began writing *Way Station*, an adaptation of a science fiction novel by Clifford D. Simak. It is a charming story about a depot for intergalactic travelers that was established on Earth during the time of the Civil War. The way station is still operating today and is stumbled upon by a young man. I loved writing this script.

Working with Joe Dante is like playing with a childhood friend. There is an aura of perpetual boyhood about him. He is inventive and enthusiastic, like a kid. *Way Station* was going to be Joe's next film after *Innerspace*, which was expected to be the hottest film of that summer. The box office failure of *Innerspace*, a Steven Spielberg Production, stunned everyone. The president of Warner Bros. announced that he would not make any more science fiction films. *Way Station* was shelved.

Luckily we had found a director for *Ghost*. Frank Oz, famed for his Muppet films and *Little Shop of Horrors*, agreed to do it. Frank and I spent a year reworking the script and beginning pre-production, only to discover that the costs were escalating and the film was getting too expensive. Paramount got nervous when Frank insisted the movie could not be done for less money. In the end there was a parting of the ways. This was a terrible shock for me. I loved Frank and his vision of the movie. We had a wonderful collaboration. But it was not to be. The search began anew for another director.

During this time the "success" of *Ghost*, at least in script form, had gotten around Hollywood. It's amazing how word travels. I am told that Jeff Katzenberg, head of production at Disney, was at a party at Dawn Steel's house and heard her talking about *Ghost*. Excusing himself, he stepped into the hallway and called my agent. Without even seeing the script, or having met me, he offered a three picture deal at his studio. In the end it was not a deal I took, but it's a good example of how "success" works in Hollywood.

For the first time I was known for something other than *Jacob's Ladder*. It was like a one-two punch. I had proven that I was not a one-script writer. This is an important perception in Hollywood. A producer's entire career depends on a writer's ability to deliver a marketable script. Producers are much more prone to go with a dependable writer than with a gifted but undependable one. To have the appearance of being gifted and dependable is a knockout combination.

Of all the new offers that reached my table during this period, the most exciting came from Harry and Mary Jane Ufland. It was an opportunity to write a film for Robert De Niro, a project in which he would star, with Whitney Huston, and co-direct with Quincy Jones. This was heady stuff for me. The fact that Whitney had never committed to the project was of little significance. We all knew she would sign the minute she read the script I was about to write.

The most exciting part of the project was spending two months researching the film, working with De Niro and Quincy, and meeting nearly every major player on the current music scene. One day I took my kids to play on the beach while I was writing with De Niro at a guest house in Malibu. I had never before been to Malibu. Madonna and Sean Penn dropped by. I introduced them to my boys, who looked at me like I was God. For the first time, I felt I was really in Hollywood.

Research is definitely the most pleasurable and entertaining aspect of the writing process. The worst part is having to sit down and write. This script, about a love affair between a has-been manager and a young gospel singer he hopes to turn into a star, was a difficult assignment for me. I realized that no matter how much research I did, I would never know the music business as well as Quincy, and the subtleties of interaction between business and talent were crucial to grounding the film in the reality we all wanted. It was a classic lesson for me. Write what you know!

De Niro, who was involved in making six films at the same time, became less and less available during the writing phase. I remember getting a call from him just as I was sitting down at the computer. "Just two words," he told me. "Fate and Magic." They were wonderful words, I thought, although they had little to do with the story.

I spent weeks trying to interpret Bob's cryptic message and finally conceived of a way to weave it into the script. I was very pleased with what I had achieved. When the script was finished I couldn't wait to get his response. "So what did you think of Fate and Magic?" I asked. "What's that?" he replied. I knew then I was in trouble.

I wrote several more drafts and finally submitted the script to the studio. MGM liked it but offered one major suggestion. Instead of focusing on the beginning of the young singer's career, I should focus on the end. I told them that was a terrific idea, but it wouldn't make the movie any better, just different. By that time, however, I was no longer available to write another draft. *Ghost* had a new director and I was obligated to rewrite the script for him.

When I first heard that Jerry Zucker of *Airplane* and *Ruthless People* wanted to direct *Ghost*, I was devastated. I cried for a month. *Ghost* was not a comedy. Although it was filled with humor, it was a multi-layered piece, with a dark side as well as a personal spiritual vision.

My initial conversations with Jerry did not help matters. While polite and careful in his words, I still sensed that he wanted to totally rework my script, to change something that "everyone" had already said they "loved." I was not happy.

Finally, one day I called Jerry and suggested we have dinner. I set one important ground rule, however: Not one word about *Ghost* could be uttered. It was, in the end, an intelligent move. That night, over dinner, I discovered Jerry Zucker. I met him, not as some crazed director waiting to destroy my screenplay, but as a warm and sensitive soul. I felt a powerful connection to him, a sense of deep camaraderie. He felt like a brother.

This sense of connectedness continued to develop over the year as we embarked upon the rewriting of *Ghost*. It was an amazing process. I wrote more than 19 new drafts. In the beginning they veered dramatically from the original script, but slowly they began to return. It was as if Jerry was using the writing process to internalize the script himself.

By the time we finished, we were not all that far from the original material. But *Ghost* had changed. We had found its commercial thrust. We both felt the script was wonderful. The studio agreed. The green light began to flash. We were in pre-production. There was only one complication.

One day, in the middle of writing with Jerry, I got a phone call from Tracey Jacobs, an agent at ICM, asking if it would be all right to send a copy of *Jacob's Ladder* to Adrian Lyne. "Are you kidding?" I said. I loved Adrian Lyne's work. I thought *Fatal Attraction* was brilliantly directed. I loved his visual power on the screen, his sense of cinematic language. But even more, I thought he had achieved a remarkable reality in his characters. I believed each and every one of them. Plus, his depiction of New York was as good as any I have ever seen, and *Jacob* was a New York film.

A week or so later I got another call from Tracey. She was panting. Adrian had just called her from France to say that *Jacob's Ladder* was the best script he had ever read and he wanted to make it. He would be coming back to the States for a brief stay and wanted to meet me to see what we could work out. I had been around Hollywood long enough to know this kind of interest is not a commitment, and that it was not a good idea to get too invested in it. Still, I was very excited.

I didn't hear anything for a few weeks. Then I got a call from two writer friends, Bruce Evans and Ray Gideon (*Starman*, *Stand by Me*). They also happened to be good friends with Adrian. They were having a party that night and expected Adrian to be there. It was, they thought, a good way for us to meet.

I was aware of Samantha, Adrian's wife, before I noticed him. Not only is she remarkably beautiful, but she dyes a part of her hair bright red. It is hard not to notice her. Adrian was sitting on the couch right beside her. He had shoulder length hair and an unshaven face that was simultaneously cherubic and handsome. He was wearing a thick leather jacket, a rumpled T-shirt, and a pair of expensive gray slacks. I realized later that this was his uniform, his trademark. There was an instant sense of the exotic about him. He was truly a rare bird.

I was about to sit on the floor, at Adrian's feet, since the couch was packed. Then, suddenly, someone arranged for the person on Adrian's right to move away. I took his place.

Adrian seemed authentically happy to meet me and began to talk about his love for *Jacob*. It was the middle of the Mike Tyson/ Leon Spinks fight, however, and Adrian's forceful English accent was punctuated with screams and cheers. By the end of the fight and our conversation, I was not sure what Adrian's intentions were regarding the script. If Samantha hadn't whispered in my ear as we were all leaving the party, "He's going to make your movie," I would have thought this was just another pipe dream.

Bruce and Ray warned me that Adrian has a chimerical quality. You cannot always get a fix on him. He is often hard to pin down. Sometimes you don't hear from him for six months and then suddenly he is on your doorstep. For the next month or so I experienced this first hand.

Not hearing a word from Adrian, I found myself having breakfast two weeks later with another Hollywood producer, Scott Rudin, who congratulated me on my deal with Adrian Lyne to direct *Jacob's Ladder*. Stunned, I asked where he had heard this. From Adrian, he said, at dinner the previous night. I was surprised, confused, and delighted. Happily, Adrian called the next day to say he wanted to get together. We arranged a breakfast at Art's Deli on Ventura Boulevard.

It was an amazing breakfast. Meeting Adrian one-on-one was like meeting an old friend. I felt an extraordinary kinship with him. We talked for two hours, mostly about ourselves. I told him how much I liked *Fatal Attraction*, especially his portrayal of the New York family. I felt he had extracted an extraordinary quality of truth from his actors. While very humble, he did acknowledge a special pride in that accomplishment.

I proceeded to tell Adrian my life story and the history of *Jacob*. My aim was to convey the huge emotional and philosophical investment I had in the material. I was willing to make significant cuts in the length of the script, but I was not willing to compromise its spiritual and philosophical underpinnings. The ending as written was the spiritual key to the work and was the one sacred feature of the script. Adrian concurred that the film, without the ending, without the understanding that the entire movie had been a projection of Jacob's mind in the last hours of his life, would lose its integrity. He said firmly that he would not make the movie unless the producing studio understood our total commitment to this vision.

Adrian told me about his own love for *Occurrence at Owl Creek Bridge* and its impact on him personally and as a filmmaker. It was one of the seminal films in his life, one he had never forgotten. He expressed how excited he was when he realized that *Jacob* was a feature length exploration of the *Owl Creek* idea. I discussed how influential the film had been to me and described the moment when I realized what my movie was about. He was impressed. He said he had read many scripts, but this was the best he had ever read and he desperately wanted to make it.

Unfortunately, Adrian's excitement could not be translated into an immediate commitment. He had arranged to direct the upcoming Guber-Peters film, *Bonfire of the Vanities* and could not sign on another project until he had seen the *Bonfire* script. I was left with the distinct impression, however, that he would opt for *Jacob*.

Toward the end of breakfast, we discussed *Jacob*'s length. We both knew that it was long at 135 pages. In the early version, which Adrian had read, I had not even bothered to follow traditional Hollywood script format. I had written it almost as a novel. I always suspected that my untutored approach to screenwriting contributed to people's fascination with the screenplay, since, without the normal INTERIOR, EXTERIOR, DAY, NIGHT, CUT TO, FADE IN, DISSOLVE TO, etc., the script was easier to read and more engaging.

I have a suspicion that no one in Hollywood really likes reading script format; they use it as a way to skip over essential descriptive passages. Without this professional shorthand, readers were forced to read all of my words. They were compelled to experience the atmosphere of the movie, not just its plot. I suspect that's why it had such a strong impact. I have since learned the commercial necessity of the traditional film form, its use in budgeting and preparing a shooting script, but I must say, I enjoyed writing free form. I felt like a real writer.

I left the meeting very excited. I called Geoffrey and told him the news. Like a good agent, he offered congratulations while cautioning me not to be too expectant. I called Lindsay Doran at Paramount. She was thrilled and hoped I would bring the package to her. I told Jerry Zucker about Adrian's interest and how incredible it would be to have two movies going forward at the same time. He did not seem as excited as I was. "Why now?" he asked. "Why not next year?" We laughed.

I had *Jacob* transferred to computer disk in order to begin the cutting and rewriting process. I also put it into traditional screenplay format. I knew this was a dangerous procedure because now I would find out how long the script really was.

It was long: One hundred fifty-two pages. A screenplay is formatted to average one minute per page. This meant that *Jacob* would be at least two and a half hours long. In fact, because so much of the material was descriptive, in real screen time, it would play even longer than that. At the very least I needed to cut out thirty pages. Ideally more.

In the early drafts of *Jacob* I had attempted to introduce a third layer to the script, the idea that Jacob's confrontations with demons might actually be connected to a larger world event, the Biblical Apocalypse. I wanted to portray the dissolution of an individual mind in the larger context of a dissolution of the entire world. For Jacob it would be impossible to distinguish between his own death and the catastrophic end of everything around him. In his internal landscape, the world would die with him.

Unfortunately, this theme had become overbearing and tended to unfocus the rest of the story. I had eliminated most of it years ago before sending Cindy the final draft of the script. Some wonderful scenes of "demons" snatching people off the street and out of restaurants, were tossed out. One of my favorite sequences, an abduction during a traffic jam in the tunnel below Park Avenue, still gives me the chills. New York friends who had read early drafts of the script tell me that, to this day, they avoid driving through that tunnel.

Still, there were residues of that apocalyptic idea in the script. I had many images of demonic forms encroaching on the city and New York did become increasingly an image of hell with denizens of the underworld crawling out of sewers and subway stations to slowly, quietly, establish their presence, taking dominion over the city.

There was, for example, a scene involving a blind newsseller named Shorty, a man whose face was covered with strange sores and bumps. Jacob, trying to buy a newspaper, runs away when he sees him. A few days later, pursuing the truth of what is happening to him, Jacob goes back to the newsstand, only to be told that Shorty had died . . . two years before.

Many of the scenes like this, I decided, were no longer crucial to the story and I began cutting them. I also cut dialogue within the scenes. I had learned from *Deadly Friend* just how painful long dialogue passages can be. Once an audience gets the message or intent of a scene, it is usually time to move on. So I was brutal. By the time I was finished, the script was down to 122 pages. It felt great.

Adrian returned from a month's holiday in Provence, and I delivered a copy of the cut version of the script. The next morning we met in my office at Paramount to talk about the changes. Adrian hated what I had done. He was aware of every cut—every omitted scene, every missing line. He thought I had ruined the script.

Grabbing the original draft, he sat down on the floor and began going over each line, restoring virtually everything I had eliminated. "I love that bit," he said as we put it back. "That's a great scene. You can't lose that." "Are you crazy? That's one of my favorite lines."

With each restoration, Adrian grew increasingly impassioned about the script. The effect was startling. Halfway through, he stopped and stared at me. There was amazing power in his eyes. "Fuck 'em!" he said. "I have to do this movie. I'm calling my agent right now."

Adrian went straight to the phone and called his agents at ICM. He explained that he wanted to do *Jacob's Ladder* and wanted Guber-Peters to know right away, before he read the new version of *Bonfire of the Vanities*. He did not want them to think he was passing on *Bonfire* because he did not like the script. He wanted it understood he had found a different project that he could not ignore, one that he had to make.

I was awed and proud. I showed Adrian a copy of the article in *Cinefantastique* that called *Jacob's Ladder* "the thought-provoking script . . . that no one dares to film." "I dare!" Adrian said, smiling. I knew it was true. And so, in cutting *Jacob*, I brought it to life. We were going to make the movie.

That, it turned out, was the easy part. What followed was more than a year of intense Byzantine drama, much of it so bizarre and convoluted that only an epic novel could do it justice.

I decided I wanted to make *Jacob's Ladder* at Paramount. Lindsay

Doran had been too important in my life not to give her studio a chance to produce it. She was very close to Ned Tanen, the president of production, and I was sure she could get the film set up there. Besides, Adrian had made *Flashdance* and *Fatal Attraction* at Paramount, films that had earned more than $600 million for that studio; it felt like a good place to be. I also thought it would be extraordinary for me to have two films being made simultaneously at the same studio. *Ghost* was looking very favorable and we were confident it would get a green light, so I asked Lindsay to show *Jacob* to Ned. He read it overnight and called her the next morning. "Buy it!" he said.

A massive negotiation began and ended in twenty-four hours. Lindsay's promise to get me "more money at Paramount that I had ever made before," came true. Geoffrey, my agent, negotiated a deal for even more money than I had fantasized about with Cindy nearly ten years before. It was a major financial coup.

Unfortunately, I neglected to tell Adrian's agents about my negotiations. When they learned the script was now owned by Paramount, they were enraged. Adrian, it turned out, had a first look deal at Columbia Pictures with Dawn Steel. It appeared that I had killed the deal.

But it did not stay dead long. Adrian wanted desperately to make *Jacob* and was willing to make it at Paramount. A lot of egos were quickly soothed and the film became a new Paramount Pictures Production.

I now had two films in pre-production, and, for the moment, on *Jacob's Ladder*, I was the sole producer. Within several months I would also be made associate producer on *Ghost.* I had never worked on the production of a major feature film before, let alone helped to produce two movies at the same time. I felt overwhelmed, totally swamped by everything that was happening. This feeling would not go away for nearly two years.

At this point I had an office at Paramount but no secretary, no assistant. Jerry and I were still fine tuning *Ghost,* and Adrian and I were trying to figure out how to translate *Jacob's Ladder* from the written word into cinematic images. I desperately needed help.

Haydn Reiss, a friend who had recently completed his first screenplay, was with me at lunch one day during this period. I alluded to my problems, especially my need for an assistant, and he immediately volunteered for the position. I thought it was a terrific idea, one of those special moments of someone being in the right place at the right time.

It seems Haydn had a knack for that. Five days after Haydn became my assistant and essentially put my office in order, Adrian announced that he, too, needed an assistant, and I suggested the possibility of Haydn working for Adrian. They both appreciated the offer. I love the way fate works. In one week Haydn went from being an aspiring screenwriter to being the assistant to one of the top motion picture directors in Hollywood. It's such an amazing town. Things like this can still happen. In fact, around Adrian, remarkable things are not uncommon. His assistant on *Flashdance*, Casey Silver, is now, as I write this, president of Universal Pictures!

Now there were three of us working on *Jacob's Ladder*: Adrian, Haydn, and myself. I quickly found another assistant, Judy Whelchel, who took charge of the office and got my life under control. For the next twenty months I worked seven-day weeks, often sixteen hours a day.

Adrian and I began an intense examination of the script. While we both agreed that it was long, Adrian did not seem anxious to cut it, at least not at this point. He knew that a script was like a complex fabric. If you pull just one thread, it could unravel with unexpected consequences. Before we took out the scissors, we had to be intimately aware of the overall design.

Despite his enthusiasm, Adrian had some major concerns. He was worried about the character of Jezzie, afraid that she would be perceived as the devil by most audiences, and he hated the idea of the devil being portrayed as a woman. I pointed out that Jezzie was not the devil but the Angel of Death. Adrian, however, regarded that explanation as an intellectual rationalization that audiences would not buy.

Another consideration was that Jacob's suffering was too relentless and that the audience would not be able to endure his constant agony. Adrian wanted to lighten him up in any way we could; at the very least to find an actor who was light and buoyant at the core. He feared that an overly intense actor would sink the film into a black abyss of despair. The audience would bail out emotionally, and not be willing to stay involved.

He was also concerned about the ending of the film: that the entire battle with Jezzie, and its resolution in the vast Spielbergian staircase of the original screenplay, did not have a human-enough face. Jacob's heaven was too impersonal. Adrian was determined to find a way to bring it back to earth.

Finally, we knew the battle between Jacob and Jezzie was not shootable as written. Adrian argued endlessly that it is one thing to say "the room crumbles beneath them and disappears into the void," and quite another proposition to come up with the image of that void on screen. He was, in truth, deeply concerned about all the visual images I had described in the script. More than anything, he feared that people would laugh at scenes that were unbelievable, images that did not seem "true."

All of these concerns, and a few others to emerge later, became a recurring theme in the many months of discussion that preoccupied us daily. The debates continued up to the time the cameras were rolling, and in some cases, even after we had finished shooting.

I first realized that Adrian and I were not seeing things exactly the same way when I showed him an illustration of "Jacob's Ladder," from the Bible I had owned since I was a child. It was a magnificent rendering of a staircase that rose far up into the heavens. Angels were moving up and down it. The image was a seminal element in the creation of the script and I used it in describing the vast imagery that occurred at the climax of the film.

The image proved to be exactly what Adrian did not want at the end of the movie! He felt it was rooted in the classical depictions of heaven that he wanted to replace. He wanted to create images that challenged or expanded those ideas.

I was very disturbed by Adrian's response, since I had been fascinated by the idea of introducing archetypal imagery into twentieth century experience. I wanted to engage the ancient images that man has played with for centuries, images out of Jung's primordial unconscious. For the first time I sensed the struggle in which Adrian and I would engage for more than a year. Perhaps the biggest problem was that Adrian did not have alternatives to what I was offering. He simply had a sense, an urge, an undefinable feeling that there was another way.

Adrian's inability to put his "urges" into words, to communicate the undercurrents of his mind, was a terrible frustration for both of us. He could never quite articulate what he wanted, only what he did not want. But I was not the only one who had to deal with this aspect of his character. Anyone who worked with him had to keep generating ideas and images until Adrian found the one he knew was right.

We began watching movies and looking at pictures in books. We watched films that had attempted to chart new terrain. We were mesmerized by Ridley Scott's film *Alien* , Jim Cameron's *Aliens*, Billy Friedkin's *The Exorcist*, Roman Polanski's *Rosemary's Baby* and Emir Kusturica's *Time of the Gypsies*. We also viewed hundreds of other films, probably every major horror film of the last ten years. Watching them with Adrian was a profound educational experience, as he would comment on the technical secrets behind every virtuoso shot and effect. He also catalogued who had been sleeping with whom and how so-and-so had an affair with so-and-so, which added background enjoyment to the viewing.

Adrian hated prosthetic make-up. Anything that reeked of rubber or latex, anything with slime running down it, appalled him. He hated its artificiality and was determined not to use anything that looked unreal or fake.

When I initially wrote *Jacob's Ladder*, Joe Dante had just completed *The Howling* and Ken Russell had made *Altered States*. Both films explored a new make-up technique in which we could watch the human body go through amazing fully-realized biological transformations. I was thrilled by this technique and wanted to apply it to *Jacob*.

The dance scene, in its original incarnation, had a room full of people transforming before our eyes into a coven of demonic beings. It was one of the most powerful scenes in the script and one that I felt "sold" the movie. Now, ten years later, the effect had been used in a multitude of films and Adrian was not anxious to repeat it. Besides, we realized after discussion with many make-up and effects artists, that to transform that many characters would exhaust the entire makeup budget of the movie!

Adrian's preference was to merely glimpse a transformation, not to study it. The horror would be enhanced the less it was seen. He used *Alien* as an example, explaining how much more horrific the creature seemed when our minds had to assemble it from the bits and pieces we were shown. Adrian had also been particularly impressed by the tiny alien that the Nostromo crew dissects on the operating table. The camera was able to hold onto it for long shots without the illusion breaking down. Only real fish and real animal parts could sustain that level of truth, theorized Adrian.

It was hard for me to give up the idea of three-dimensional transformations, but Adrian insisted that cinema was about the power of illusion. Not everything has to be seen. When special effects are seen, however, they had better look fantastic.

Adrian was evolving an aesthetic for the film based on authenticity of imagery. Its most profound expression came in Adrian's perception of the demons. He hated my idea of classical Bosch-like creatures, part toad, part fish, part bird, part man. He despised the image of devils with horns and pointed tails. He felt that people are too familiar with the classical renderings of the demonic soul. We see demons in their classical costumes and poses, and we classify them instantly. They are familiar to us and, therefore, not threatening. They are easy to dismiss, and therefore, not demonic.

Adrian wanted demons that you could not dismiss, that you could not hide from. He wanted demons that approached you from the inside, that emerged from your own consciousness. He wanted something that expressed the demonic in human terms. We began to focus on people's endless attraction to and repulsion from human deformity. There is a kind of perverse interaction between well-formed and deformed human beings. The eye does not want to look, but cannot pull away.

Suddenly the word "thalidomide" emerged in our conversations and we realized that we had discovered a term that perfectly defined the image of the demonic that Adrian had been searching for. Rather than show a creature with wings, Adrian envisioned a creature with a growth emerging from its back, an extra flap of skin. The audience should be able to look at it for a moment without understanding what it is. And then, suddenly, it should dawn on the viewer that he is looking at a wing. Strange bony protrusions on the skull should suddenly be perceived as horns. A long fleshy growth extending from the backside could be viewed as a tail. And then all the parts would begin to coalesce, as a word forms and rises into our consciousness, the word "demon." By this time, Adrian theorized, the audience would be in a state of primal terror.

This was great stuff for me. I was sold. While part of me was still deeply attached to the idea of intersecting biblical and modern day imagery, the thalidomide conclusion seemed brilliant and set an entirely new tone for *Jacob's Ladder*.

We began casting. I thoroughly enjoyed this phase of pre-production. It was wonderful envisioning actors as the characters I had written. Each person gives you a different slant on the material. Adrian has a tendency to see everybody in town and it takes him a long time to make up his mind about everything. Casting went on for almost the entire period of pre-production, which in our case was almost a year.

Tim Robbins and Elizabeth Peña were among the first actors that we saw. Something about both of them was especially compelling and we could never get them out of our minds. Quietly, almost subliminally, they were the actors against whom everyone else was compared.

Tim was the only actor we met who both Adrian and I could see instantly filling all three aspects of Jacob's character: a Doctor of Philosophy, a Vietnam vet, and a postman. We watched all of Tim's previous movies, paying close attention to his performances in *Bull Durham*, *Five Corners*, and *Miss Firecracker*. His screen presence was always magnetic. He drew your attention in every frame. And one sensed, deep down inside him, an innate goodness and the light-heartedness that Adrian had always required for the role.

Elizabeth turned us on immediately. She was charming, sexy and seductive. But she also had an edge. There was an undercurrent of danger inside her; the unexpected. I had never visualized Jezzie as Hispanic. I had always seen her as a midwestern farm girl. But Elizabeth left an indelible impression that grew and grew over the many months of casting. In the end, we always came back to her.

After a few weeks in the new offices at Paramount we began to receive our first feedback on the script from the remaining studio executives. *Jacob's Ladder* was not universally loved. There were reasons that it was one of Hollywood's best "unproduced" screenplays. Many of Paramount's executives didn't like it.

The studio divided into two polarized camps with no one in the middle. People either hated it or they loved it, and both sides seemed passionate in their view of the film. Some executives wondered why we would want to make another Vietnam picture at this stage of the game. Other executives argued against them, saying the film was not about Vietnam. Some felt cheated that the entire movie's experience had been in Jacob's mind. And there were those who loved it exactly because of that. There were execs who found all the twists and turns too confusing; others reveled in the mystery of having the rug pulled out from under them again and again. There were those who thought we were making an Agent Orange movie and those who considered it a profound journey through the soul of a dying man. It was a terrible dilemma—how to bring these divergent opinions into one converging sensibility.

The general view was that Jacob's journey needed to be more personalized. Adrian suggested that we give Jacob another son, Gabe, a son who had died. At the end of the movie the boy could lead Jacob into heaven. This would have a profound emotional effect on the audience and hopefully make the movie satisfying for everyone. A lost child would give Jacob something to long for during the movie, something he could want, and attain, by the end of the film.

I had mixed feelings about this. I was concerned that the addition of Gabe might affect the very delicate balance of the film, adding one too many elements, and throwing everything off kilter. Still, I could appreciate the studio's attraction to the idea and was willing to try it.

Originally, Gabe was introduced at the beginning of the film, while Jacob read a letter from him in Vietnam. Later, we decided Gabe's presence at that point seemed to confuse the opening thrust of the movie and we pulled it out. Instead we introduced him in the scene where Jezzie drops all the photos of Jacob's past onto the bed and Jacob reviews his life.

The photo worked here; the revelation of a son who had died was emotionally effective. Unfortunately, when Jezzie subsequently threw the photos into the incinerator, she then appeared even more evil than she had in earlier drafts where she was simply getting rid of the "garbage."

Jezzie's character began to shift. Adrian was concerned that people would hate her and we would never engage them in the film, let alone in her relationship with Jacob. We fought for weeks, trying to fit Gabe into the script while defining and redefining Jezzie's persona. Jezzie needed to be a woman who could be perceived as both angel and devil; making her too evil or too good would compromise the balance of the work.

During this period I began to realize that the ending of the script was eroding. My attachment to the visual fireworks, but more importantly, to the spiritual and philosophical basis for those fireworks, was being called into question. Adrian and I entered into profound spiritual discourses on the nature of death and dying, and we battled over the symbolic content of the last ten pages of the script. This was especially agonizing as we became more entrenched in our positions. We would repeatedly return to Jacob's death and resurrection in the battle with Jezzie. In my view, Jacob must learn that he has been doing mortal combat with his own fears, his own demons, throughout the movie. The only way to overcome these demons is to embrace them, to essentially recognize the enemy in himself, and surrender the absurdity of the struggle.

In the original draft, Jacob experiences Jezzie as a trickster. The more he tries to hold onto her, the more she changes her form and appearance. At one point he finds himself choking his own son. By finally "letting go," Jacob frees himself from the entire struggle and accepts the inevitability of his death, of death itself. At that moment his body is engulfed in flames and, like a Buddhist monk, he sits down and allows himself to be consumed by them. The screen goes dark. Gradually there is a sense of dawn. A charred mass becomes visible before us: the remains of Jacob Singer. It is a grotesque sight that grows stranger as we notice that in the area of his eyes there is movement, life. At that moment, Michael Newman appears as if from heaven and approaches Jacob, instructing him to get up. Jacob's flesh, Michael says, can't hold him any more. He reaches for Jacob's blackened body and pulls at the dead skin. A beam of light shoots out. Michael tells Jacob that he is free, he has won the battle. Full of light, Jacob emerges from his lifeless flesh a new being. By accepting death, Jacob is born into a new triumphant life. His soul is free.

Obviously, this is not your traditional Hollywood theme. This movie, of course, was never traditional. But now Adrian was expressing difficulty with the image of Jacob emerging from the charred mass of what was once his body. There was no way Adrian could visualize the scene without seeing it as a trick, an assembly of bad special effects that would have the audience rolling with hysterical laughter in the aisles.

Over and over I redesigned the scene to avoid the special effects problem, but never to Adrian's satisfaction. Finally Adrian advised me to surrender to reality; there was no way he could shoot this scene. As we eliminated the sequence, I saw the entire philosophical base of the film eroding irretrievably. I was terrified the movie would become something else, that its whole purpose for being, from my perspective, would vanish.

Adrian tried to reassure me that it was going to work. We would find the equivalent to my images in some other cinematic motif. We looked at thousands of photographs and paintings. The walls of the office became a gallery of powerful images.

The work of H.R. Giger, the man who had inspired Ridley Scott during the filming of *Alien*, became very significant early in our research but was gradually replaced by other new-found images. Joel Peter Witkin, a photographer with a powerful and terrifying vision of the world, inspired many dialogues and impressed us tremendously.

In time, the paintings of Francis Bacon emerged as an undismissible force. They haunted all of us. We began to understand the look of the film. What had begun in my mind as a hybrid of Bosch and Blake was now moving into the contemporary realm epitomized by Bacon's work. His suggestion of the demonic was, for Adrian, a stunning corollary to his own visual sensibilities.

Brian Morris was hired as our art director. Brian was responsible for some of Alan Parker's films, most notably *Angel Heart* and Pink Floyd's *The Wall*. With his presence, the look of the film truly began to emerge.

We submitted the new draft of the script to the studio. Although very little had really changed and the earlier script was mostly intact, the subtle changes introduced by the addition of Jacob's son, Gabe, threw everyone off balance. The response was disastrous. Even some of our earlier supporters were now disaffected.

Somehow the introduction of Gabe cast an even darker tone across the screen; and the movie was already perceived as being pretty bleak. Adrian, however, remained undaunted. He essentially told the studio to trust us; we would get it right. I went back to the drawing board.

Meanwhile, Paramount was going through a secret but profound change of management at the top. Ned Tanen, president of Paramount and our primary supporter, had long been talking about leaving the company. Rumors were flying that his departure was imminent. He assured us that if anything happened, he would remain an ardent and vocal supporter of the film. Well, things did happen, and he did remain ardent and vocal, but unfortunately, his departure left us in an unexpected void. The new Paramount executives, after much wringing of hands, decided that *Jacob* was not for them. We were put into turnaround.

This was a stressful period. We received word that Paramount was dropping the film just two hours before we were due to leave for London and Zurich in search of special effects personnel. Adrian was staggered. *Flashdance* and *Fatal Attraction* had made a fortune for Paramount and he could not believe they were going to reject *Jacob*. But a shocking loss of faith is not an uncommon occurrence in the movie business. Many films begin their lives at one studio and get made at another. Now our goal was to quickly find a new studio to take us on.

For about two weeks, it looked like no one would rise to the occasion. The majors were frightened off and it looked as if *Jacob* had become, once again, the script no one dared make. And then suddenly things changed. We had a fateful luncheon with the heads of an independent company, one that was rapidly becoming a new power in Hollywood: Carolco.

Mario Kassar and Andy Vajna had turned a small company into a giant corporation by making a string of films for Sylvester Stallone and Arnold Schwarzenegger. The *Rambo* films alone had reportedly filled the company coffers with more than $400 million. Our luncheon was unsettling for me. The players were intimidating and the stakes were very high. Jeff Berg, president of ICM and Jim Wiatt, his executive vice president, joined us at the table of a fancy Italian restaurant, along with Mario and Andy. Nobody ate.

The luncheon conversation, while polite, seemed unguided. For a long time no headway was being made. Then Jeff Berg took charge. It was amazing to watch a real pro go into action. I sat with my mouth open as he explained why Carolco had to make *Jacob's Ladder*. If I had had $25 million in my pocket I would have given it to him. In the end, that is essentially what occurred. Before I even understood what had taken place, we were all shaking hands and the deal was made.

Except for one thing. Upstairs, in the ICM offices, I was told that there was one impediment to the deal. Andy and Mario felt I was getting too much money for the script. I was told that if I did not cut my fee by one quarter before 5 p.m., there would be no deal.

I was stunned and desperate for advice. I tried calling my agent. He was with his wife visiting the wine country in Napa Valley. I called Lindsay Doran at Paramount. She was out Christmas shopping. I called my lawyer, Charlie Shays, in New York. The office was closed. He was not at home. I tried calling every advisor and confidant I could think of. Not a single one was available. Finally, I realized that this was the entire point of what was happening. I would have to decide by myself.

I agonized for a long and troubled hour and finally came to a decision. Screw 'em. If they wouldn't pay me my money, they couldn't have the script. I called Adrian to say I was sorry if I had killed the deal but that what they were asking was wrong. He said I didn't need to apologize to him. He thought I was doing the right thing.

I called Jim Wiatt and told him my decision. He said I was a fool, I was destroying a major opportunity and that I would regret it. "So be it," I responded.

An hour later we closed the deal and not another word was ever said. Soon afterward, each of my advisers returned my call and each one said I had made the right decision. It was a great lesson for me. I knew now that I was playing hardball in the big leagues and that I'd hit a home run.

The deal at Carolco was wonderful. There were very few executives at the company and agreements were completed quickly. The only problem was that I had to give up my executive producer credit and take associate producer instead. Andy and Mario executive produce every film they make.

We moved into new offices at Carolco about the same time *Ghost* moved into production offices on the Paramount lot. I now had to run all over the city to meetings. It was becoming increasingly difficult to be in two places at the same time.

I asked Jerry to which film I should devote most of my time. He was emphatic. "I need you and Adrian doesn't," he said. Jerry invited me to join him in all phases of production, to be with him during casting, on the set, and to stay with him until the film was done. It was a wonderful offer.

Then I spoke with Adrian. He was also open and honest. Essentially, he had never had a writer on his set before and said that it would not really be a comfortable arrangement for him. I was welcome to visit whenever I liked, to hang around as much as I liked, but I would not have a real producing role. That position went to Alan Marshall, a producer whose work I had long admired and whom I had suggested for the film.

Alan, like Adrian and production designer Brian Morris, was also British. He had worked with Alan Parker, producing virtually every one of his movies. In fact, they had made *Angel Heart* together for Carolco a few years earlier, so Alan was right at home with Andy and Mario. Alan was a powerhouse of a producer, a gentle man with a not-so-gentle demeanor, who galvanized us into action. Our relationship was difficult at the start but soon became warm and respectful. Except for Haydn, I was now surrounded by Brits. The film was scheduled to shoot in early September, with six months of preproduction.

Philosophical discussions raged anew. I found myself becoming increasingly isolated in my point of view, with Adrian, Alan, and even my old friend Haydn often allied against me. While the discussions were always very polite, almost friendly, there was a growing sense of entrenchment on all sides. Adrian would begin every sentence by saying, "With all due respect," and he was, in fact, always respectful. We just saw things differently.

Soon I was aware, however, that I also had to contend with a chorus of critics made up of secretaries, assistants, and anyone else who might just have a passing comment on *Jacob*. Adrian was very open to all comers, which in many ways was to his credit. He did not want to get stuck in one viewpoint or perspective. As the director, he needed to be like an intelligent sponge, absorbing many ideas and points of view. While I respected his approach, this was a trying and painful period for me.

Adrian was sensitive to my discomfort. He bought me a wonderful present, a copy of *Heroes of the Kalavalla* by Babette Deutch. He knew that *Heroes* had been the basis of the first script I had ever written, as a child in elementary school. Inside the book was an inscription written by the author, and below it, a loving note from Adrian. Essentially, he asked me to trust him and not to worry: "It'll all come out in the wash."

As we continued our work, many of my fears did go away. Studying the storyboards for the visionary sequences, I began to glimpse the power of Adrian's visuals. Directing is in many ways a task of translation; the director must take the force of words and turn them into the power of images, and Adrian was a master at this.

We began to cut the script. For a long time Adrian and I did a kind of dance. I would cut scenes and he would restore them. But now we were at the point where some cuts had to stick.

The first major cut was in the opening of the film, the Vietnam sequence. The key to the scene was the revelation at the end that American soldiers, not the Vietcong, were attacking and killing each other. Adrian felt that revelation was so important it should be saved for the end of the movie. I argued that by keeping it up front we set up a mystery that would hook the audience for the entire film. Adrian thought they would be hooked just seeing the soldiers flipping out as the battle began. Finally, I decided not to worry about this since, with editing, we could change the placement of these scenes in the final version of the film. On paper, however, the scene seemed seriously weakened.

The next major scene cut was with Professor Stern. I initiated this one, so I should not complain. Adrian fought for it for a long time. But in the end, the film could not stand still for a five-page scene between Jacob and his former college professor talking about mythological and theological demonology. I loved the scene and it gave a fuller dimension to Jacob as a character, but it simply did not belong in a Hollywood movie. It was a literary moment, not a cinematic one. And so, with the push of a button on my computer, the scene was gone.

For the original of *Jacob*, I had labored on the character of Professor Stern for weeks. Cindy had demanded that I rework the scene many times until Stern had the authentic voice of a wizened academic. I also used Stern as a voice for my own personal philosophy and tried endlessly to squeeze in volumes of metaphysical truths. In the end, one truth survived: you cannot use film as a teaching tool. Audiences are not there to learn. They are there to be entertained. If you can successfully get one idea across in a film, you have achieved something monumental.

The dance sequence in Della's apartment originally read beautifully and was truly frightening in its evocation of demonic transformation. The new version of the scene was less literary, but we were long past the point where anyone cared how something read. Adrian needed to know just what each image in this scene would look like and how it would be achieved. We spent a long time on the dance scene and in the end it was more successful in the story-boards than scripted.

The scene where Jacob wakes up and finds himself in bed with his wife Sara and talks about dreaming of Jezzie was always the riskiest and certainly the most confusing moment in the film. It had equal potential for brilliance and for disaster. By adding Gabe to the equation, I worried that we might tilt the balance into total confusion. But if Gabe did work here, we could feel Jacob's deep connection to his youngest son and his presence at the end of the film would be made that much more effective. When I first wrote the scene, I knew that it was a gamble. I knew even as we were deciding to shoot it, that it would remain a gamble until we could see it on the screen.

The hell sequence, where Jacob is taken to the hospital and finds himself on a journey into the inferno, was the occasion for one of Adrian's masterstrokes. In the original script, Jacob, lying on a stretcher, begins to see an image of hell materializing on the wall before him. Demons emerge as if from the molecules themselves and wheel him through the wall into the fiery pit. As usual, Adrian was totally unsatisfied by my classical interpretations of hell. I showed him engravings by Gustave Doré, but they did not enthuse him. Hell had been tamed by familiarity. He wanted something contemporary that would burn itself into the audience's consciousness.

Then Adrian hit upon using the hospital itself as a manifestation of the underworld. He envisioned Jacob on the stretcher being wheeled down to X-ray, but never getting there. Instead, the hospital would grow increasingly horrific, tapping into deep, universal fears of the hospital experience. The stretcher's wheels spin aggressively, hypnotically along the hospital floors. The surface changes from bright tile to rough cement. Small pools of blood appear in the cement and coagulate against the floorboards. I was sold.

A number of scenes were cut involving Jezzie's wilder, more demonic aspects. We were going to spend a long time with Jezzie, and Adrian feared that no one would want to spend it with a shrew. I contended that her dual angelic/demonic nature established the necessary set-up for the film's final sequence. That complex nature also allowed Jacob to ask Jezzie the essential question, "Who are you?" That query would foreshadow the moment when Jacob discovers that Jezzie is neither angel nor devil, but his own creation.

Among the delicate nuances of the movie, Jezzie's character is the most fragile. If she is too demonic or too angelic, she loses her believability as an inhabitant of the real world. If she is too much of a harridan, we wonder why Jacob is living with her. If she is too sweet, she loses her power in the final confrontation with Jacob.

The last third of the movie underwent the most continual rewrites. We tried endless variations, taking scenes out, putting them back, trying them in new configurations. A scene wherein a demon emerged from a wall and tried to suck Jacob in, came and went over and over again. Ridley Scott told Adrian that this was one of the scenes that had most affected him, which encouraged Adrian to keep it. The article in *Cinefantastique* had even featured illustrations depicting this scene. But ultimately the scene simply didn't belong any more. The film was changing.

I was able to support nearly all the transformations the film was undergoing, but finding a new end sequence became a torturous experience. Through many variations, I struggled to maintain two key elements. I was determined that Jacob would do battle with the reality and the illusion of Jezzie and discover that he was fighting himself. And I was determined that Jacob would experience a resurrection, an awareness that he had transcended death, to show that there was no absolute finality to human existence, that biological death was not an end but a transition. I wanted to affirm the survival of the human soul. In my movie, I wanted to see the spirit of a man escape the duality of human existence, the complexity of good and evil, the enthrallment of light and dark. That's why I had written the film. It was the whole reason for its existence.

To me, *Jacob's Ladder* was not simply about one man's struggle, but everyman's struggle. Learning to let go of life is, in biblical terms, the key to infinite life. I wanted to dramatize what Louis tells Jacob when discussing the teachings of Meister Eckert, the German mystic and theologian. Heaven and hell are the same place. If you are afraid of dying, you experience demons tearing your life away. If you embrace it, you will see angels freeing you from your flesh.

In Eastern religions, it is not the body that dies, but the illusion of the body. Death is an experience of ego loss. One loses the sense of separation between one's finite self and the larger universe. In Eastern terms, this separation is illusory and death is a disillusioning experience. It is a moment of truth. You become aware of your oneness with all existence, a oneness that has always been there.

If you are not prepared to be stripped of your illusions, death will be a painful process. If you have spent a lifetime angrily fighting with the world around you, you may not enjoy discovering that you have, in fact, been doing battle with yourself. You will fight this knowledge. You will see terrifying visions. Hell will become a real place.

If, however, you have loved life, if you have learned to remain open to it, then death is a liberation, a moment in which you recognize that there is no end to life. You are one with it in all its finite and infinite manifestations.

These are the underlying themes of *Jacob's Ladder*. They are the reasons I refused to let anyone direct the movie until the right person came along. I always felt that I was better served letting the film sit on a shelf, than having a movie made that betrayed these ideas.

You don't get a lot of chances in Hollywood and I didn't want to blow this one. Of course, I knew that any film production was a gamble and that you opened yourself up to innumerable forces when you engaged in the extremely collaborative process of making movies. But I also knew that with the right director I would need to trust those forces and Adrian, to me, was that director. I was willing to trust, but I was not prepared to diverge so strongly with him over the end of the film.

Adrian's argument with me ultimately rested on one question, "Who are you to presume that your view of death is any more true or relevant than anyone else's?" This, of course, is a difficult question. I have very deep and real reasons to feel what I feel and believe what I believe. But whether I am right or wrong is really not the issue. As an artist, I create out of my own vision, my own personal sense of the universe. Of course Adrian has a right to do the same. In Adrian's conception, heaven is a place of reunion. He told me that his relationship with his father had been difficult, and that he hoped heaven would offer an opportunity to see him again and set things right. In a sense, our two concepts collided regarding the end of *Jacob's Ladder*. In filmmaking, it is hard for one singular vision to prevail, especially if that vision belongs to anyone else but the director. In truth, a movie is an amalgamation of many ideas and perspectives, and the writer, although the original visionary, is not the final one. Even if you direct your own movie, many other forces are at work, from studio executives and costume designers, to the response of test audiences. Film is probably not the best medium for people with deep convictions and personal visions. On the other hand, if and when your concepts survive the assault of the filmmaking process, the opportunity to share yourself and your ideas with the world is unparalleled.

Unable to walk away from my film and from Adrian, I worked feverishly to find an ending that would satisfy us both. I already knew that I would not communicate the full range and depth of my ideas to an audience; now I hoped to salvage its basic thrust. I wanted people to understand my belief that there is a journey into death, that the spirit freeing itself from the body experiences a battle between the forces of heaven and hell, and that liberation came simply from the ability to stop struggling, to let go. If this idea endured through the final manifestation of the film, it would still be a worthy creation.

One image, inspired by Bacon and Witkin, recurred throughout our discussions: the blurry image of a man in torment, in endless movement, whom we began to call Vibroman. None of us was quite sure why he was there, but Adrian was deeply committed to the image and it surfaced throughout the film, in the dance at Della's apartment, in the car with speeding demons, in the mirror in Jacob's apartment. To me, it seemed a symbolic presence with no symbolic meaning.

I never understood or really cared for Vibroman, but knew that he was somehow important to Adrian's vision of the film. One day I came across a suggested storyboard for the end of the movie. I was shocked by it. Although it resembled my final scripted version, it was also very different. Vibroman was now a key element in the scene! But for me had no symbolic stature. He was simply a repetition of earlier images.

I felt that the ending was fast deteriorating into mindless metaphors with no ultimate statement and no real purpose. I told Adrian how much I hated what was happening. I felt as impassioned as ever and did not care at that moment if I was asked to leave the project. But Adrian never flinched. He, too, realized that we were not yet there and asked me to try and fix it.

During this final attempt, it all came together. I realized for the first time the instinctive undercurrents in Adrian's creative process. Vibroman was not a meaningless image simply thrust into the fray; Adrian was groping with something he could not articulate but that had real, enduring, emotional power. I suddenly saw Vibroman as a vision of the unknowable, the unthinkable, the ungraspable. He was the vision of death.

Throughout the film, Vibroman had appeared and frightened

Jacob, but we had never brought him to dramatic conclusion. Now it all seemed clear. It was Vibroman that needed to become Jacob's final test. By conquering this dark and terrifying figure, Jacob was confronting his greatest fear. By peering into the heart of this ultimate force, he would accept his own death.

It was a tremendous revelation. My subconscious and Adrian's had come together and given us a symbolic presence to ground the movie, a presence that had been emerging for a long time but that neither of us had before been able to fully grasp. Adrian's relentless pursuit and determination had brought us to a single image that could satisfy Adrian's need for closure on the script and my own.

I wrote the new ending and Adrian was excited about it for the very first time. I was excited, too. I knew that the film would not have the breadth of my original conception, but that it would have its own truth.

This was a remarkable time for me. *Ghost* was ready to start production. The studio was excited about the script and we had a wonderful cast: Patrick Swayze, Demi Moore, and Whoopi Goldberg. We began shooting on July 18, 1989. I remained in Los Angeles, working closely with Jerry, while Adrian and the *Jacob's Ladder* group moved to New York. Tim Robbins and Elizabeth Peña were cast as Jacob and Jezzie, along with Danny Aiello as Louis, the chiropractor.

It was amazing, having two films shooting simultaneously. I would be on the set with Jerry in Los Angeles and get a call from Adrian in New York, asking about a line change or a new take on a scene. My mind would be constantly jumping from one film to the other. It was like a schizophrenic condition.

In October, *Ghost* moved to New York and for five weeks I had two films shooting in the same city at the same time. I would take a taxi from one film location to the other. It was an astounding experience. At night both *Ghost* and *Jacob's Ladder* showed their dailies at the same film laboratory, Technicolor, on West 44th. *Ghost* would screen from 7:00 to 8:00. Then I'd say good night to the *Ghost* crew and the *Jacob's Ladder* people would come in. It was an unparalleled time in my life.

Watching the filming of *Jacob* was a revelation for me. I saw Adrian in action and for the first time I fully comprehended his genius. He was a man whose creativity came alive in the presence and production of images. Ideas that had failed to make it to the page were now there on the screen.

I was in love with what I was seeing. There were images of Jezzie's divided personality seen in fragments of mirrors, not obvi-

193

ous and overstated, but subtle, probing, and thrilling. Shots lingered on actor's faces waiting for the right moment to emerge, tiny glances, inner thoughts. Each frame had textural and psychological potency. The acting was masterful.

One day we were shooting in the hell-hospital. The camera was mounted low, just behind the wheels of the gurney carrying Jacob across the hospital floor. This was the image which had excited Adrian and initially suggested the feeling for the entire sequence. It was a dramatic shot but Adrian was not happy. He puzzled over it for a few moments and then rigged the gurney so that the wheel would wobble as it rolled. It was a tiny adjustment but its dramatic impact was astounding. It made the scene real. It gave it urgency.

Jacob's battle at the end of the movie was staged in an apartment with a domed ceiling. Flashes of lightning outside the window exploded across the dome and for moments the ceiling became the sky. Inner and outer worlds were merged in a rush of climatic ingenuity. All the special effects in the world could not have accomplished this moment so simply.

Adrian's use of light and shadow astounded me. They were living forces. The film was heightened, alive. I was awed and full of excitement. This was remarkable filmmaking. I knew that there had been a reason that Adrian and I were brought together to make this film. I knew that there was a reason to trust this difficult but extraordinary process. I was thrilled.

The editing process began on the first day of shooting and I was occasionally able to view the new-cut footage. Tom Rolf, who had worked with Adrian on *9¹/2 Weeks*, was the chief editor and his work was brilliant. His sequences were comparable in artistry and subtlety to Adrian's own direction.

The pace of my life continued to intensify. The home we had purchased with money from *Deadly Friend* was now being torn down and rebuilt with money from *Jacob's Ladder*. In March, I spent a month in Wilmington, North Carolina re-writing a film called *Sleeping with the Enemy* for Twentieth Century-Fox. The film, starring Julia Roberts and directed by Joe Ruben, was scheduled to begin shooting within three and a half weeks. The pressure was enormous but thrilling.

One day Jerry Zucker called me in Wilmington with good news. *Ghost* had been screened for the Paramount executives and the response had been overwhelming: They loved it. His call was followed by others from each of the top brass, all confirming what Jerry had said. They insisted that we had a huge hit on our hands.

When I returned to L.A., we began test screenings for *Ghost*. Again, the response was extraordinary. Paramount moved up the film's release date to July 13, 1990 to take advantage of additional summer playing time. In a season filled with action films, *Ghost* was the only romance. Still, if anyone had told me that *Ghost* would end up as the biggest grossing film of the summer, beating out such heavyweights as *Dick Tracy*, *Total Recall*, *Die Hard 2*, and *Days of Thunder*, I would never have believed them. It was an amazing experience. I was on the telephone for four hectic weeks with people I had not heard from in as long as 30 years, calling to express their compliments and congratulations. *Ghost*, it seems, touched a universal chord. I was very moved by the outpouring of affection the film elicited from so many people.

In August, I saw the first half of *Jacob's Ladder* at a small screening. I loved what I saw, and the response of the invited audience was wonderful. Two weeks later, I viewed the rest of the film, up to the last reel. It had a powerful, almost religious quality that took me by surprise. I felt great surges of emotion surfacing from unknown depths and was moved to tears several times during the screening. The performances were superb. Tim's performance as Jacob was especially moving, and he also demonstrated the buoyancy Adrian had desired and believed he would bring to the role.

Only one element of the film shocked me. Adrian had never shot the heaven sequence, the section that followed the antidote scene where Jacob overcomes the onslaught of his private demons to break through the void and gain a glimpse of heaven, an archetypal Edenesque landscape, the doorway to a new world. I had always envisioned the imagery in traditional, even clichéd terms: a peaceful kingdom of extraordinary beauty. I did not want to reinterpret heaven; I wanted to reflect the archetypal conceptions people have of such a place.

It is intriguing to me that very few artists have tried to envision heaven. Other than images of Christ's transfiguration and some Tibetan iconography, I have rarely seen satisfying interpretations of the heavenly realms. Gustav Doré's engravings for Dante's *Paradisio* are probably the best realizations of angelic space I have seen. Interestingly, hell seems never to have been as difficult for artists to envision.

I loved the challenge of realizing heavenly imagery in cinematic terms. Few filmmakers have attempted it and I was looking forward to seeing how Adrian would meet the challenge. He and I had discussed this sequence often, but I knew that we had not yet found anything to satisfy him. The closest possibility was an image of Jacob floating in a body of perfectly still water, with a golden light reflected in his eyes and playing on his face. While this evaded the actual depiction of heaven, at least it was suggested in reflective terms.

The longer Adrian waited to shoot this scene, the more I suspected it would never be done. Then, one day, Alan Marshall confirmed my suspicion. Heaven, he and Adrian decided, did not need to be shot. We already had it on film. Heaven, Alan said, was home. Jacob's return to Sara's apartment would be his entry into heaven.

I can't say that I was overjoyed by this announcement; it seemed a simplistic interpretation of my original script. Still, there was an inherent logic to the choice and in screening the film (without the last reel), it seemed to play. I was nearly a convert.

Jerry Zucker told me that a film has two halves: everything up to the ending constitutes the first half, and the ending itself is the second. I saw the "completed" *Jacob* for the first time in late August. Only ten minutes had been added to the film, but they changed everything.

For me, the battle with Jezzie had always been the climactic moment of *Jacob's Ladder*, the point at which Jacob becomes his own hero, not by attacking the demon before him, but by embracing it. His true victory is in accepting the futility of his struggle and in letting go of a life that has reached its end. Unfortunately, the battle did not work on film. It seemed that Adrian had never embraced it conceptually and therefore did not develop it thoroughly in the shooting. I was present when the scene was being shot in New York but left for L.A. before Adrian had finished. I could not be sure just how much of the scripted material made it onto celluloid.

I knew as I screened the last ten minutes of the movie that the battle was not working. There simply was not enough filmed material and what had survived of my scene was now confused and without thematic relevance. It seemed an intellectual exercise, and a poor conclusion to a movie that was otherwise a deeply emotional experience.

In the scene as shot, Jezzie appears in Sara's apartment to tell Jacob that it is all over. She repeats this statement many times from many locations throughout the room, confusing and frightening Jacob. He yells out, "Who are you?" and she answers, "You know who I am!" As he approaches her, she begins to go through a series of spectacular transformations that last for but a few seconds and end with the appearance of Vibroman. Jacob reaches out to this vibrating figure, pulls off what seems to be a mask, and sees his own face staring back at him. A tear falls from his eye and we cut back to the stillness of Sara's apartment. Jacob now sits on the living room couch, and hears Gabe in the distance calling him to the staircase for his ascent into heaven.

The battle lasted barely a minute and left me totally confused. I, the author, had no idea what had happened. I could find no meaning in the sequence and, since it was the ultimate moment of the movie, I could find no meaning in the film. I felt devastated, especially knowing that up to that moment the film had been so extraordinarily brilliant. All of my worst nightmares were being realized as *Jacob* came to an end, and it all dissolved into meaninglessness.

I didn't really need to express my feelings to Adrian — he could see them on my face. And I knew he felt the problem too. Suddenly, everything went into high gear. Adrian, Alan Marshall, and the editors began to work around the clock to fix the ending of the film. A few weeks later I was invited to another screening. I have made some radical changes, Adrian said.

Radical was the appropriate word for it. Instead of altering the battle with Jezzie at the end, Adrian had cut it out entirely. Based on suggestions by Mario Kassar, the president of Carolco, Adrian had also removed the antidote sequence, the scene in Grand Central Station, and Michael's death. Now when Jacob learns the truth of his death from Michael, it is this that sets him free. He jumps in a cab and asks to go home, back to Sara's apartment, back to the safe haven he has been searching for, the place he has needed to go all along. Sitting in his old living room he hears Louis' voice repeating Meister Eckart's words: If you are afraid of dying you will see devils tearing you from your flesh; if you've made your peace, you will see angels freeing you from the earth. At last, Jacob understands and ends his struggle. Memories of his life flash past him until he hears Gabe inviting him to climb the stairs, up Jacob's ladder, into heaven.

It was for me a truly shocking ending. But the biggest shock was that it worked. The film had discovered, or rediscovered, its own integrity. The image of heaven as hearth and home had been Adrian's aim all along, and now that he had delivered that ending, it fit. It was in truth the only possible satisfying culmination to the film he had made.

But this was not the end of it — there was one last flurry of activity. Tom Rolf re-cut the Jezzie transformation. It was wonderfully cinematic, but no one was certain if it would add to or subtract from the emotional impact of the film. The studio loved the sequence and wanted us to use it. They felt its pyrotechnics were appropriate to the finale of a commercial movie. This was a torturous decision, since we knew the film was working without it. Reinstating the sequence was a terrible risk. As of this writing, the decision has not been made.

There is no more difficult moment for a writer than the revelation that films are not ultimately works of pen and paper, but works of celluloid. What plays on the page may not always play on film, and in the end, a movie must be constructed from cinematic blocks, not literary ones.

*Jacob's Ladder* was no longer the film I had originally conceived, but in a sense it was the film it needed to become. I was enthralled by what I saw, a simplicity and elegance to the final work I had never anticipated. In earlier versions the weight of Jacob's suffering had overwhelmed the film. Now, having excised many of the final scenes, the film found its appropriate balance, its proper weight. While it was painful to lose the antidote scene, one of the most brilliant sequences Adrian had shot, it was a necessary sacrifice. The resulting film was a stunning interpretation of the original script; I was moved and humbled by its power.

I will always wonder if my vision for the end of the film could ever have worked: the huge, almost biblical battle with Jezzie; Jacob's resurrection; the mythical staircase. I will always wonder how these elements might have made a difference. Of course, I will never know and this will be a lasting frustration. Such will always be the lot of screenwriters.

I know the creative team behind *Jacob's Ladder* brought their full talents to this production and I am deeply indebted to them all. Together we have participated in a vast undertaking of great uncertainty. Whether the final film triumphs or falters, I believe we have made a movie worthy of our time, our energy, and our love. No matter how the public receives *Jacob's Ladder*, I will always be proud of the film it has finally become.

*Bruce Joel Rubin*

# JACOB'S LADDER

## AN ADRIAN LYNE FILM

Co-Starring
VING RHAMES
BRIAN TARANTINA

### Cast

| | |
|---|---|
| Jacob | TIM ROBBINS |
| Jezzie | ELIZABETH PEÑA |
| Louis | DANNY AIELLO |
| Michael | MATT CRAVEN |
| Paul | PRUITT TAYLOR VINCE |
| Geary | JASON ALEXANDER |
| Sarah | PATRICIA KALEMBER |
| Frank | ERIQ LA SALLE |
| George | VING RHAMES |
| Doug | BRIAN TARANTINA |
| Rod | ANTHONY ALESSANDRO |
| Jerry | BRENT HINKLEY |
| Elsa | S. EPATHA MERKERSON |
| Hospital Receptionist | SUZANNE SHEPHERD |
| Group Leader | DOUG BARRON |
| Santa | JAN SAINT |
| Street Singers | KISHA SKINNER |
| | DION SIMMONS |
| Taxi Driver | SAM COPPOLA |
| Drunk | PATTY ROSBOROUGH |
| Sam | EVAN O'MEARA |
| Tony | KYLE GASS |
| Mrs. Carmichael | GLORIA IRIZARRY |
| Jacob's Doctor | LEWIS BLACK |
| Policeman | RAYMOND ANTHONY THOMAS |
| Field Medics | CHRISTOPHER FIELDS |
| | JAIME PERRY |
| Field Doctors | MICHAEL TOMLINSON |
| | A.M. MARXUACH |
| Woman On Subway | ANTONIA REY |
| Army Officers | JOHN CAPODICE |
| | JOHN PATRICK McLAUGHLIN |
| Emergency Ward Nurse | BELLINA LOGAN |
| Resident Doctor | SCOTT COHEN |
| Evil Doctor | DAVIDSON THOMSON |
| Jed | BRYAN LARKIN |
| Eli | B.J. DONALDSON |

| | |
|---|---|
| Doorman | THOMAS A. CARLIN |
| Nurses | CAROL SCHNEIDER |
| | BECKY ANN BAKER |
| | DIANE KAGAN |
| Della | BILLIE NEAL |
| Field Sergeant | MIKE STOKIE |
| E.M.T. Bearer | JAMES ELLIS REYNOLDS |
| Attendant | DENNIS GREEN |
| Orderlies | BRAD HAMLER |
| | BYRON KEITH MINNS |
| Partygoers | REGGIE McFADDEN |
| | STEPHANIE BERRY |
| | CHRIS MURPHY |
| | JOHN-MARTIN GREEN |
| Paul's Wife | ARLEIGH RICHARDS |
| Mourners | ANN PEARL GARY |
| | BARBARA GRUEN |
| Street Kid | JOE QUINTERO |
| Machine Gunner | JOHN LOUIS FISCHER |
| Masked Man | ALVA WILLIAMS |
| Hospital Patients | ELIZABETH ABASSI |
| | NORA BURNS |
| | ALISON GORDY |
| | JESSICA ROBERTS |
| | HOLLY KENNEDY |
| | BLANCHE IRWIN STUART |
| Jacob's Assailant | PERRY LANG |
| Stunt Coordinator | PHIL NEILSON |

Stunt Players

| | |
|---|---|
| DANNY AIELLO III | JIM LOVELETT |
| GARY TACON | BILLY ANAGNOS |
| DEBORAH WATKINS | DANNY DOD |
| GENE HARRISON | DON PICARD |
| PETER HOCK | PETER BUCOSSI |
| CYNTHIA NEILSON | DAVID S. LOMAX |
| ANDY DUPPIN | MANNY SIVERIO |
| JEFF WARD | GREG SMRZ |
| MICK O'ROURKE | MICHAEL C. RUSSO |
| JOE FITOS | JOEL DAVID WEBSTER |

Production Manager
CLAYTON TOWNSEND

| | |
|---|---|
| First Assistant Director | JOSEPH REIDY |
| Second Assistant Director | VEBE BORGE |
| 2nd Second Assistant Director | DEBORAH LUPARD |
| Special Prosthetic Effects Designer | GORDON J. SMITH |
| Principal Art Director | JEREMY CONWAY |

Production Sound Recordist.............................................TOD A. MAITLAND
Camera Operator...................................................... CRAIG HAAGENSEN
Additional Editing .............................................. PETER AMUNDSUN
                                                                              B.J. SEARS
Associate Editor............................................................... VICKI HIATT
Production Accountant ......................................................JANE TSIGHIS
Production Office Coordinator .........................................INGRID JOHANSON
Assistant Coordinator ......................................................ALEXIS ALEXANIAN
Art Director...................................................... WRAY STEVEN GRAHAM
Assistant Art Director..................................................CHRIS SHRIVER
Art Department Coordinator ............................CLAUDETTE DIDUL
First Assistant Cameraman..............................VINCENT GERARDO
Second Assistant Cameraman..........................WILLIAM GERARDO
Standby Cameraman ............................................... GABOR KOVAR
"B" Camera First Assistant...........................JOHNATHAN ERCOLE
"B" Camera Second Assistant .....................ANTHONY CAPPELLO
Camera Trainee ........................................................ FRANK RINATO
Still Photographer .................................................. ANDY SCHWARTZ
Location Manager ............................................... PATRICIA DOHERTY
Location Coordinator ....................................................JOSEPH IBERTI
Script Supervisor................................................... COREY YUGLER
Set Decorator..................................................KATHLEEN DOLAN
Lead man.................................................................JOHN OATES, JR.
Swing Gang........................................................CONRAD BRINK, JR.
                                                                              PAUL WILSON
                                                                              RAY MURPHY
                                                                              GLENN JONES
                                                                    HAROLD McCONNELL
Special Effects ........................................................CONRAD BRINK
Special Effects Assistants .......................................MICHAEL MAGGI
                                                                    WILLIAM BISHOP
Make-Up Artist........................................................ RICHARD DEAN
Hair Stylist .......................................................LYNDELL QUIYOU
Boom Operator ................................................TERRENCE J. O'MARA
Sound Technician............................................... RICHARD MADER
Post Production Supervisor................................ MICHAEL R. SLOAN
Post Production Coordinator ..............................NOORI DEHNAHI
Assistant Editors ........................................................JOE SHUGART
                                                                              RACHEL SHAW
                                                                              DONNA STERN
Apprentice Editors......................................... JENNIFER DAVIDOFF
                                                                    STEPHANIE MITCHELL
                                                                    JACKI REISMAN-WERNETT
Supervising Sound Editor................................ MILTON C. BURROW
Sound Editors .........................................................NEIL BURROW
                                                                    RICHARD BURROW
                                                                    SCOTT BURROW
                                                                    GORDON DAVIDSON

| | |
|---|---|
| Sound Editors (Cont.) | MARK GORDON, M.P.S.E. |
| | EDWARD SANDLIN |
| | GARY SHEPHERD |
| | CHESTER L. SLOMKA |
| ADR Editor | ROBERT HEFFERNAN |
| Foley Editor | SOLANGE SCHWALBE BOISSEAU, M.P.S.E. |
| Assistant Sound Editors | SCOTT BOYD |
| | JIMMY SANDOVAL |
| | KAREN MINAHAN |
| Apprentice Sound Editor | DAVID AUGSBURGER |
| Foley | TAJ SOUNDWORKS |
| Re-Recording Mixers | ANDY NELSON |
| | STEVE PEDERSON |
| | MIKE GETLIN |
| Re-Recording by | TODD-AO/GLEN GLENN STUDIOS |
| Music Editor | DAN CARLIN, SR. |
| Assistant to Mr. Jarre | PATRICK RUSS |
| Music Contractor/Coordinator | LESLIE MORRIS |
| Music Recorded and Mixed by | SHAWN MURPHY |
| Synth Ensemble | MICHAEL BODDICKER |
| | MICHAEL FISHER |
| | RALPH GRIERSON |
| | RICK MARVIN |
| | JUDD MILLER |
| | NYLE STEINER |
| Special Sound Effects | STEVEN DEWEY/MUSIKWERKS |
| Voice Casting | BARBARA HARRIS |
| Assistant Costume Designer | CYNTHIA HAMILTON |
| Costume Supervisor | MICHAEL DENNISON |
| Head Costumer | DANAJEAN CICERCHI |
| Costumer | MARY GIERCZAK |
| Costume Shop Manager | SALLY LESSER |
| Property Master | THOMAS WRIGHT |
| Propertymen | THOMAS McDERMOTT |
| | TRAVIS WRIGHT |
| Illustrator | ANTHONY WRIGHT |
| Construction Coordinator | LOUIS SANCHEZ |
| Carpenters | RICHARD TENEWITZ |
| | BOB ZETTERBERG |
| | ANDY GANGLOFF |
| | RICH KAMIN |
| | MOSHE RABINOWITZ |
| Head Construction Grip | RALPH FRATIANNI |
| Construction Grips | JOSEPH B. DONOHUE, JR. |
| | JACK PANUCCIO |
| | DON ZAPPA |
| Scenic Chargeman | JOSEPH GARZERO |
| Assistant Scenic Chargeman | RALPH CAVA |

| | |
|---|---|
| Scenic Artists | KEVIN GOLDEN |
| | DOMINICK DIRENZI |
| | CATHY IPPOLITO |
| | PAUL TAPPENDEN |
| | MATHEW LOEB |
| | PETER GARZERO |
| Standby Scenic Artist | EDWARD GARZERO |
| Chief Electrician | JAMES "PACKY" DOLAN |
| Best Boy | JAMES P. DOLAN |
| Electricians | ROBERT SCIRETTA |
| | ROBERT McGAVIN |
| | CHRISTOPHER DOLAN |
| | RICHARD DOLAN |
| | GREGORY QUINLAN |
| | BRIAN STOCKLIN |
| Generator Operator | RONALD DOLAN |
| Rigging Electrician | JOHN "JACK" FINNERTY |
| Shop Electrician | CHARLES MEERE |
| Key Grip | MICHAEL MILLER |
| Best Boy | THOMAS "CASEY" JIRGAL |
| Dolly Grip | RICHARD GUINESS, JR. |
| Grips | JAMES FINNERTY, JR. |
| | JAMES V. MILLER |
| | JAMES McMILLAN |
| | ROBERT "PETE" MILLER |
| | JOSEPH FINNERTY |
| Assistant to Mr. Lyne | HAYDN REISS |
| Assistant to Mr. Marshall | MARIJKE KOLSTEEG |
| Production Assistants | DEDE DENNEHY |
| | CHRISTIE COLLIOPOULOS |
| Set Production Assistants | JUAN ROS |
| | ELLIE SMITH |
| | CHRIS SWARTHOUT |
| | MIKE VIGLIETTA |
| Assistant Accountants | MARGARET McCOURT |
| | MARA HADE |
| | JAN NIZEN |
| Accounting Assistant | CHRISTOPHER GRAY |
| Art Department Assistant | EDWARD IOFFREDA |
| D.G.A. Trainee | HARVEY EPSTEIN |
| Casting Assistant | SUZANNE SMITH |
| Extras Casting | NAVARRO-BERTONI CASTING |
| Production Runner | JOHN FISCHER |
| Location Assistants | CORINNA OTT |
| | DARREN WISEMAN |
| | MICHAEL NICKODEM |
| | JUSTIN COOKE |
| Craft Services | SUE JONES |
| | LYSBETH HOPPER |

Shop Manager.................................................................................ERIC ZOBACK
Shop Assistant .......................................................SARAH PRESCOTT
Medical Coordinator ............................................KATHY COSSU, R.N. E.M.T.
BENNER MEDICAL PRODUCTIONS
Video Playback Operator......................................................RONALD MADER
Parking Wrangler.............................................................RICHARD TEDESCO
Unit Publicist ............................................................................REID ROSEFELT
Publicity.................................................................PEGGY SIEGAL COMPANY
International Publicity...............................DENNIS DAVIDSON ASSOCIATES
Animals Owned and Trained by ..................DAWN ANIMAL AGENCY INC.
NEW YORK
Transportation Captain...............................................EDWARD O'DONNELL

Drivers

| | |
|---|---|
| THOMAS BUCKMAN | TOM FORD |
| ED FANNING, JR. | MIKE CONNELLY |
| TOM WALSH | JAMES GIBLIN, JR. |
| DENNIS CURRY | ROBERT BUCKMAN |
| ALMONT JENKS | JAMES CLARK |
| TONY LOPES | ROBERT COLLINS |
| PETE CASSELLA | ROCCO CURATOLO |
| JAMES MAHR | JAMES SWEENY, JR. |
| RICHARD S. KORNAK | TOM KEARNS |
| HENRY AVELIN | STEVE HAMMOND |
| FRANK BEGGINS | KEVIN FINNEGAN |
| GARY MAHR | PHILIP FORD |
| KEN EHRHART | JAMES WHALAN, SR. |
| LOUIS VOLPE | RICHARD CLARK |

PUERTO RICO UNIT

Location Manager .......................................................JEFFREY FLACH
Unit Accountant................................................... ROBERT GRINDROD
Location Coordinator .......................................... JUAN HERNANDEZ
Production Office Assistant...........................DELPHINE KILIANSKI
Military Consultants................................................ WARRIORS, INC.
CAPT. DALE DYE, USMC (RET)
CAPT. RUSSELL RAY THURMAN (RET)
MIKE STOKIE
Helicopters Provided by ........................... COLONY HELICOPTERS
Head Pilots............................................................ROBERT SMITH
BEN OLIVER
Pilot-Production Liaison ................................... JOSE MALDONADO
Crew Chiefs..................................................JOHNNY MIDDLEBROOK
ROGER BACHTOLD
Set Decorator...................................... LETICIA STELLA-SERRA
Construction Coordinator...........................................CLIVE BROWN
Head Carpenter ..................................................... TOM SHORT, JR.
Carpenters...............................................SANTO JORGE GRULLART
JOSE CALDERON OQUENDO
MARTIN CALVILLO

| | |
|---|---|
| Construction Laborers | LUIS PADILLA |
| | ELIAS RIVERA MELENDEZ |
| | JULIO ROMAN SOTO |
| Scenic Artist | DIANA DAVILA |
| Painters | JUAN CUIN |
| | JOSE ALEMAN |
| Vietnamese Technical Advisor | TRONG NGUYEN |
| Steadicam Operator | LARRY McCONKEY |
| Steadicam Assistant | LARRY HOUSTON |
| Camera Assistants | ENRIQUE PUIG |
| | RAFAEL AMARAL SEIN |
| Electricians | RAFAEL MOLINARY MACHADO |
| | PEDRO PABON |
| | ANGEL PASTRANA |
| | JOSE HERNANDEZ |
| | GLENNIS BURK |
| Grips | LESLIE COLUMBANI |
| | ERNESTO CASIANO |
| | RICKY VALENTIN |
| | PEDRO JUAN LOPEZ |
| | MIQUEL ANGEL LOPEZ |
| | FREDDY HERNANDEZ |
| Sound Assistant | ANTHONY ORTIZ |
| Special Effects Assistant | FAUSTO FERRER CRUZ |
| Wardrobe Assistants | CESAR HINOJOSA |
| | ANGEL E. VAZQUEZ |
| | VIVIEN E. MARTINEZ |
| | JUAN VIDAL SERRANO |
| | JULIO A. SOTTO |
| | MARI SOCORRO PEREZ |
| | WILLIAM BADILLO |
| Assistant Accountant | MARIBEL AVILES-VEYE |
| Extras Casting | ZORAIDA SANJURO |
| Craft Service | JOSE CRUZ ROBLES |
| | FERNANDA ROBLES |
| Key Production Assistant | VINCENTE JUARABE |
| Production Assistants | JUAN PEREZ RIVERA |
| | ROSA RIVERA |
| | HECTOR ROBLES DIAZ |
| | JORGE IRIZARRY HERNANDEZ |
| | NOEL SERRANO COLON |
| | ABDIEL ANGLERO |
| Location Assistants | GASPAR PONCE |
| | JORGE MALDONADO |
| First Aid | IRMA RIVERA PARRILLA |
| Mechanic | ANTONIO CARMONA ORTIZ |
| Picture Car Wrangler | MIGUEL CASTANEDA |
| Transportation Coordinator | RAUL RIVERA |

Drivers

| | |
|---|---|
| HIRAM ACEVEDO | MARGARITA SERRANO |
| RAFAEL MARQUEZ GONZALEZ | ROSARIO CRUZ ORTIZ |
| PABLO DIAZ RODRIQUEZ | MANUEL CRUZ NEGRON |
| MICHAEL FERNANDEZ | ANGEL ANTONIO GARCIA |
| MANUEL GARCIA RODRIQUEZ | JUAN RUIZ CONCEPCION |
| JOSE L. MONTALVO | MARCOS MONTES |
| JOSE HERNANDEZ | JUAN TAVAREZ-FALCON |
| DUAMEL GONZALES | HIERSON GARCIA |

Special Prosthetic Effects
FXSMITH INC.

| | |
|---|---|
| Head Mechanical | JAMES GAWLEY |
| Head Sculptor | EVAN PENNY |
| Head Painter | TOM CZARNOPY |
| Office Manager | NOELLA NESDOLY |
| Prosthetics | BILL STURGEON |
| Special Make-Up | DON McLEOD |
| | ARLENE SMITH |
| Special Props | HOWARD MUNFORD |
| Special Mechanical | IAN BIGGS |
| Sculptors | RUSSEL CATE |
| | RAYMOND MACKINTOSH |
| | JOE VENTURA |
| Mixer | SANDRA GALLOWAY |
| Modelmakers | LORNE BARRIE |
| | JAY D. McCLENNEN |
| | MICHAEL SHERWIN |
| Machinist | KEN PEARCE |
| Buyer | ERIC BELDOWSKI |
| Studio Assistant | BILL FRANCIS |
| Special Make-Up Assistant | GIONILDA STOLEE |
| Negative Cutting | DONAH BASSETT & ASSOCIATES |
| Color By | TECHNICOLOR |
| Color Timer | BOB RARING |
| Dailies Advisor | JOEY VIOLANTE |
| Titles and Opticals By | CINEMA RESEARCH CORPORATION |
| Dolby Stereo Consultant | STEVE S.B. SMITH |
| Cameras, Grip and Lighting Equipment Supplied By | GENERAL CAMERA |

This Motion Picture was made with the help of the City of New York Mayor's Office for Film, Theatre and Broadcasting, New York City Health and Hospitals Corp., Seaview Hospital, Home and Color Hospital, New York State Governor's Office for Motion Picture and Television Development, and The New Jersey Motion Picture and Television Commission. Special thanks to Budge-Wood Laundry Services, Inc., United States Post Office, the Williamsburgh Savings Bank, and the Puerto Rican Institute of Arts, Cinematographic and Television Industries.

Financial Services
FRANS J. AFMAN

Completion Bond Services Provided By
COMPLETE FILM CORPORATION

Production Insurance Provided By
ALBERT G. RUBEN & COMPANY, INC.

Media Investment & Services Provided By
MEDIATORS PICTURES CORPORATION/STERN-HERMAN

"LADY MARMALADE"
Written by B. Crewe/K. Nolan
Published by Kenny Nolan Publish-
   ing/Tannyboy Music/Stone
   Diamond Corp. (BMI)
Performed by LaBelle
Courtesy of CBS Records

"PLEASE MR. POSTMAN"
Written by R. Bateman/G.
   Dobbins/W. Garrett/B.
   Holland/F. Gorman
Published by Jobete Music Co., Inc.
   (ASCAP)/Stone Agate Music
   (BMI)

"WHAT'S GOING ON"
Written by R. Benson/A.
   Cleveland/M. Gaye
Published by Jobete Music Co.., Inc.
   (ASCAP)/Stone Agate Music
   (BMI)
Performed by Marvin Gaye
Courtesy of Motown Records

"MY THANG"
Written by J. Brown
Published by Unichappell Music
   (BMI)
Performed by James Brown
Courtesy of Polygram Special
   Products

"SONNY BOY"
Written by B.G. de Silva/L.
   Brown/R. Henderson/A. Jolson
Published by Warner Bros. Music
   (ASCAP)
Performed by Al Jolson
Courtesy of MCA Records

"HEARING SOLAR WINDS/Part
   3: Arc Descents"
Written by D. Hykes
Performed by David Hykes and
   The Harmonic Choir
Courtesy of Ocara/Radio France

Original soundtrack album available on
Varèse Sarabande Compact Discs and Cassettes

(Varese Sarabande logo)

"To Tell the Truth"
Courtesy of Mark Goodson Productions

Read the screenplay from APPLAUSE THEATRE BOOKS